THE CONVERSATION

THE CONVERSATION

CANDID PERSPECTIVES ON FUNDRAISING AND ADVICE SHARED BY DONORS AND NONPROFITS

EJ JACOBS

to my mum and to Amy

Acknowledgements

The old adage that begins, 'It takes a village…' could not be more appropriate in describing the process of birthing this baby to full term. But it is a bit difficult to give proper acknowledgment when all of the participants except me are anonymous. That being said, I will effort to do my best.

This project could not have happened if not for the extraordinary amount of individuals who lent their time, thoughts, experiences and eagerness to see a change in how we speak to each other as people, representatives of people and representatives of resources. Just over one thousand funders, including foundation staff of all sizes (private, corporate and family), philanthropic advisors, and high net worth individuals from hedge fund titans to celebrities and athletes were contributors. While the majority of contributors are from North America, it is a very slight majority, with nearly half representing philanthropy in Europe, Africa, Asia, South America, The Middle East and Australia. I sadly could not find an Antarctic philanthropist to make this properly global, but not for lack of trying.

The wealth of voices from all across the nonprofit sector who also participated provided a pivotal anchor to this book. As global as their philanthropic counterparts, the collection of mostly grassroots, national and regional contributors also cover the ground in every continent, except the elusive Antarctic, who seems keen not to be a part of this in any way.

Whether it was a sentence, a paragraph, a question, an answer or an in-depth discussion, the influence and importance of all involved cannot be overstated. I humbly thank you all, as I am sure those who will benefit from your contributions thank you.

This book is not meant to guarantee funding, even with all the wonderful contributions from both donors and nonprofits. Organizational readers are not going to find a pot of unrestricted gold on the last page. Apologies in advance. What readers will find is a better understanding of the donor and nonprofit perspective, which can be worth its weight in gold in the right hands.

Table of Contents

Introduction

Introduction

With absolutely no experience in philanthropy or even the nonprofit space, I was understandably somewhat nervous during my first proper meeting with a fundraiser as a gatekeeper of those funds. Despite no evidence to be found in my bank account, I was in the role of donor, even if only by proxy. It could not have started any worse. In an attempt at small talk, I was asked about my professional background. I said that I was a journalist and editor prior to joining the foundation, with no real prior experience for my current position.

The grant-seeker, who was also the Executive Director of the organization for which he was seeking funds, did not hide his disappointment at my lack of history in the space. He openly bemoaned how I might not fully understand the landscape in which his organization operated, missing key intricacies of their efforts. He preemptively suggested a follow up meeting with my boss before our meeting had even begun. I immediately felt like the emperor who had suddenly realized that the too good to be true deal on invisible clothing was neither good nor true. I apologized profusely for my own apparent inefficiencies and promised to ask if a follow up meeting would be possible after we had finished ours.

Then we got down to the meat of the meeting and something funny happened. Although I was in a completely new career path, I did what I had done naturally for several years prior to joining the foundation: I asked questions. I didn't just ask questions that the materials he brought with him could have easily answered; I asked questions on methodology, decoding data, implementation and the inclusion of beneficiaries into the organization outside of the clearly edited testimonials. Instead of hearing answers that were way above my head or beyond my scope of understanding, I instead heard, 'That's a good question that I really don't have an answer for now,' or 'No one has ever asked that of us before, so we don't really have information on that.'

I also made suggestions, ones which the ED wrote down furiously while genuinely thanking me. With all his technical gravitas and wonderfully color-coded graphs, he turned out to be the ill-equipped one. Considering this was my first proper meeting at a foundation, I would have remembered it, had it gone smoothly or not. Overall, it went quite well for many reasons, including a strong reminder not to doubt myself and of what I can bring to the table with my own experience and acumen.

Now this is not a story of self-praise or how my first experience led me to have an underlying distrust of grant-seekers or nonprofits. Quite the opposite. Those who know me professionally would hopefully agree that I am not just a donor, but a true nonprofit ally. If I am a fan of an organization's work or an initiative, even if my foundation cannot support that work, I will eagerly try to put that work in front of those who can. This has resulted in tens of millions of dollars in financial support separate from our own foundational giving. I've never braced myself for a repeat of the behavior from my first encounter; I've judged each grant-seeker based on their own presentation, merits and passion.

In many ways, I was grateful for how my first engagement went nearly a decade ago. Rather than form a negative opinion based on this one experience, I saw the dangers in this particular experience and have wanted to guide any would-be fundraisers from making comparable missteps, especially if their work is too necessary to be the victim of unfortunate presentation or engagement. The phrase, 'You only get one chance to make a first impression' is magnified exponentially in the donor world, as every missed opportunity can represent significant sums of money lost. And donors speak to each other.

Apart from my first experience, some of the more common missteps that I've directly encountered have been the use of language that assumes too much upon the donor, an inability to explain an organization's purpose and goals, ignoring our foundation's mission or regional focus to force a partnership, and making comparisons to work that our foundation supports without explicitly explaining how funding both would not be redundant. I should add a distinction for the last example that a fundraiser may think he/she has made a clear distinction between his/her organization and one we support, but it is not always clear to me. This is something that many donors and foundation staff agree upon. A good way to lessen or avoid such a conflict is to run your pitch by an unbiased source with knowledge of the work, including a current donor.

Missteps are not limited to the fundraising side by no small measure. And the impact of donor bad practices can be equally, if not more harmful to the charity space, regardless of organizational size or wealth. I remember a conversation I had with a high net worth individual and friend, where we were discussing our funding focus. He said he had switched his philanthropic giving from one area of Human Rights to another. When I asked why, he said he was dissatisfied by the work he supported. It yielded few results and left him feeling like he would have to fund possibly for decades before seeing a win, and he wasn't interested in waiting that long.

I then asked how he picked his implementing partners, if he put out calls for proposals or joined working groups on the topic. He said he didn't accept unsolicited proposals and relied on recommendations from the few donors and colleagues he knew that had some knowledge on the topic. The organizations he decided to support were mostly international nonprofits (INGOs) or organizations that operated on a larger scale. As a private donor, he thought this was the best way to be effective without increasing his bandwidth.

Familiar with his former focus area, I rattled off some organizations I knew of that were quite effective and produced strong results, including a few that continued their work despite being underfunded. He had never heard of any of the organizations. Not that his new philanthropic focus didn't need his funding, but he had chosen a very myopic approach to grant-making in an area in dire need of attention, advocacy and financial support, only to immediately jump ship when his approach failed, laying the blame of that failure at the feet of the nonprofit sector's perceived ineptitude.

He is hardly the first philanthropist to use this type of funding ideology, only to chastise the nonprofit side as a whole for the failure of unrealistic expectations put upon a sample set of the organizations that may or may not be equipped to address those expectations. Many of those donors do not have the benefit of fearless criticism or advice on their strategies from implementing partners. Most foundations do have recurring internal discussions to address and improve strategy, but if the problem is in the ideology—or worse—the paradigm, then how effective can that process be?

There are forums that are meant to bring donors and nonprofits together to collaborate or improve how both sides work, together and individually. The limited success of many of these types of convening are not too difficult to diagnose: you represent a nonprofit and get an opportunity to engage with a donor who may be able to directly or indirectly support your work. Would you take that short moment to educate the donor on better practices that could also be construed as alienation or would you spend that time trying to create a relationship that would be more beneficial to your organization?

Conversely, as a donor or donor representative, attending some of these forums can be an inundation of in-person proposals or requests for meetings, instead of an exchange of ideas or practices. What is meant to be a learning opportunity quickly turns into a Pavlovlian exchange of business cards and little else. Even the most patient and well-intentioned donor will suffer from fatigue, especially with no real filter in place. Having attended my fair share of conferences, I can attest to the overwhelming mélange of limited time and limitless requests for that time.

While attending one conference a couple years ago, I had over 90 requests for a meeting and in one day, I took 26 of them. I openly tell people that was easily the most mentally exhausted I had ever been in my life, professional or otherwise.

The easy response is simply to say no, but while a few people did abuse the parameters I set, something substantial came of almost every meeting, including direct funding relationships, partnerships and connections to other partners in order to further their organizational missions. Although I would never do that again, ever, ever again, it is hard to ignore the need for resources and the ability to help. I remember relaying my experiences to a fellow donor at the end of that conference and she revealed that she had about fifteen more meetings overall. Clearly, this is not healthy behavior for either of us, and while I have the ability to limit my engagement, nonprofits who rely on foundations like mine for survival are not afforded that luxury.

I've advocated to some conference to build a better platform for grassroots organizations with no real bandwidth to reach out to donors beyond their borders with minor exceptions. But how do conference organizers increase their own bandwidth to identify those more obscure organizations with any efficacy? It feels as though some answers beget more questions.

During my time in philanthropy, I have been able to create many friendships, partnerships and better understanding of how nonprofits and donors of all sizes work. I have been able to see how both sides engage, what works, what doesn't, and what has no place in engagement. These experiences, along with too much anecdotal advice from those outside of philanthropy led me to examine the best way to deliver concrete advice to the people who need it most from the people who understand this sector the most.

In preparation for a session on fundraising I had planned to host at a conference, I reached out to about thirty donor colleagues for their advice, with a twist: I asked them for at least one 'do' and one 'don't' that they believed every nonprofit should know before engaging a donor, but the advice would be completely anonymous. If they had extra time or more to say, they could also give a memorable experience—

good or bad—with a fundraiser. The result was a PDF that became the basis for a significant portion of this book. When given the opportunity to educate on the best ways to engage, donors responded honestly from a clear, personal, informed and informative perspective.

Moments before the session was set to begin, it was apparent that there was a genuine hunger on both sides to discuss engagement honestly and frankly. Twice as many people as anticipated turned up, with some people choosing to sit on the floor when all the chairs were taken up, instead of attending another of the many great sessions occurring concurrently.

As a handful of these tips were read aloud, along with the experiences, I noticed more than a few red faces and nervous glances at the ground. Among the many donors in the session, there was some head-nodding and a look of relief that the words were finally spoken and not directly out of their mouths. What happened after laid the groundwork for the rest of this book.

We had a conversation. Donors, nonprofits, consultants, interested parties, people in chairs and even those on the floor all came together to discuss, offer and evaluate next steps for better engagement. With only two hours allotted for the session, we could not delve into the genesis of bad engagement, so we rolled up our sleeves and went to work on how to best represent the causes we supported both with our work and our financial capacity, as well as how to best make the other side of engagement understand each other's perspectives and complexities.

We also addressed the advice graciously offered from anonymous donors. It also helped immensely to have donors in the room—including a few who contributed to that list—to provide context. After hearing the list, the most common question from nonprofits was if there was a way to reengage if someone was guilty of committing one or more of the dreaded 'don'ts.'

Prior to the session, I had feared that my co-host and I might be made responsible to respond to all the inevitable questions that the list would induce, but as the session progressed, we mostly did little more than facilitate, as the donors in attendance tackled the bulk of the questions with calm and insight. For the first time in my experience with such a robust group, the opportunity to create better practices and understand each other more had superseded the self-promotion that habitually made its presence felt.

Fundraisers spoke from a place of vulnerability and frustration about their own experiences with donors. They addressed—not attacked—

the power dynamic that exists between the donors and nonprofits, the varying guidelines that each donor sets up in order for the conversation around funding to even begin, and the unrealistic expectations on a small organization and its Executive Director's time and availability. Some spoke of situations they currently were dealing with and sought guidance from fellow peers and donors in the room.

Donors were just as active as their nonprofit counterparts. One donor shared how an organization representative had thoughtfully engaged her, but she did not see a fit with the organization at the time of initial engagement. She did invite the person to keep her informed on the organization's work and progress, which the person continued to do without pushing the pitch. After a few years, she was able to see a path to partnership, crediting the person's patience and professionalism.

Finally, after we had all rolled up our sleeves, we switched roles, professionally. I instructed all nonprofit attendees that they were now meant to represent a grant-making institution of their choosing. All the donors had to play the ED of their favorite organization that they supported, with the thought that they would be able to represent those organizations well enough in a short and short-notice role play. We also saw this as an opportunity for donors to exhibit the best practices that had been discussed throughout the session. The 'new' donors had to meet with at least six non-profits and after all meetings were concluded, pick two organizations to support, while letting the others know that they would not receive a grant and why.

The results were beyond expectations. In what we thought would be an educational experience mostly for nonprofits turned out to be an equally significant teachable moment for all parties involved. Donors who only had to play the role of fundraisers for about 45 minutes realized how absolutely difficult it was to fundraise and to speak to someone knowing that the livelihood of the organization relied upon that support. When faced with the same questions and comments that nonprofits often hear and were keen to repeat, some donors were at a loss for a response.

An example of such a comment is one that I had previously given to a nonprofit ED who was in attendance. Upon our first meeting, I said quite frankly, 'My foundation does not support work in your region or scope, so we will most likely not fund you, but I am still interested in learning more about what you do and why.'

Knowing that the pressure was off to deliver the perfect pitch or find a way to fit a square peg into a round hole, he spoke more freely about his organization, his methods and his reasons for entering the space.

Although we did not immediately become direct funding partners, we became friends and I became an ambassador for his work. I offered advice and opportunities for funding where I saw them and when the moment came to provide some sort of direct support, I seized it.

Fast-forward to the session, where he decided to pose the same comment to another donor. That donor-turned-fundraiser went silent for the first minute or so before trying to recover in the allotted time provided for the pitch. Now far be it for me to fault any donor for not being able to come up with the perfect response during an impromptu role play lasting only six minutes. In the debrief following the role-play, that donor and others expressed their newfound empathy for nonprofits, who they previously felt should be prepared for all situations.

Since that session, I am aware of at least two other instances where that role play has been repeated by others with similar results. This illustrates the need for all sides of philanthropy to foster a better understanding of each other in a more nurturing way. So when I was approached by one of the original contributors and was asked to turn that list into a book, I was apprehensive. While a concise document providing insight into what donors want and don't want proved its merit, I had no interest in creating a large scale talk-down to nonprofits, as if the funder side was infallible or immune to criticism.

Figuring out how to effectively reach donors is a constant struggle for nonprofits. There are valid fears of donor fatigue, foundations with non-solicitation policies and increasing competition from new and existing nonprofits. Trying to fundraise under these conditions is daunting, often leading to desperation. And people do questionable things when they are desperate.

Once I decided to take on the task of expanding that session into a book, creating a deterrent to that desperation became the main focus. I spoke with well over four hundred fellow donors from the public, private, corporate, governmental and individual areas of philanthropy within the first couple years. By the end, that number had surpassed one thousand. I asked them—continuing the shield of complete anonymity—to speak unfiltered about how they thought those who look to fundraise should approach them and how they shouldn't. Many offered their dos and don'ts, but I saw value in the full conversations with the donors who truly understand the struggles of their implementing peers. In fact, with the exception of a few obvious chapters, much of the advice given was done in person—often on the spot—without the ability to self-edit or consult notes. The goal was authenticity.

Knowing what donors want and don't want is integral to successful fundraising, but it is only one large piece of the puzzle. Where do nonprofits take this information and how do they implement it in a way that helps their organizations, the people and/or causes supported by their organizations, and their relationships with potential donors? What are the questions from the nonprofit sector for donors that they are either too afraid to ask or cannot get answered? What are steps that philanthropists can take to improve engagement and, ultimately, the results of nonprofits?

The Conversation is an examination of all these facets and more, in order to leave as few questions unanswered as possible surrounding donor and nonprofit engagement. Not every question has a pleasant or satisfactory response, but operating from honesty will help how we operate in the long run. I remember reading an article by the Nonprofit Quarterly, titled Scaling the Wall: 5 Ways to Get Unsolicited Proposals Heard. One of the suggestions was to 'send a Letter Of Intent (LOI),' even if a foundation explicitly says it doesn't take unsolicited proposals or LOIs. Now this may work for a few people, but should we endorse behavior that will most likely not work for a nonprofit and could even result in a bad reputation with the funding institution?

Nonprofits have been accused of not speaking together enough, but such is not the case with many donors. The last thing a nonprofit wants is for its name to be mentioned between donors in a negative way. My suggestion for dealing with a foundation that does not accept unsolicited proposals (and you will read other suggestions later, including from such foundations) would have been to investigate connections between those unsolicited foundations and ones that already support your work first. Ask if they believe there might be a fit and if so, would they be willing to make a recommendation or possibly a referral. If your funding partner agrees that the work is worthy of an introduction, they may be willing to do this. This may yield the same results as the one proffered in the article, but it also eliminates possible alienation.

For my part, I am open to receiving proposals via third party introductions, but there are certain types of unsolicited proposals that I will not even entertain. There are tell-tale signs of proposals sent from people who thought doing their homework on whether our foundation would be a fit meant a quick internet search for contact information. They could not be more wrong.

Conversely, the overwhelming majority of grants that I endorse for funding come from introductions and recommendations from both fellow donors and friends on the nonprofit side. That includes grant-ees and colleagues who we may not directly support, but still maintain a good relationship. The advice I offer is advice that I know for a fact can work, because it is advice I incorporate and from which I have already benefitted. It is important for me—beyond the purposes of this book—to equip the people who are doing good with the best tools to continue to make their good work great.

Although this book is titled, The Conversation, there have been so many conversations with donors, nonprofits, philanthropic governments, startups, consultants and the beneficiaries of all their efforts. As much as we try to deny or ignore the power dynamics, it is rather difficult for the donors and nonprofits to speak candidly without some form of apprehension. The goal of this book is to coalesce all of these discussions into one, so that the information is not only representative of what readers want to know, but also representative of what readers want to express, truly making it a conversation.

1

First Things First, Why Are You In This?

Statistics can be used to shape, if not manipulate a narrative. The narrative within this book is meant to be shaped by experience and expertise. That being said, there are a few stats that are vital to share before venturing into any conversation about engagement. According to the National Center for Charitable Statistics (NCCS), there are more than 1.5 million nonprofit organizations registered in the USA alone as of 2015. This huge number does not even take into account the hundreds, sometimes thousands of new nonprofits that are created every month, again just looking at the states. This reminds me of one of my favorite quotes, 'No individual raindrop ever considers itself responsible for the flood.'

Almost every person on the nonprofit side with whom I have spoken agrees there are too many non-governmental organizations (NGOs). However, it would be rare to find a nonprofit that would admit to contributing to the flooding of the charity sector, and yet the sheer volume of the crowded space places more pressure on each organization to prove it is necessary or at least complimentary, and not redundant.

There are nowhere near as many new philanthropists that enter the space on an annual basis, even on a global scale. Although this number can be a bit inflated due to local efforts, the amount of new philanthropy is not growing at a level to sufficiently support existing nonprofits, let alone the continuous cycle of new additions. This increased competition for donor dollars means that nonprofits must find a way to stand out more in fundraising, while having the mission and results to maintain a relationship beyond initial interest.

The deluge of nonprofits also places great strains on the philanthropic sector to navigate its own resources through an uncharted route in hopes of creating actual impact. It's a bit like the reality TV show, The Bachelor: dozens of suitors in various forms and backgrounds present themselves in ways that range from the well put together to the less refined. All claim to be worthy of a rose from someone they've spent very little time getting to properly know. While some who fail to gain a rose are graceful in the face of rejection, others are angry, feeling as if they were not given a fair shot by someone who has had limited time and familiarity in making that decision.

In fundraising, having only twenty competitors might be considered an advantage. And instead of a rose, the life or death of an organization is at stake. As much as there is a need to take the time to learn more about the grant-maker, there is a serious need to self-reflect and be able to successfully answer one question: 'Why are you doing this?'

What may seem like a simple question on the surface has confounded many working in the nonprofit field, and not for the seemingly obvious reasons. The first mistake many make in interpreting this question is that they confuse the need for a personal story that connects to their work with why their work is best suited to address the issue at hand. So which course is the right one? Short answer: both.

We speak a lot about donors and nonprofits, but we cannot leave out the people and causes that inspire our work. Primum non nocere, which, in Latin, translates to 'first, do no harm,' is seen as a guiding principle for healthcare workers around the world, but this must also lead the path of every NGO, irrespective of size or focus.

There is quite a bit to unpack there. Putting aside the personal aspects that connect the work, the importance of personal and professional due diligence cannot be overstated. By personal due diligence, I mean taking a full self-examination into the motives you have for wanting to involve yourself into the existing crisis. Do you view the problem you wish to confront with maternal eyes, wanting to give the problem a great big hug and make the pain go away or do you view it with social eyes, pushing for a solution to the problem that would benefit the beneficiaries in a way that you would want it to benefit you if ever in a similar situation? Though both come from a place of love, it matters greatly if the relationship you have with the recipients of your work is as a parent or a peer.

The most significant hindrance of the parental nonprofit approach is that it too often tends to be narrow in vision, scope, methodology, implementation and, ultimately, impact. Depending on the cause and region, it can also reinforce many stereotypes of western interventions. Again, this particular area is not about what donors want, as monies can be raised to support just about any endeavor. This is about what beneficiaries need, not according to you, but according to them, according to the research and to the results of real homework. Personal due diligence should help you find out if your heart, intentions and mission are all aligned in the right place.

Professional due diligence is no less important if the aim is to help without harming. I've witnessed people speak about some horror they learned of from the news and was moved to consider starting a charity to help 'in some way.'

This form of helping is akin to seeing someone bleeding to death in the street from a gunshot wound and instead of ringing the police or emergency services, someone decides to start a medical response team to treat the victim. The majority of people who say they wish they could help in some way will probably never actually start a nonprofit, but there are already plenty in existence born from a similar premise.

Due diligence should not end at whether you are the only actor or the only one performing a certain function in the space. There may be a reason no one else is doing what you're doing where you plan to do it. A review of the area, the responses (both current and prior), the results of those responses and input from those affected should be done well before you begin choosing the words to create the coolest sounding acronym of your organization.

Along those lines, I've noticed that some nonprofits have shown more foresight for the organization than for their beneficiaries. This is especially troubling when the nonprofit only offers niche services. There is a lack of a plan for when beneficiaries fall out of the service pool. If an organization is mapped from A to Z, where A is the target problem, Z does not represent the nonprofit's solution; Z is—or should be—the stage where no additional support is needed by the beneficiary at all.

I could open a state of the art soup kitchen that provides full meals and comfort to the poor, as well as job training and psycho-social support. However, if it is only open two days a week and I supply no information to connect those people to an alternative place for supplemental assistance for the remainder of the week, my biggest success might be getting my hand completely around my shoulder in order to pat myself on the back, while the people I claim to care about receive uneven support. There may be legitimate reasons why this fictional soup kitchen could only be open for two days, but that does not excuse my inability to better inform on additional support, nor does it feed them when my soup kitchen can't.

A nonprofit should not be a vehicle of good intentions, but of good investigation that ventures beyond any self-styled relevance test. If an NGO lacks a clear connection to another organization that addresses obvious support gaps, funding consideration drops dramatically in favor of those who have it. Some get around this by promising to identify these partners once projects are fully funded and running as intended, but if they don't deliver, it is difficult to continue investment.

Engaged donors with smaller portfolios can push their implementing partners to secure the necessary partnerships that were promised early in the partnership. Inundated donors, as many are, may ask for a progress report once or twice and choose not to renew the grant if no clear partnership for beneficiaries has been established. They may also cite this reason to other prospective donors who query about the funding experience. Bottom line: the reason why you're in this has to be more than just your introduction to the issue, but the journey it has taken you and your organization.

But...you need a story. For every donor who wants you to lead with your impact, there is another who comes to the meeting with Kleenex in hand, wanting to be ugly-cried into loving your work. And of course, there are many donors in between who want to hear your story as a way to assess your commitment to your work, so they know you are as invested as you want them to be.

There are stories I have heard that I will never forget and, to be quite honest, have kept me involved with an organization longer than I may have been without the story. So as not to appear hypocritical, I should clarify that those organizations had also done the personal and professional due diligence. Their stories moved me from making a grant based solely on mission and effectiveness of implementation, to helping them find other resources to further implement that mission. That is the power of a good story.

I have spoken to numerous colleagues and friends in the nonprofit space about developing not just a story, but their story. They struggle mightily with this for various reasons. Many are introverts or have no experience in talking about themselves in such a way. For some, the story is too personal and telling it more than once is either too difficult or feels exploitative, so they shy away. Others feel they have no story to tell. Executive Directors or senior staff brought into the fold may be great at retelling the founder's story, but fail to properly merge their personal journey with the path of the organization they now represent.

While there are donors who understand new staff may not have a similar connection to the work as the founder or original staff, there will still be those who want to know how you align with the mission other than accepting a job opening. Remember, for many donors, making a donation is a deeply personal act and they want to see a reflection of that from the person making the pitch. Perfecting the story is not the point, though that will be covered later; this is about understanding that a story needs to exist and why.

Remember the personal due diligence bit? If done properly, your story should be an organic byproduct as a result. Your story is a personal story, but is not just about you. It is also the story of those who cannot court the necessary audience as you do or hope to do. If their story doesn't resonate in yours, we may know why you are in this, but not why it matters.

Having a story is quite different than telling that story. The delivery of that story is also crucial, whether in-person or written. It doesn't need to have the length or plot of a novel. It needs to be concise and heartfelt. As later chapters will show, this is something most donors agree upon. On the topic of storytelling, while donor fatigue gets most of the focus, I've never heard anyone properly touch upon storytelling fatigue. Storytelling fatigue occurs most when nonprofit founders find themselves having to explain their inspiration for starting their work multiple times to those who can potentially support that work.

I've witnessed storytelling fatigue several times, most recently when meeting with the founder of an organization that had come highly recommended by a colleague. He came to our meeting well equipped with graphs and PowerPoint printouts. When I asked him what made him choose his cause and the country of focus, he sighed, as if he were a celebrity who had been asked for his autograph for the hundredth time that day. Then he muttered a response that sounded as if it were a passage from a book he was called upon to read aloud in class. I found his response somewhat discouraging. Not known for my meekness, I openly asked him if he was tired of telling that story. He replied no, but his body language indicated that he was embarrassed I caught how he wished he could just push a button and have a recording recite his story with the same passion as the first time he shared it.

I get it, but other donors who ask about your story may not. The best suggestion I can offer is to treat your story like the baby photos all proud parents love to show to anyone who inquires about their child. It should be your source of pride, not a nuisance or at least it should not be conveyed to others that telling it inconveniences you somehow. That is harder to do if the story is linked to pain and possibly unresolved issues. In those cases, be up front and say that is difficult to fully discuss, but you would be willing to discuss the parts that don't retraumatize.

This question of why you are in this field is not meant to only be a nonprofit exercise, but something donors are equally, if not more responsible for answering. Nonprofits, for all their well-intended bad ideas that could corrode the progress of an entire sector or for their strokes of genius that can elevate an entire population out of a predicament, can accomplish very little without donors, small or large.

And yet, not all donors acknowledge the enormity of their power. There are donors who don't believe they should feel pressure for the mistakes made by their grantees. Not that they don't feel sympathy or anger when an organization fails to deliver on its promises, but they believe the responsibility for these failures rests squarely with the implementers and should not affect giving strategies. One donor compared the unpredictability of grant-making to giving a much smaller, on the spot amount to a beggar on the street.

'You give with the assumption, with the hope that he or she will take that money and put it towards food, but you know that there are many other ways for that money to be spent, good and bad. Feeding a child or feeding an addiction, but you give because you hope the money will be used for good. It's the risk you take in giving.'

It is worth pointing out that these remarks were made during a conversation on the paradox of risk philanthropy, but it does highlight the view of the philanthropist, in this case, of the individual donor. As nonprofits would reaffirm, foundational and especially government philanthropy is rarely as simple as a good faith grant based on hope in lieu of evidence. Sometimes, good faith can be a bad practice.

While hardly any nonprofits would complain about a donor giving a good faith grant, the problem resides between those direct flights from one extreme to another. Donor gives a bad organization a grant while preforming zero due diligence and when that decision proves itself to be unwise, donor demands a good organization jump through a million hoops and stretch itself beyond its means in order to prove it is a good organization. Donors like this hear terms like monitoring and evaluation being tossed about in discussions of best practices and apply them with neither context nor nuance.

This is why it is important for donors as much as implementers to have an understanding—intrinsically and overtly—of why they want to be a part of any solution. Poor choices by philanthropists are capable of slowing progress or impeding it altogether. Before the philanthropic advisors or the daughter of that distant cousin who runs an obscure charity working on something you've never heard of in a place you know nothing about gets a hold of you, it is best to examine the moment that made you want to donate money for more than the tax benefits. This understanding is critical in establishing the role you want to have in the nonprofit space, as well as the expectations you have of the efficacy of your grants.

Is it tied into your own personal experiences? Shared experiences? Professional experiences that you believe can have an impact in areas of need? In the end, it is your contribution, so there should be a reflection of you in it. It doesn't have to be all about you, nor should it. This gives those who will want to collaborate with you or seek your resources an authentic indicator of where you want your place in the field to be. The beauty of individual philanthropy is that it can remain personal with no outside mandate attached.

Having a relationship with the work also provides better insight into to those who make the effort to connect with you. In many instances, keeping their work alive means keeping people alive. One nonprofit participant poignantly said during our discussion, 'If I make a bad impression, if I mess up when speaking to a donor, some girl who could have been rescued is now strapped to a floor, brutalized, and then sold for cows and goods. It's just that raw, and when you are that involved in it, you can't run away from that feeling, and yet, you can't say any of that to donors you meet either. I feel that responsibility directly and every time I put myself out there to ask for a major gift, I feel so vulnerable. Then I meet a donor who has no clue about the enormity of this meeting for me. It's tough.'

This is the donor importance through the eyes of a nonprofit, and what is on the table for the people you meet. So even when there is not an alignment, if you are in touch with what you're trying to accomplish in one field, you can show that same respect for others trying to make a similar impact even if it's in a dissimilar field.

This also doesn't have to be limited to one area of focus. If your philanthropy allows you to affect more than one area of need, then explore it. They do not have to overtly overlap either. The Arcus Foundation supports the rights of both the LGBT community and Great Apes. On its face, there is no direct correlation, but knowing the story of the foundation's founder provides the answer, as well as the context for how his foundation wants to interact with both causes.

Taking a multiple focus approach doesn't have to be restricted to the causes with which you are familiar. While there is an entire section of people much smarter than me offering advice to donors, I would be remiss if I didn't use this moment to suggest that if you do have that ability to focus philanthropy in multiple areas, choose at least one area with which you have little to no familiarity, which is desperate for a philanthropic interjection.

The causes that are nearest to our personal experiences tend to be the fruit hanging so low that it's practically scraping the ground, and are often overfunded. Crises too foreign to land on our radar, but too important to be ignored are, in fact, ignored. Supporting these kinds of causes may take a bit more time and homework on our part than others, but then that takes us back to the original question: Why are you in this?

And individual donors are not the only ones responsible for being in touch with why they chose to play a part in working in philanthropy. Programmatic staff of institutional and corporate foundations have the same obligation, even if they represent preset funding mandates, possibly more so than individual donors. Program Officers have the task of explaining institutional decisions to their implementing partners and applying them with thoughtfulness, while providing an accurate landscape to senior staff or trustees of what is truly needed on the ground, so the role cannot be minimized to just being a mouthpiece of a board. There is power in that position, the power of persuasion and justification.

All the experiences that factor into the story of the individual donor and even the implementers are just as relevant to institutional donors. They not only affect how funding mandates are carried out, but how they are shaped and amended or even abandoned. A family foundation executive told me of when he arrived into his current position, how the foundation had set funding mandates that were in place for many years, despite not yielding desired results. His experience, both professionally and personally, led him to a different vision for the foundation.

He was able to introduce a new direction that made sense, while pointing out areas where the impact of granted resources could be felt, as well as measured. He assuaged fears of going out on a limb by providing evidence of a need for intervention and identification of the right partners to lead that intervention. He spoke openly of what factors contributed to how he wanted to carry out his philanthropy and used that to the benefit of his foundation, but also to the benefit of the communities that would now benefit.

It seems odd to think that Executive Directors of a charity should come to a meeting ready to share many personal parts of themselves in order to create a significant relationship with someone who is not willing to be put in a similar position. This in no way means every meeting between donors and implementers needs to resemble an episode of Oprah, but if you are planning to ask the why, be prepared to offer your own answer as well.

Ultimately why you are in this goes beyond you. The actions we take to improve situations in the world are second only to the mindsets that help to manifest those actions.

2

What Are We Talking About?
Defining The Language We Speak

Jargon. Acronyms. Stats. The new tenets of modern language. FYI, we can now LOL our way through many written conversations. In a sport like baseball, fans go back and forth about ERA, OPS and RBI with ease. Fortunately for those of us fluent in millennial or baseball, these expressions have clearly objective meanings with little room for speculation. Not every shortcut in the rest of our communication properly represents its intended purpose. Ever notice how the use of 'ASAP' seems more urgent or even ruder than the long form of 'as soon as possible,' despite both having the exact meaning? This happens less within the language spoken by subsets of society, like the sport-lovers, gamers or foodies.

There is a luxury in the language of niche groups where terms foreign to others actually make communication much easier. This could not be further from the truth in the nonprofit sector. There are so many complications and contradictions that even the most fluent speakers sometimes have no idea what the hell they are saying. The language struggles with being both too academic and too condensed in how it is communicated, which sometimes forces words and phrases to take on ill-fitted meanings. Words that should elicit clear definitions are instead shackled with several inferences that can lead to multiple interpretations, including misinterpretation. Much of the nonprofit jargon can be summed up in one word: okay.

No, I am not saying that nonprofit jargon is okay; I'm saying much of it has been defined the same way the word 'okay' came into existence.

Some might think that OK is a derivative of okay. In reality, OK is short for an early 20th century term, 'oll korrect,' which was a deliberate misspelling and mispronunciation of the term 'all correct.' It was created using a very popular form of slang of that era and is the only surviving term of its time. But over the decades, OK took on its own meaning and, for the sake of ease in pronunciation, was given the long form version of okay. So…"okay" is a made up word to help define a made up acronym for a term originating from the way a select group of people used to, but no longer communicate. Sounds confusing? Sounds familiar?

The difficulty of nonprofit jargon is that it is limited in vocabulary, but represents a sector that is limitless in scope. People organize to celebrate the beauty in life or to protest against its destruction. There are organizations for health, education, science, nutrition, peace, conservation, governance, racism, gender-inequality, anti-trafficking, fair labor practices, children, elderly and the arts. These are wide-ranging topics and yet, they are meant to fit all of their differences into the same small packet of words and terminology.

And not speaking the language can prove disastrous for those who take baby steps into the nonprofit space, no matter what they do or how well they do it. I've personally seen good nonprofits be dismissed because their brilliant efforts were lost in translation. So the importance of the nonprofit lingo is evident, even if its efficiency remains up for debate. To explore this further, I asked scores of speakers fluent in nonprofit from both, the philanthropic and implementing sides, to finally put faces to the names we often hear and think we know.

I purposely chose a wide array of people, including domestic and international donors based in the United States, as well as donors from the Global South and Asia. I also sought inclusion of people I know rely heavily on their prospective grantees having a grasp of these terms, as well as those who claim to despise it. On the implementing side, I also received input from a globally diverse field, but I also wanted to include those who I knew had mastered the lexicon and those who have masterfully found a way around it, all while still finding success with donors.

Funny enough, as the definitions were given in real time, some of the people who I thought were most comfortable with the jargon had the more difficult times providing their definitions. Although this exercise was meant to provide guidance for those who are still struggling with nonprofit jargon, it was also a way to shed some light on the inconsistencies and outright contradictions between what we believe and what the people with whom we partner believe when speaking the same words, but not necessarily the same language. We also cannot forget that these differences have a significant bearing on the communities we condense into our jargon.

The importance of forcing participants to speak and not skillfully craft their responses in written form was to level the playing field a bit. There is an expectation that nonprofits know the jargon in both written and oral form, but we rarely ask the architects of much of the language to do the same. I thought it would be a good exercise to put donors through a similar constriction, even if it might be uncomfortable. And that's okay. (See what I did there?) These definitions are not meant to be contenders for entry into the Oxford dictionary. They are insights into how the people representing each field internalize them and use them to guide their journeys.

Of the terms up for definition, one word is not among them: empowerment. It could be argued that all of the nonprofit terms are useless, but the ones included here have roots in something tangible. Empowerment does not, despite what others in the field might say. When I think of empowerment, I think of an experience I had with my wonderful mother when I was just a child.

At around eight years of age, my mother sat me down and explained that when she felt I had done something wrong, she now wanted to give me the chance to defend myself, like in a court of law. In her lawyerly way, she explained that she wanted to give me the opportunity to plead my case properly in situations where I faced a possible punishment for something I may or may not have done wrong, or if I wanted permission to do something she was hesitant to allow. Her objective was twofold: The first was to make sure I understood in a more comprehensive way why she would say no or why my (very rare) bad behavior justified grounding. The second was to let me know that even as a youth, I had power, and this was her way to 'empower' me.

Of course, every time we had such deliberations, my mother won. I was a kid after all and was new to this approach of trying to get what I want. I immediately longed for the 'cry until she caved in' approach I had been employing with much more success. Then one day, a few years into this method, something happened. I wanted to have a sleepover on a weekday (for what reason I can't remember) and asked my mother. She said no and I asked to present my case. Smiling, she said sure. I gave all the reasons it should be allowed, but this time, when she came up with strong arguments as to why it wasn't a good idea, I had a good counter argument. I could see her face go from brimming with pride at my good rebuttals to frustration that she wasn't 'winning' this particular case. When I made my final point—rather successfully, I thought—I waited for the seemingly inevitable verdict from my mum.

No. She said no. When I asked what logical reason she could possibly have for denying my request, she said rather exasperatedly, 'Because I said so.'

My little world was crushed. I thought I had power, because my mother's experiment succeeded in empowering me, but not in giving me any real power. My mother still had all the power and she allowed me to think I had power. It all worked fine until my feeling of power went head-to-head with her actual power. Actual power won.

This is the problem with the use of the nonprofit's use of empowerment. There is no mystery to its actual meaning, unlike the other words defined in this chapter. It is a feeling of power or a sense that one has the resolve to accomplish goals previously thought to be impossible. But whenever empowerment is spoken from the nonprofit side, there is an inference of a clear cause and effect that empowering beneficiaries somehow yields real power that makes them less immune to their circumstances. Empowerment is only about feelings. The words below are not about feelings, but about how nonprofits and the people who support them work together. So on to the jargon that was actually defined.

Participants were asked to define these terms in any way they chose. From those responses, below are five of the strongest from donors and implementers each. By strongest, I don't mean the most concise. Not even close. I could see people cringe after giving answers and then cringe even more at the thought of it being included in a book. They may cringe further if they continue to read on. And yet this was the point in people giving on the spot answers instead of emailing more manicured responses.

One particular donor who had contributed, but was unhappy with his definitions, had asked a couple days later if he could get a redo. I politely refused. When he asked me why I would not grant his request, I explained that as a donor who has been a vocal proponent of the jargon within the field, he had to put his request in the context of the nonprofits who meet with donors very much like him, if not him. As mentioned before, they are not afforded an opportunity to hit the reset button when they struggle to define their work within these often restrictive terms. I also assured him that as much as I was seeking the clearest definition of these terms, if they existed, I was less impressed with how pretty they looked on a page and more on how they fit into the spoken vernacular of engagement.

Considering there are seventy total definitions of the same seven terms, there might be an urge to skip ahead to the engagement piece, but I felt it important to show how the experts and veterans of the field navigate but also struggle to articulate the cornerstones of their own lexicon, especially when examples were given. I also found interesting is how often people used one bit of jargon to define another, further proof of how limiting the language can be. I may have also included examples I thought were the strongest evidence of my hypothesis that sometimes, we don't know what the hell we are saying. That is not to shame participants at all. I'm so grateful to those who lent their voices to possibly the hardest part of the conversations we have in our field: defining the words in which we speak it.

●●●

Sustainability

Donor 01 (US-based Africa donor)

Unfortunately, after years in the field, I think sustainability is the word funders say to organizations when they want them to not need funding anymore, which is an unrealistic expectation in most cases unless the organizations are built to generate significant revenue. It's the kind of word that causes nonprofits to then start these projects like chicken farming that are never particularly successful, all in an effort to become sustainable.

In the development sense, I would take sustainability to mean the longevity of the impact of an intervention. But I think that it has become this term that means funders don't want you to always need grants so figure out a way to find other money.

Nonprofit 01 (US based international focus)

Sustainability I would define as a much more complex word than it seems. It is a process and a goal. It is a way of protecting the integrity of people, places and planet for an amount of time that is too difficult to define.

Donor 02 (Africa based international donor)
It means producing more with no more investment. Donors like to ask about sustainability in terms of what will happen when we leave, but this is a bad question. We are already here and are here to perform a function that has been established that the government cannot or will not do. Based on this logic alone, sustainability is a very stupid concept, at least as a panacea.

Nonprofit 02 (Grassroots African organization)
To me, sustainability means people on the ground gaining full ownership—whether it's a project or an action—so that it remains, producing the fruits that they think will help and improve their lives. The ownership stays with them. They improve it. It goes according to their own plan and they control its movement to where it has to be.

Donor 03 (Asia focused donor)
Making services last. Making sure that the work gets picked up by local actors and local communities to ensure that it will be ongoing.

Nonprofit 03 (Asia & US based organization)
Sustainability I think for a lot of funders, means having financial diversification and moving away from foundation funding, at least this is how it is explained to us. When we think of sustainability, it really is more about the sustainability of the work, in terms of how it can go on and how the impact can deepen and scale. So sometimes there is a disconnect when there is too much focus on sustainability from a diversity of funding, there is tension with the impact.

To make the idea more concrete, we have foundation funding to build our platform and reach more students sooner and faster. However, there are other donors who are more interested in us finding other sources of funding beyond donations, but that doesn't always keep with the ethics of our mission. So there is tension that builds when this comes about. I think of sustainability as something entrenched in the community and the movement has taken off. I know that eventually I will have to not rely on foundation funding, but when I have to take time away from focusing on implementation to focus on that, I think of sustainability as a loaded term.

Donor 04 (US based global donor)

Sustainability has to do with the revenue or the long-term viability of a business model for an organization. It doesn't need to be 100% earned revenue, but it does mean that there is certainty for the future and cash flow of the organization. I often think of nonprofits as running two businesses: one is the programmatic business. It could be health, education, youth development, clean water, etc. The other business is running a fundraising shop. So for me, sustainability is tied to the future revenues and financial longevity of an organization.

Nonprofit 04 (Africa-based, social enterprise hybrid)

The initiative at hand is able to deliver its core programs without the need to raise external forms of funding. In my head, I went straight to financial stability. Because we have a built-in enterprise, we have a view of financial sustainability and nonprofit sustainability. Financial stability that the initiative raises is equal to or more than the amount that the initiative needs to continue running and delivering.

For nonprofit sustainability, I would say substitute finances with external support. So an initiative can continue to run without the continued and sustained impact of external resources. Even as a not for profit, I am not just thinking on behalf of my entrepreneurs. As an entrepreneurial not for profit, sustainability looks like being able to—through our core competency—raise revenue that covers our core operations and all program costs. Taking the financial focus out of the equation, sustainability means that fundamentally, things can run without external inputs.

Donor 05 (European-based international donor)

Interesting, our foundation is asking this question actually. I guess I would define it in many ways. Sustainability is having some long-term stability to be able to provide some significant investment in an area to make a change. I've heard it since the beginning of my career and I've never heard anyone answer the question about how you do that.

Within the concepts of sustainability, there is also always a need for some kind of a reliance on either donors or success of a business if it's financed through a for-profit means.

To me, as a grant-maker, sustainability means to have some sort of stability in order to not focus on the survival, but to focus on actually doing the work of your mission. It means enough stability over a period of time to focus on the mission vs. survival. If more than 70% of your energy is going into fundraising and keeping everything afloat, you can't actually invest in moving your mission. I think there should be sustainability of leadership. For me, sustainability goes beyond an organizational question. It can also be through leadership and allowing people the space to be able, again, to carry forward their mission vs. maintenance or survival.

Nonprofit 05 (US & Europe based international nonprofit)

Sustainability is more about mission reach and the idea that, whether in the short or long term, there is an opportunity to reach a given particular mission. –I'm so thrown off— (I assure the person that it is not the first time it has happened and to continue if comfortable.) I think sustainability has a lot of things tied into it. It depends strongly on the audience. I've been in groups where sustainability was focused on environmental sustainability and often times, human sustainability was left out of it. And yet the converse is true. When I hear human sustainability discussed, it is often devoid of environmental sustainability. It seems the conversations around sustainability are isolated. I think sustainability implies a longevity, which is not always what it should be about.

When you're thinking of sustainability from a donor perspective, it's more about whether or not an organization can sustain itself. But at the same time, if impact and mission are met, then is sustainability even relevant? Sustaining a program that has already served its purpose drowns the community when another sector continues to be neglected.

Impact

Donor 01 (US based Africa donor)

I'm an M&E (monitoring and evaluation) person, so impact to me is the very long-term effects of an intervention on a community or beneficiary group or whomever that intervention was meant to effect. I think that often when funders talk about impact, they actually mean outcomes. Outcomes are usually in the two-to-five year realm. You do a job training with a young adult and in two to five years, they're employed and that's an outcome, but that's really what funders are looking for, but they often will say impact instead, which is more like twenty years from now there are more jobs for young people. So what happens is you see organizations being pushed to measure their impact and it stresses them out. These organizations are thinking, 'How are we supposed to measure something that hasn't happened yet, because it is ten years down the road?'

What they really need to be looking at are their intermediate outcomes, which are closer at hand and a bit more tangible.

Nonprofit 01 (US based international focus)

I think the way we use the word is with the assumption that impact will be beneficial to all parties in a way that those parties would wish to see impact. I think part of the conversations that we leave off too often centers around the unintended consequences from working and creating impact. I think defining and measuring what we consider impact is not an easy task.

As practitioners, especially those who are stretched for resources and capacity, then it is a challenge to find that balance between investing time and money in defining impact and actually doing the work and hoping it creates the desired impact. I think we have to realize that the examples that we hold up as examples of good impact may be too subjective, but are being presented as objective and achievable, especially in the short-term.

Donor 02 (Africa based international donor)

Quantifiable, short, quick way of understanding what has worked. Sometimes it can be somewhat nebulous because impact only has meaning to donors. Working in a grassroots nonprofit before, we came to understand this word meant nothing. It is code for what a donor wants to see to justify a grant.

I want to see how many girls were put into schools. I wanna know how many textbooks were provided, but I don't wanna know what they are learning or if they are learning. I don't wanna know if a vaccine I paid for was the only thing needed or if it served as a pathway for other goods and services to enter into the community.'

So impact, most of the times, is looked at only one way and that way is beneficial only to donors.

Nonprofit 02 (Grassroots African organization)

Impact is any action or activity that brings the change that people on the ground want. It makes everything that they worked for or needed to a level that produces the desired fruit, desired outcome.

Donor 03 (Asia focused donor)

Impact is measurable, but should not be measured in the short-term. You have to come back five years or more after the model has had time to be fully implemented before you find out what has worked and what hasn't. This is the best way of measuring if impact has occurred. Also there is a learning of what is happening throughout the process that you can feed back into the process to have better impact.

Nonprofit 03 (Asia & US based organization)

For us, impact is very clear in terms of testimonials from the people we support. Our work relies heavily on ground-level feedback. But impact defined beyond our work tends to get very technical. We have donors who come in and say, 'I'm going to have you talk to our M&E folks,' and we have to make sure those conversations are about measuring impact and not measuring sustainability.

Luckily, I have a close enough relationship with our primary donors to push back and say, 'Look, sometimes when there is a staff of four, there is going to be a tradeoff between improving good work and growing good work. Do you want to have anecdotes about how the line is moving in the right direction or do you want to have deep work to measure the impact? What is it that you want us to do, do the work or measure the impact of us doing the work?'

Sometimes it becomes an intellectual exercise, where we are chasing elusive 'key performance indicators' and we're trying to track them without looking at the best uses of our time. So you have to present the donors with questions of what impact and at what level of measuring they expect. It doesn't matter how much funding is given if it still goes beyond the capacity of our staff and the program parameters.

There are a lot of funders who like to talk about the logic model, which focuses heavily on inputs and outputs and outcomes, but although it's called the logic model, it comes across like a logistical model. For us, the way to measure our impact is done through surveys that are very expensive that many donors will not pay for and we can't afford.

Donor 04 (US based global donor)

You ask ten people, you get ten different answers, which you're probably getting with this. For me, impact is changing the trajectory of a target constituency. If you're an organization, it's important for you to define who you are trying to impact and what type of impact you want to have. I don't like that I defined the word using the word, so I would say impact is changing the trajectory of a life based on some type of intervention. It is important to measure impact. It's important to understand what it would cost to deliver that impact or change.

I think impact is possibly the most challenging word in the social sector. I really do believe that no two people would define it the same way, but at its core, impact is meant to explain how an intervention changes a life, in its simplest form.

Nonprofit 04 (Africa-based, social enterprise hybrid)

(Long pause) A situation or a person or a subject being better off after something has been invested into it than how it started. In my view, I would say impact is an improvement of a human's wellbeing.

Donor 05 (European-based international donor)

Making a difference. It's really making a difference. For me, it's been usually for the good (laughs), but it could also be making a difference not for good.

Nonprofit 05 (US & Europe based international nonprofit)

(Laughs) With impact, so much is tied to data and numbers. I recently attended a session that mentioned the term, 'anecdatal,' and I really loved it. Especially with social entrepreneurship, there is always the pull between the business impact and the human impact and which one matters more. There is a balancing act, but if it is not viable from a business perspective, can there be any impact? And if it's not viable from a human perspective and creating change, is it an impact we want to represent and promote?

From a very generic economic perspective, impact could just be change over time that varies based on where it sits on the balancing seesaw of business and human perspective. And I love the anecdatal term because, in some ways, it's the idea that the data needs to change over time, but at the same time, it's the story. It's the micro-level story, not the macro data that really shows impact. So, you can have changing numbers at any particular given time and data can be skewed at any way shape or form, but if you have those micro-level stories that show there is change, then I think you can feel that impact is happening.

I also think impact is very difficult with the timeframe, too. Similar to sustainability, the timing and timeframes of this jargon are important to the definition and to their success, but are not factored into the definitions or the expectations. When we talk about impact, what is the timeframe? Are we talking about six months, three months, a year or year over year? But how many years and what type of impact is happening? When you are taking an anthropological or cultural perspective you might think you're having an impact in the short-term or you may be thinking you're having an impact, when that might not be the case.

Someone I know had gone to a country in Africa on a mission to adopt a child. She was a white woman who had gone through the process before, but without success. She then found in a newsletter this child she wanted to adopt. However, because she was a foreigner, the orphanage where the child lived reached out and found the child's father for permission. The child was then given back to the father, despite their formerly determining that he was not in a good place to care for the child. The father then turned around and tried to bribe the woman for money in order for her to adopt the child. It became a huge situation that ended with the adoption not happening.

From this woman's perspective, she thought she was going to make such a huge impact in the life of this child, which she did. This child ended up back in an abusive family. So how does impact look in this particular situation, especially four years down the line? On a macro level, there are many occurrences of this type of situation, obviously on a much greater scale.

I can give you a more personal macro example in my work. In one country where we work, we have a wonderful big name vendor who has partnered with the local community. They have built an amazing factory and have built up this entire village of people, employing men and women—primarily women—in a way that had not been done prior in this area. On the surface, it seems so wonderful and inspiring.

The flip side to this is that they are the sole vendor of the entire factory. They are the lifeline to the village. They have made this entire community completely reliant upon them and only them. What does that mean in terms of impact? In the short-term, it's great. They can feel good about it. They can market it and really feel good about it, because they are providing impact in the form of income, which is one of the best possible ways. But how does this look in five or ten years from now? What if the company folds? What if the company is bought out? What if they find more attractive locations that are better for their business proposition?

I think timing is an integral part to consider for impact. It also begs the question of if you are doing it to feel better about yourself or doing it to create sustainable impact in the community. If you don't have a viable long-term strategy then is the work really impactful or just a prolonged blip?

Capacity Building

Donor 01 (US-based Africa donor)

This is a tough one. Capacity building... (short pause) and this is anonymous? (I give assurance that it is) Capacity building in its truest form should be about organizations identifying needs and accesses resources that help them to address those needs. They are typically around systems building or advancing their mission in some way. Sometimes capacity building can become a way to make international grassroots organizations look more western. And it becomes not really in their control and not something they would choose to do on their own. Capacity building programs could really be about just making these organizations look like good western NGOs vs. taking them from where they are and letting them lead their own capacity building.

Nonprofit 01 (US based international focus)

The investment in the structures and talent in order to produce optimal work. I think that can come in many different forms, from human talent to functioning printers to having sufficient funds for partnership building and learning and growing and professional development. It's really a struggle to find that type of investment and it's very frustrating because you know deep in your soul that if you were fully funded to your fullest potential, it would result in making the area where you work a much greater place. So capacity building for me would be about funding potential and 'getting it.'

Donor 02 (Africa based international donor)

Oh wow! I love that. I loved that you asked that. It was the first on my list. Capacity building means…I've been very cynical with my other answers—and I don't want to be—but it is difficult not to be cynical with this one. Capacity building? Whose capacity are you building? The question of who and the assumptions around capacity building have been so wrong.

There was a huge mess created by international development partners in the 1980's and 1990's working on nonprofit reforms. There was nothing sustaining the reforms and the assumptions behind the ideology were wrong. Today, people are talking about capacity building to address that mess. But the philanthropic response to this mess has made me cynical, even though I find myself on the philanthropic side now.

The current ideology is that the one with the money has the power, which may be true, but not the knowledge. We still allow an ideology to permeate that is influenced by money instead of acumen and thoughtfulness. Then we demonize those who don't understand what capacity building means and discount that the people on the ground are actually smart and more connected, just in ways we may not understand. They actually have more capacity than they know—than we know—but are told their capacity must conform to a more western standard, even if that standard creates missed opportunities.

Nonprofit 02 (Grassroots African organization)

Capacity building for me means that people on the ground look at what they want to do and see what they lack in accomplishing the goals they have set for themselves. Then they seek somebody or something or a method that can help them reach that level in order to accomplish the task at hand that can give them the results they want. It is looking in their toolbox and adding the tool that is not there to complete the work.

What it doesn't mean for me is somebody thinking, 'Those people lack the capacity to build on their own, especially in handling the resources that I am giving them. Therefore, I will come in and direct the capacity building.'

When this outside method fails, that same person goes back and says, 'I built your capacity and you failed.'

The second thing it doesn't mean is, 'I'm going to give to technical support, but not give you the money to accomplish the task.'

Capacity building is not a top down approach. It is a mutually collaborative process. When I hear capacity building mentioned by donors or at conferences I attend outside of Africa with donors, I shiver because it implies they are bringing impact from the Global North to the Global South. They can bring the money and resources, but they cannot bring the impact. The impact can only happen locally. It is not just the donors at conferences. They come visit a project, stay in some nice hotel, have a driver, go visit a few places and give some money that is restricted or say some words of encouragement, but not give real resources, nor the time to listen to the people they have the opportunity to meet who can tell them how the capacity should be built. Then when something goes wrong, they say, 'I did something for you. Why couldn't you do more with what I gave?'

What I really think capacity building should be is a mutual process where the people on the ground are giving capacity, but also knowledge in what needs to be done without fear of their ideas being rejected for not being sexy enough. It also means donors building the capacity for honest dialogue with an organization before building the capacity of the organization.

Donor 03 (Asia focused donor)

Capacity building is building the know-how and knowledge of either yourself as an organization or more importantly, of your partners, to more effectively address certain issues or topics.

Nonprofit 03 (Asia & US based organization)

I think capacity building is very important. We think about capacity building in terms of how do we get the beneficiaries of our work to take the message forward and create a ripple effect, because we know we will not be able to reach the same amount of people with our limited staff. This happens by making sure the services they receive are at a caliber that will make them want to share their experiences with others.

Beyond the borders of our own organization, I think there is a broader definition of capacity building for nonprofits, which is also vital to the organization's growth. This includes board development, skill development and leadership development. We're an all-woman team. We are all women of color and varying ethnicities. We're also very lean, so there are some dynamics in place around the type of leadership expected of us and the types of circles we're supposed to congregate in. Those dynamics go more to promoting our diversity and leanness, but how does that build our capacity? How do we even fundraise from this dynamic? It can get tricky.

Donor 04 (US based global donor)

What really comes to mind with regards to capacity building is when I think of nonprofits, social sector organizations or social enterprises, I think of them as really focused on refining their program model. Very much trying to change a life through the various causes in the social sector. However, I think most NGOs spend most of their time and dollars exclusively on program activities and not nearly enough on non-program activities such as accounting, IT, finance, and development/revenue generation. When I think of capacity building, it feels like a term that a funder uses to describe a certain grant that goes to a grantee organization.

The big lead up is that I think NGOs and funders agree that most NGOs need to step up their game from a portfolio support perspective, if they want to scale as an organization and reach more people. Capacity building could be making sure an organization has good M&E. It could be hiring more folks to the development team. It could be profession-alizing a business plan. I think capacity building primarily—but not exclusively—tends to be related to non-programmatic activities for a nonprofit that are services being provided by someone from outside of the organization. It could be a current funder or future funder.

Nonprofit 04 (Africa-based, social enterprise hybrid)

The improvement of somebody's skills, knowledge, understanding or competence. From my view, I look at capacity building from the heart, the head and the hands. The heart being the passion and the vision, the head being the intellectual knowledge or concepts, and the hands being physical skills. For me, capacity building lies between the sec-ond two, being able to further build or develop someone's intellectual capacity or practical tools. So the output of capacity building would be a better version of someone or something after the investment has been made, and in my view it would lean more toward a knowledge program rather than an improvement of a physical skill.

Donor 05 (European-based international donor)

Education and education and education. Capacity building is recogniz-ing the importance of education, but education with purpose. Also ed-ucation for specificity of implementation or for operations or what-ever an organization needs.

Nonprofit 05 (US & Europe based international nonprofit)

It's the idea that there are all these amazing organizations that are started and there are incredible visionaries and leaders who are working towards something, but the reality is that they might not have the skillsets or opportunities or access to the information, edu-cation or expertise needed to really build up the business.

Even within our own organization and the people and businesses that we serve, capacity building is really around building up the organiza-tion in order to scale and increase its impact. This is more of a per-sonal perspective, but even if you're trying to maintain the status quo, capacity building still needs to happen. As times change and you need to refine and adjust a business model, capacity building is necessary in terms of building out new technology platforms, building out a physical location or even reducing the size of a project or staff. This can be seen as capacity building through refinement. Understanding where resources are best utilized and cutting instead of expanding for the sake of project or mission growth. I think capacity building is critical in terms of increasing impact, not always increasing scale.

Scale

Donor 01 (US-based Africa donor)

(Sighs) Scale. Again this is a word that I believe should mean finding your organization's greatest breadth of impact and that looks completely different for every organization. It becomes problematic when we think that you can copy and paste a solution to create scale, especially this idea that you can copy and paste from country to country in the developing world, particularly in Africa. You would never tell a great nonprofit in the US, 'Why aren't you scaling to Canada,' so I'm not sure why we do that in the developing world.

Nonprofit 01 (US based international focus)

I haven't wrapped my hands—or my head—around scale, just the pressure to scale. I just haven't, because there can be so much growth in a project you're doing or in one specific partnership and you see the improvement, but how do you put that in terms of scale? Is it a matter of reaching more people or going deeper and making more meaningful gains with the same population? I also think numbers can be so misleading.

I think the starkest example of that is creating free primary schools for thousands of children. So now you have thousands of children technically in school, so you can tick those boxes and say, 'increase in numbers means we've scaled,' but how do we know that the scale has resulted in the same high-level education of the pilot project or are they getting educated at all? I think I understand why it's become sort of important, but I still don't understand my so much value has been placed upon scale. The way I interpret scale and many around me do is that it is an empty numbers game. Yeah, can't wrap my hands around it. How's that for being honest with a funder?

Donor 02 (Africa based international donor)

(Laughs) You know, I'm a different type of donor. First, I am African and have worked for nonprofits on the continent and in the United States before working for a donor. It took some time for me to see that these words we use are there behind the curtain with the 'Great and powerful wizard.'

Really, they mean nothing, but it frustrates me that we are not allowed to define them as donor-driven, but create a nebulous meaning that gives nonprofits and recipients false understanding while absolving donors of their roles in the confusion.

Scale is a very fancy sophisticated word designed to scare some and make others sound smart. Personally, I don't understand the concept of scale as we commonly use it. What do you scale? There is no silver bullet. If scale means reaching out to more people with more services then yes, that's fine, but that is not how we really define scale. We don't want to put real money behind providing more services, which is the practical meaning of scale, we want to put less. We don't consult governments either and I don't believe you can have true scale without government involvement.

I laugh at some of my western counterparts when they talk about scale. I remember once I asked a New Yorker if he was from Texas and he was offended. It's the same country and he wants to explain to me the differences between the two states in one country, but fails to understand the diversity between two actual different countries within Africa, where there aren't just cultural differences, but serious linguistic and economic and philosophical differences. But we talk of scale without taking any of these things into account.

Scale is something that works for the private sector, because you are dealing with goods, not people. When people are involved, they are consumers. With nonprofits, people are not equated to the consumers, but to the goods. What does that say about our approach, about our ideas of success? When there are problems with goods and services within a business, there is usually a contingency plan in place. Human beings are too complex to create any similar kind of blanket template plan. But we continue this approach and wonder why we fail.

Nonprofit 02 (Grassroots African organization)

Oh dear. Scale...I have never known any community on the ground that talks about scale. It is a word I hear at conferences. It's a word that means multiplying things so they become bigger. To me, scale is doing something, looking at it and knowing how deep you can go, not just always how wide you can go. Scale indicates numbers for counting people, but not accounting for them.

The numbers scratch the surface of the work, but if you want to have an impact, it has to have a depth and a breadth, but always with a Reflection Action Process. Reflect on the original goals and on the current status. Act where is necessary and reflect again accordingly. Plan and acknowledge mistakes in order to not repeat them. Grow in maturity as well as organizationally, not just adding numbers because that is what you are told should be done.

What I hear in conferences is donors saying they want to fund a project that has scalability. Their definition of scale sounds like growing the people being served from 100 this year to 1,000 next year. If it is not going in that direction, then it is not scale.

The growth may not be in the number of people, but in the strengthening of the services they receive. It may be that the scale occurs in allowing the community to become more self-reliant. The funny thing is that there is something ironic, almost hypocritical in the donor approach. When we want to hire new staff to help with new projects or implement elements of a new approach to a project where we currently are unfamiliar, donors will say no. It is better to train our core staff on what they don't know and not bring in new staff when a project may be finite.

But then the same donors push us to scale the numbers of the people we help in the community, sometimes to other communities, where we have little data on whether our approach is needed or will work. When we try to implement the same process of strengthening what exists and not needlessly growing the numbers, we are told this approach is wrong.

So I am still a bit confused about the meaning of scale, because I think the people who talk to me about scale are also confused.

Donor 03 (Asia focused donor)

Scale is more of a market systems approach that has been proven effective to bring projects to a larger scale. Scale is the quantitative outreach of reaching thousands and millions rather than, in your pilot phase, reaching one hundred, and learning what's working and what is not.

Nonprofit 03 (Asia & US based organization)

Scale I think I have to view from an American point of view, since our nonprofit mainly raises money from there, and perhaps it is the same general view in philanthropy. It seems as though scale is always a success indicator. But sometimes you have to think about depth versus scale. I think scale is very important. There are many ways programmatically, for example, I should scale or partner or collaborate, but sometimes the efficacy of, 'go deep, but prove something for the sake of scale and not the sake of impact," is questionable.

I'll give a concrete example, if that's helpful, from a project we were doing around sexual reproductive health training for local workers in a community. There was pressure from some of the funders who asked us how we could commoditize the model so that we could reach more women. But this is very difficult work in the cultural context and, in many ways, getting our access to care once we've done the trainings was more important than simply focusing on the numbers. For us, scale meant growing the effectiveness of the training, but it was made clear to us that scale to them meant reaching more women.

Donor 04 (US based global donor)

If impact is the toughest word to define in the social sector, then scale is probably 1A. Scale for me means further reach of a program. Most organizations start by having a direct intervention with a defined constituency. Scale is discovering how you have a greater influence over that target constituency, but not necessarily doing it from a direct basis. You could, though. Scale in it of itself is just doing more programming or delivering more of something to a larger number of people. There are certainly efficiencies and inefficiencies in terms of scale.

Scale is not necessarily to me just meant to be replication or blowing out an existing model; it means having a greater influence in the problem that you're trying to solve. Scale starts with a basic understanding of how large the problem is that you are taking on and understanding the NGO's ability to tackle that problem. From there, you can determine if you are in a position to get further and further into being the longer term solution of a problem. Scale then becomes the aspirational term to having greater impact.

Nonprofit 04 (Africa-based, social enterprise hybrid)

The growth of an initiative that increases its impact and increases the number of beneficiaries with whom the initiative is working. So if there is a target beneficiary group or, in my case, with enterprises, a target market, scale would continue to resemble the same target market, just with increased services and support.

For me, instantly when I think of scale though, I immediately begin to think of systems. I think of other players that are able to take a foothold in an initiative and also be drivers. So government comes to mind and actually the private sector can play a part, too. Scale is not just about the target market, but also the type of influencers that are choosing to get behind and drive an initiative and drive outcomes. I like these terms.

Donor 05 (European-based international donor)

Scale is leaving no one behind. It's ensuring that if something really works and everyone should have it or if it should reach everybody, then that's where we need to head.

Nonprofit 05 (US & Europe based international nonprofit)

Scale. Scale, scale, scale. It's the big jargon word. Well, it depends. I have a different perspective on this and I guess it's based on passion point. I think the definition is limited only by the person defining it. Scale for some could mean completely changing the lives of a few people, and the personal relationship with the beneficiaries is enough for someone to feel like enough has been done. If it's a personal mission, as opposed to a large scale focus, then the passion behind the mission will shape the outcomes differently.

To scale, for me, means being able to utilize your model and obviously replicate it for impact—I'm gonna use all the jargon now (laughs)—to impact change over time in a way that's sustainable and longer lasting. With scale, the most important thing is not scaling for scale's sake. Not everything is meant to be scaled. At all. Scale is only relevant when there is an existing need. So if your organization or purpose is particular to a localized mission, geography or issue, then it could be done. Then it relates back to the timeframe.

You can accomplish something and that's great. And then you can move on to something else. Nonprofit leaders don't always understand this. Your organization doesn't need to be in existence forever. And that's success. Moving on sometimes is seen as failure even when the mission has been accomplished, just because it hasn't been scaled, but if the original community was served as wanted, scale should not be the indicator for success.

Organizations should only be driven to scale when they see a clear need for macro change and not because the donors mandate it within their giving guidelines. So if you find that there is a model, a module, a service or an intervention that can support a need across geographies or populations or even timeframes, then that warrants scale. From a socially responsible perspective, that is when you should feel motivated to scale that work as a global citizen. You shouldn't horde what you're doing like a secret sauce out of fears over ownership, but really be able to offer it up to others.

I'm proud of how we have scaled at our organization, because it is not us seeking new partnerships that only benefit numbers on an annual report; we're working at multiple sites globally and what has driven our scale is that over 500 businesses and potential partners have contacted us over the course of one year saying, 'We need your programming. Please help us with your expertise and services.'

At that point in time, you think, 'Holy shit! What are we doing to accommodate these requests from businesses and from high level vendors?'

This is when it kind of hits us over the head that we need to scale the services. There is an obvious need and we have to be capable of fulfilling that need. And it's better for us to go to a donor and show the need and the interest instead of creating gaps where there are none for the sake of scaling the donor's demands.

Monitoring (or Measuring) & Evaluation – M&E

Donor 01 (US-based Africa donor)

So, measuring and evaluation is—or should be—an organization's ability to learn from what they're doing and, by learning, improve their work. What it tends to mean when it's gone too far in one direction is the system in which you report to funders. What it really should be about is what data does the organization need in order to learn and to improve? What data is also there to prove that the hypothesis and theory of change are true? If you have good funders, that should also be the same data your funders need, but that is not always the case.

Nonprofit 01 (US based international focus)

I think that there are certain things that can be measured and there are certain things that cannot be measured. There are certain things that can be measured objectively and others, subjectively. Although we can't always objectively measure or evaluate something doesn't mean there is no value in a subjective approach even though it may be a bit messier and a bit greyer. Getting a sense of what resources and expertise exist and are making a difference or improving a situation is extremely important.

For me, M&E indicates if your inputs and efforts are bringing more dignity and quality of life to the people you help. I think it's a really hard balance to know what gets invested into that, such as money, time and the actual work at hand. This is an area we are just getting into as a community. I know it's something we need to do, but I don't know how we will best approach it. I hope that we are thoughtful and that it is allowed to be a continual learning process in terms of how to implement it across the sector. I hope we are not lured into unstable reasoning on what we need to do to make this M&E a success.

I have a deep respect for the human element and any kind of measuring means interacting with people. I would want to ensure that these types of interactions, although done for evaluative purposes, also take into account possible traumatization and retraumatization of victims or survivors, all in the name of data. We don't want the people we help to ever feel like research subjects. I think the human piece—where applicable—cannot be forgotten.

Donor 02 (Africa based international donor)

Systematized learning and application. It's informing outsiders on key specific areas that they don't understand, but they need to know more about. I believe in this one, but I still find, when discussed in the sector, it is deprived of the human element. People are people and react in different ways that may one day seem to follow a specific trend, and the next look completely random. Monitoring and Evaluation is a good term, but the way that it has been used in development lately pushes it into the same category of buzzwords.

It's unfortunate, because M&E is necessary. As a nonprofit, you need to know how what you're doing is performing, if you are spending your money correctly and if that can be improved to benefit the work and the people. You should have a good understanding of what are your indicators and a shared definition of success, not only with a donor, but most importantly with the community.

Nonprofit 02 (Africa based organization)

Monitoring and evaluation is when the people on the ground who are doing projects or activities begin to take a hard look at all the key factors to determine what works and what doesn't work. The best kind of monitoring and evaluation is the self-reflective organizational kind, again going back to the Reflection Action Process. Having an eye of openness to critique and learn. Also, we have to be careful not to create a dependency on a program that needs to stop, and I mean this for both the donor and the community members.

But when monitoring and evaluation comes from the outside, what I have noticed as a person working on the ground is that there's a performance. People perform for the donor because they know what the donor expects and only cares about seeing, but they see that the donor indulges in the performance. The donors come with a checklist based on numbers and meetings and if the donors provide them with this list, they only show what's on the list to maintain favor with the donors.

To me, monitoring and evaluation personally means you want the programs to have a staying power that improves community or whatever it is we are trying to do. It only comes when you own it, when you are not afraid to make mistakes, and when you are open to new learning. After that, you can monitor and evaluate for the right reasons. People fear that they will be punished by donors, so they make up stuff in the monitoring and evaluation that they haven't done just to adhere to the checklist, but it just makes projects fail.

Donor 03 (Asia focused donor)

If you don't measure your work, then what do you do? You just don't have a clue what you're actually doing. M&E identifies the quantitative and qualitative results of what you do and looks at whether you have done what you said you would do by evaluating the sustainable impact of the results.

Nonprofit 03 (Asia & US based organization)

I think of monitoring and evaluation as a way to hold ourselves as an organization up to a mirror. It is a very important part of our strategic planning. We want to know how many campuses we are going to reach, how many live events, how many people we can connect with our movement and how much content we are going to generate. Then we measure the possibilities of our estimates and evaluate what can be done within our means.

It's interesting that for us, we speak of measuring and evaluation the way donors speak of scale. I don't know who is right or wrong, but it definitely highlights a disconnect. I do think that each donor has a different way about how he likes to measure or think about monitoring and evaluation.

The conversations about this can be cringe-inducing and sometimes worrying. It should be a useful tool to have so that we—we as in the nonprofits—are having the impact we need to have, but it shouldn't be a policing of the organization or of the spending by donors. M&E shouldn't turn into asking how high when the donor says jump or says scale. It should be spoken in a language that makes sense to us, instead of us appeasing the metrics based on what everyone wants to hear.

Donor 04 (US based global donor)

Monitoring and evaluation or measuring and evaluation. You can call it data collection or aggregation analysis as well. Whatever you want to call it, it is hugely important. It is measuring the impact of an organization. What I mean by that is M&E captures multiple data elements around an intervention in order to understand the true impact of that intervention.

M&E is needed especially when you are trying to attract later stage funding. It's that independent objective resource to measure the effectiveness or ineffectiveness of an intervention. It should be a function that all early stage organizations should strive to have at least a basic aptitude of carrying out. There should also be a third party evaluation of the organization as well, in order to validate the results and the organization's ability to deliver them.

I'm a big believer in doing early stage monitoring and evaluation to understand if the problem an organization is trying to solve can be done with their method. M&E helps us see if they are getting closer to their mission goals. I don't want to hamstring an organization because of positive or negative externalities, but M&E has to be an alignment of who you are trying to influence at a later stage. If you are trying to influence big aid or foreign governments or indigenous people, the types of information that you capture and share are going to be markedly different. I know people say that M&E is too often done for the donor and should be for the nonprofit itself, but really, the last mile influencers are why M&E is needed most.

Nonprofit 04 (Africa-based, social enterprise hybrid)

Oh gosh. They get worse! I feel like it's overused. I feel like donors often need to justify giving a grant to non-established, non-INGO, who are not asked to go through the same hoops as larger nonprofits. Yes, we need M&E to be able to step back and ask ourselves if we are, at the end of the day, achieving the reason why we exist.

A hybrid like ours, we look at two things to hold ourselves accountable to the mission. We look at how many jobs we have created and how many individuals within the low-income market have improved their lives based on our involvement. For us and for our beneficiaries, it is important to know that. In this way, M&E is a good thing, because it holds us accountable and lets us know if we are just doing things or if we are contributing to the reason why we exist and this much larger vision that we often define, but rarely track.

In theory, I very much like the idea of M&E, in its purest form. It should be done in real time. Let's get real time feedback, let's not wait until the program is over to see whether or not things are going well. I feel like in its actual form, it is overused and a waste of resources for a lot of organizations that already have limited resources. They should be directing those resources to deeper programmatic interventions, as opposed to really, really, really vigorous monitoring and evaluation. I understand that donors have to justify why they give their funds, but it is done either as a one size fits all blanket policy or done to give the appearance of everyone keeping busy.

I don't know if I have actually defined M&E, but if I had to give it a textbook definition, it would be the process of monitoring more of the ongoing action to see if it is working with an overall analysis of the objectives of the initiative. For example, in our work, we ask our entrepreneurs to pay a small amount to our program. Therefore, our M&E of seeing if we are delivering on what we want to do or what we say we are doing occurs more innately. We make it easy for our entrepreneurs to call us out and hold us more accountable, because they are not getting something for free. They have a larger stake in the quality of our services and provide us the feedback when our program has worked for them and when tweaks might need to be made.

We have the mechanisms in place for them to confidently and confidentially say, 'Your organization did or did not build a really strong marketing campaign for my new healthcare insurance that I'm marketing to pregnant mothers and I've paid you X amount of my revenue to get that service.'

We can measure our success in their success, while evaluating our strategies based on their inputs. Real M&E can be integrated into the fabric of how the organization runs, where we are ideally more beholden to our beneficiaries instead of our donors.

Donor 05 (European-based international donor)

It is hugely important to measure to know how we are doing, but at the same time, keep in mind why we are collecting that information. Sometimes we tend to use monitoring and evaluation systems that are not applicable or realistic for the real-life implementations and priorities of programs. Sometimes we are stuck with the models because donors are feeding into poor monitoring and evaluations systems. We do not allow nonprofits to have the flexibility to discover something new that may still lead to progress, but not the way it was laid out in the original proposal. Nonprofits are also at fault. They tend to stick to something that doesn't work just because, in their proposal, they decided this would be the way for evaluating their project.

Monitoring and evaluation requires thinking and should be modernized. We still use really old methods of how we do it.

Nonprofit 05 (US & Europe based international nonprofit)

I think that monitoring and evaluation is so incredibly key. Personally, having been on the giving side of philanthropy, as well as working for bad nonprofits before, I think it is so, so, so key. I think it is necessary and great that grants and donors demand this, because it's the diligence they need to do and the education the nonprofit needs that it may not otherwise get if never asked to analyze the merit of the work.

I think this is where the balance of human and business also comes into play, where nonprofits don't make a dollar at the end of the day, but they have to address what they seek out through their mission. If they don't have metrics or data collection in place to assess their work, then there is no indicator for if change is taking place. I believe nonprofits should have the freedom to refine their programming without fear of poor outcomes resulting in funding cuts, but they need to measure something in order to know what to refine or change.

Without monitoring and evaluation, it's just assumptions. It isn't accurate or real in any definitive way. Nonprofits often times try to tick off what grant-seekers are asking for versus really thinking about their programming and what they internally need. There's a lot of fear around M&E, which leads to tweaking the data, to have the data make the nonprofit look attractive or to collect the data for grant reports, but not program refinement. There's fear of program refinement that if the program is seen as not working via the data, the nonprofit will look vulnerable.

But I think it's incredible to be able to refine and assess, to reach a goal and move on to the next thing or dissolve the organization knowing the purpose was fulfilled, which I'm not sure everyone else agrees with, but that's my feeling. M&E needs to happen and happen regularly. It needs to be collected appropriately. It needs to be communicated with the beneficiaries of the work and with the donors, but driven by the organization. It should be core to the programming functions and not core to the development. Unfortunately, M&E often falls into the hands of or is directed by development departments and not the program team where it belongs.

I also think—ok, I know I'm really venting now, but—program staff and social entrepreneurs are not trained in M&E and the importance of it, how to collect it and its implication in their work from a business perspective, and not just a feel good human perspective. I think this is something that needs the most investment from donors, but also from the organization in terms of education.

If more grantees were willing to, in addition to grants, add a request for M&E funding, whether it's training and support, this would improve the mission. I hate consultants, but that's a whole other piece. I think they have a pretty set template—and it depends on who you get, obviously—but can be a poor fit for a nonprofit already on low funds who may have wasted funds to have the organization taken in the wrong direction.

So I wouldn't promote hiring consultants, but to have donors provide external support for M&E training would be key to organizational growth and mission reach. For a donor, this is one of the best investments, because after the donor leaves, the organization will now have a skillset that will last beyond the donor's grant.

Theory of Change

Donor 01 (US-based Africa donor)

Gosh, you're hitting all my jams. A theory of change in its simplest form is a hypothesis about what you think will happen when you do the intervention or the work that you plan to do.

Nonprofit 01 (US based international focus)

So I got asked this in a grant application not too long ago and I felt like I was out of the loop. I mean, I could take my interpretation of it, but I felt like it was something that other people had probably been more officially and efficiently trained in answering. I felt an implication that no matter how well I thought I could answer it, there was a secret code or a response that needed to be included that I did not know, because I didn't have the sufficient professional development or training. Nor did I have the time or research to go and ask others, 'What do you think is meant by theory of change?'

So I made what I thought was a common sense approach or my interpretation of it, but I...I was lost. They even gave an example to reference and I did all that, but I still felt like I was flunking the test. And if I am having this much trouble with it, imagine those who have to answer the same thing where English is not a first language or when this kind of verbiage is completely foreign, like smaller grassroots organizations. I think even asking the question can potentially create an uneven playing field. I think the idea of theory of change had some logic to it amongst its creators, but it was not a logic or theory that was shared as robustly as it could have been with those who have to live with it.

(Out of interest, I asked this person to provide the response to the grant application question, as well as could be remembered offhand)

I feel like I handled it OK, but I am not very good at gusseying up language when I feel I should be more obvious and pragmatic. I feel sometimes we can get caught up in feeling forced to speak in a way that's too esoteric. My answer was not complicated and I kind of feel like I was being called to give a complicated answer. I essentially repeated our mission statement, which I think already highlights the change we want to make.

Donor 02 (Africa based international donor)

I'm probably the worst person to ask to define this one. For me, it's really one of the most ridiculous terms. If I have to define it, I would say it's the sector asking, 'how do you resolve the mess created through previously funded programs that didn't make sense to have or support,' and sound smart doing it without really changing much. Donors are basically asking, 'How do we create a narrative and document the work we want to see without investing more money?'

Donors claim that theory of change is a way to clarify the timeline between the points of entry to the end result, but it comes off as a pretentious way to describe aspects of basic programming. The theory of change is the way people move from point A to point B with what resources they have and under the assumptions of their hypotheses. This sounds good if we are talking about goods, but again, we are talking about people. For me, theory of change is a way of forgetting about the basics and making things sound unnecessarily complex. Wanting to address a problem and having a good plan to do so does not always require a theory of change, but a theory of success.

For me, it's a very confusing term for people who are running programs day-to-day, from a basic standpoint, who are fighting with issues that they know how to address and do it with little or no money. We don't ask them enough in a thoughtful way, 'What do you need?'

Instead we ask them, 'What is the theory behind the change you are already making and can see, that I may not fund unless you sound more convincing in your response than in your work?'

All these words can be really confusing and, in this case, really counterproductive.

Nonprofit 02 (Africa based organization)

Theory of change would be the long-term vision of transformational impact to be achieved in the lives of beneficiaries and your methodology for achieving it.

Donor 03 (Asia focused donor)

Theory of change is a really important model to plan out and know where you are going in order to define outcomes and outputs.

Nonprofit 03 (Asia & US based organization)

(Long Pause) I think it would be a principle agreement and understanding of how an institution should develop and what essential components of the institution should remain over time.

Donor 04 (US based global donor)

Theory of Change is understanding the North Star of an organization. It tells me the purpose of why an organization exists. Theory of change should be an understanding by a social entrepreneur of a social problem and his or her potential solution to that social problem. There are a couple parts to theory of change.

There's the understanding of the direct impact and there's an understanding of the social impact. One of the clear examples of theory of change and how it ties to a mission or vision statement is Teach for America. Teach for America has the aspiration that one day, all children will be afforded the ability to quality education. Their theory of change is twofold: One, if you pick smart talented teachers and give them a bit of training, it will result in a better economic outcome for students. You may or may not believe that, but it is part of their theory of change.

The other part is that Teach for America believes that introducing new young teachers into an environment where the impact of their work is most evident, even for a short period of time, creates a higher level discourse on education reform in the USA. Then you can look at the intricacies of using alumni as change makers on whatever platform they choose to operate and feed back into the improved learning. You can see that Teach for America is single-focused in its objective, but multifaceted in its approach and the long-term impact it wants to create and maintain. Theory of change is an explanation of what you're trying to accomplish and how you plan to accomplish beyond programmatically.

Nonprofit 04 (Africa-based, social enterprise hybrid)

(Makes a face) Oh God. I take that back. I don't like *all* of these terms. I, straight away just, nonsense. When someone says theory of change to me, I immediately question their...path in this space and the incentive for why they are asking about that, especially after I have or some other organization has already explained why it exists.

We have already laid out the end cause of the organization and the modalities we're investing in to get there. To me, it feels like it is...an ineffective way and sometimes an intimidating way for people to over-intellectualize a situation and for people to use their upper hand of possibly having more academic or theoretical experience in this space to overcompensate for not having experience on the ground.

I rarely ever hear practitioners in the field talking about theory of change. But, if I was to describe it after my rant, I would say it was an organization asking, 'What are the beliefs and the assumptions that we're making that are going to create the immediate outcomes, as well as the much larger scale impacts?'

There is a sliding scale of when impact is going to be created tangibly, how much of the time before impact is done laying the groundwork for that impact and how much time after is used fruitfully to sustain and possibly grow that impact. You have to identify that critical path that takes you from immediate action to the larger vision. Theory of change is each step you take along that path that happens in between.

An example of this would be an organization saying, 'We believe that business development services are going to create less poverty within Tanzania. So to prove that hypothesis, we believe that investing in business advice, loans and proper working spaces, and all of the other vital inputs will result in better informed businesses. Better informed businesses will run as better situated commercial entities. That will make them more profitable and create more jobs. More jobs will lead to people being able to have financial stability and equity in their lives, in some areas for the first time ever. Financial stability means that people will be able to have and create more choices around health, education, family planning and contributing to the economy. Those choices will result in a higher standard of living for the population and growth of Tanzania as a country.'

So the theory of change is basically a mapping of your mission statement and the critical path to account for the ripple effects and ultimate change you hope to see, even though there are parts you just cannot be able to see. Overall, I think it's very silly.

Donor 05 (European-based international donor)

It's a theory. It's, how should I say this? I don't want to call it bullshit (laughs), but...it's another one of those fashionable terms. It's really about finding and detailing the way to make the difference, building on evidence and bringing that evidence to the community to show that your work is more than just a guess. There is some work, some data behind the guess, so that it is a very educated guess.

Nonprofit 05 (US & Europe based international nonprofit)

I hate this one. It just reminds me of theory of everything. OK, I'll be totally honest. I think theory of change is really bullshit and I think it's basically whatever the visionary believes and as soon as the visionary is paired with someone who is more of an implementer, that theory of change may change as soon as a strategic plan is put into place. I think the theory of change will change again when a major funder comes into play with a different giving guideline. Theory of change is essentially the scale of the model or the program itself. It's just a fancy term for how we address the mission we have.

Systems Change

Donor 01 (US-based Africa donor)

What I want systems change to mean is a changing of power dynamics. I think we can too easily believe (as donors and nonprofits) that just scale or just getting big enough or proving something in some randomized control trial—even though humans are not a petrie dish—is enough. We want to believe that we can find a solution to something that we can scale up and that magically, governments will take it on and then ta-dah! Systems change.

But what systems change at its core should actually be about is a power dynamic that is always increasing the power of the marginalized and decreasing the power of the oppressor, in my opinion.

Nonprofit 01 (US based international focus)

I believe it has something to do with very structural change at high levels of governance or economy or societal organizations. It is more of a structural view of society. How a society works versus how it can work and identifying the players who can make that change, with respect to governance, policy and the economy, as well as the rule of law. This can also be done through disruption, by putting an entrepreneurial lens on it.

Donor 02 (Africa based international donor)

Systems changes means how do we align funding dollars with leaders running programs to take over the role of the government where there is a void. It's a plan of how to create change without involving the government at a level comparable to if the government were involved. It is how a donor uses grants to change systems and processes and the status quo. All this, without involving the government, which is ironic since the government often creates the framework for how change can be implemented or expanded.

I know I came off as cynical in my responses, but many people who become cynical while doing this work leave. They can't take the bureaucracy and self-imposed obstacles associated with something as simple as wanting to improve the world or the lives of the most underprivileged in the world. I remain because I see hope in the work. My cynicism is with the language, not the work. I do my best to support good work, needed change and tear down the systems preventing that change. Can that be my definition of systems change?

Nonprofit 02 (Africa based organization)

Many times, our communities or our brains have been set up in a way that makes us think that this is how things need to be. Because we believe that, we find ourselves always doing the same things cyclically without challenging this process. So from this point of view, systems change has two meanings to me.

The first meaning is to have a view of how things currently are and understanding how they need to be disrupted for the sake of progress. I like the word disruption. I work with many youths who have no history of college education in their families and the only images of black youth they see in movies and also on the news are negative. So we changed this view by not only providing the education and explaining its importance, but introducing that missing piece of the example of college-educated black people for them to see that it could be done.

Have them interact to see that their paths were not entirely different. To me, this is the disruptive systems change I support.

The second meaning of systems change to me is more of a system of change. When a community comes together after identifying that something must change in order to treat an issue or improve conditions, the entire community assumes roles to facilitate that change. They become the system for change, by identifying what is wrong with the current system and how they can be the best agents of change. In this meaning of systems change, it is completely a community effort, not something external. As a community, in order to create systems change, we have to be fully immersed in both the present conditions and the consequences of the interventions, both good and bad.

The worst consequence for an external organization applying a program that is not beneficial to a community is that donors will no longer support it and have them divert funds or resources from those programs, but the nonprofit can pack up and go home if unsuccessful. A community does not have the same luxury. The consequences mean everything to its members, so the systems change starts with them or has to start there.

Donor 03 (Asia focused donor)

Oh my gosh. (Laughs) I'm laughing just because everyone always uses these words, but they mean something different to so many people. Ah, systems change. Often to me, systems change depends on whether you're talking about an actual change of a system or an approach. When I think of systems change, it's much more of an approach. What it implies is that you think very holistically about how inputs or changes affect an overall dynamic as opposed to one piece of a puzzle. You can't have an impact on one piece, whether it's an organization or a national policy or a national response to a social issue.

When I think about systems change in my work, whether it is within the context of either community or national level, it is about change across a variety of different components that make up the whole. You may...ah even with this one, I am finding it hard to articulate. I guess I would say systems change would impact (pauses) more of the whole than just part of the whole. It means some sort of shift on how the response is being done on a policy level, on a finance level and on a capacity level to really make a significant change.

If you're talking about a national response, systems change is going to require a significant shift and alignment between the different components that make up that response. A policy on its own is not going to make a difference if there is no funding behind it, and that's not going to make a difference if there is no capacity behind it. There also has to be real political will behind it, which would tap into the informal systems that drive social norms. Otherwise what you have is a beginning of a shift, but it won't be complete enough to have an overall systems change.

Nonprofit 03 (Asia & US based organization)

In philanthropy, a lot of terms just become en vogue. Systems change is the latest term that is going to save everything. Every couple of years we have new terms that we love that don't seem to mean much, which is how we arrive at systems change. Thinking about systems changes and trying to get a nonprofit to reach that level is, in some ways bullshit, pardon my language.

In some of the communities where we work, like one region in Asia, the reason we are there as an intervention is because the policy and the government are not there. There is a lot of corruption, or legal enforcement isn't there, so we are often a stopgap measure for when things don't work. To artificially turn us into equations where people plus communities is somehow meant to equal systems change without accounting for the complexities is nonsensical. It is about recognizing the complexities and unpredictability of the world in which we live, not fitting it into a pretty little diagram on a flowchart. To us, systems change is just the pretty little diagram with no real-world application.

Donor 04 (US based global donor)

When I think of systems change, I think of solving a problem or thinking of a problem from a holistic perspective. I believe that most nonprofit organizations, at some level, should have a goal to change a system. There are cultural norms. There are expectations that exist today and when you start to talk about systems change, you have to look at how a community operates differently in order to have an impact on the constituents in their community. In many ways, systems change is the exit strategy for a number of nonprofits.

It starts with direct impact, meaning an organization delivers a program directly to a set of constituents. The next evolution is finding implementing partners to deliver your curriculum. Perhaps a third would be policy or advocacy work. At the end of the day, the effort for most social entrepreneurs and nonprofits is to fundamentally change a system. Systems change for me is very much the end-game for the nonprofit sector.

Nonprofit 04 (Africa-based, social enterprise hybrid)

I actually really do like this one, because I believe that anyone within the impact space should be thinking about systemic change, especially sustainable systemic change. We are not going to rework too much in silos. The nonprofit sector is too ego-driven. That is not the only problem, but the ego-centric nature just facilitates more work in silos instead of less.

If we're going to be ambitious—no, it isn't even about being ambitious—if we're going to be real about sustaining the impact of our initiatives, we need to be looking at how the system that we're working within, the system that has created these challenges we have come in to address, can be altered to accept and maintain the change we have deemed necessary. We're essentially putting ourselves out of work and returning the responsibility of sustaining impact back in the hands of government or newly established actors

For me, systems change is capacity building or influencing an infrastructure that is high level or a system that can alter its existing state of being or existing characteristics. In my context, it is about working with the government of a specific African nation to inform them on how to invest in more Small and Medium Enterprise (SME) growth. We are working with them on that already, but the systems change we want to accomplish is visible when we work with the Ministry of Education and advise them on how to create an entrepreneur curriculum that is now being developed and implemented within the educational system of the country.

If that system creates more entrepreneurs and, in turn improves the economy, then we will feel as though we have not only accomplished our mission, but made our mission obsolete, because the system we were fighting to change has been changed.

Another example of systems change is looking at creating more angel investors within the country, such as large corporations or high net worth individuals that drive corporations. We can provide the guidance for them to be the new change agents within the country and not deplete government resources. It also reduces dependency on international philanthropic grants and moves the model smartly towards investment. There is not just one way of creating systems change.

Systemic growth should fundamentally be, I feel, a requirement of impact work. If there isn't an ambition to work at a systemic level, then individual initiatives, in my opinion—and I know this is ambitious—should group within a larger consortium that is leveraging the core focus better. They should be collating their efforts to drive a much larger level of change. Otherwise, we're just busying ourselves in the short term.

Even if impact and sustainability are achieved, for example in a school that has managed to bring top level education to serve a population of over 2,000 children and managed to make itself sustainable. That is very genuinely impressive and commendable, but when success like that exists in a silo, no matter how large the bubble, there are missed opportunities that possibly millions of others in need are not benefitting from who could.

The reason for this disconnect could be that ego of the nonprofit leaders I mentioned before, not wanting to either cede any power or recognition for the work or not looking at the problem systemically, with no connections to the people best positioned to change a system in which they operate. A seismic change is not being required of nonprofits. Systems change is about slightly shifting the needle of the context that frames the problem.

Donor 05 (European-based international donor)

That's my favorite. My favorite is really building systems, systems for action, systems for working. Of course, systems have to evolve and have to build on new technology. To give you a practical example, we have enabling technologies, such as smart phones, which maybe two years ago could not have been used to show videos to people who are illiterate. Now, if you can use those videos to train people in remote villages to save a life or if you can use those videos to teach children how to read in a more functional way, you should be doing it.

This is creating technology that enables...I don't want to say enables a system, because it's systems by system, but it's building those networks that can improve the quality of whatever we do. While at the same time, and what I love about it is that having the system is creating a way of monitoring that system. That's a gain where we have unprecedented opportunities with the new technology. We're just not smart enough to use all the data that already exists that we don't even know that we collect. So we have to learn how to find new ways to build systems and find new ways to evaluate the system.

Nonprofit 05 (US & Europe based international nonprofit)

Systems change is actually a great one, because systems, from my perspective, have existed since the start of civilization. Systems have always been created and systems need to be adapted and refined, the same way any organization or any human being would have to adapt and change over the course of a lifespan. This is more of a macro or meta perspective of it, but I think systems change really needs to happen more.

I think systems change is something really important for all nonprofits to consider because, at the end of the day, you have a mission that you are trying to achieve and, for the most part, the reason an obstacle is in place or a need exists is because the system in place is creating that in some way, shape or form. It is essential to acknowledge that system responsible for the obstacle in order to create a realistic mission statement with an end goal. It is also needed to identify if that systemic obstacle is being addressed by another organization, institution, government or external party, because these will be your partners in accomplishing your goals even more than a donor.

Identifying the current system doesn't mean that the organization should be built to take on the system, but it should be built with an understanding of the system in which it operates, if for no other reason than to know how much progress the current system will allow for the mission intervention to have. Applying a mission to a system to which you are ignorant is sort of like picking out an outfit for an event that you know nothing about. You're basing your success on luck versus preparation.

An organization needs to understand the root cause of the reality it is trying to improve. Systems change is looking at the macro cause of a problem, even if the organizational programs are structured to help individuals. It is the obligation of the nonprofit to see how the system is perpetuating a problem before it can draw conclusions about its own work. If there are gaps in the system, see if your organization can fill them. It may not be about a systems change, but systems identification is crucial.

For our organization, we are trying to do capacity building for businesses in remote areas. One huge roadblock for a business to be sustainable in the long-term and to scale is market access. You can create an incredible website or incredible presence at a trade show or sales strategy or pricing or buying relationships. If a large scale brand does not feel comfortable sourcing from homeworkers or decentralized producers, if that's the way the system, which is in place—very high risk, there's no compliance, there are a lot of issues in place with so little visibility—then those large scale brands will never buy or increase the percentage above their comfort zone. Change will never happen at a high level. There will be change, but it isn't going to be systemic.

As an organization, we have realized that reality. When you look at systems change, you have to look at all stakeholders and all partners involved within the system. They all need to come to the table in order for a change to occur. We were approached by a corporate stakeholder who pointed at these things in a heartfelt way to tell us why they were not sourcing from these communities. They had made a tremendous commitment to pledge from decentralized producers, but said they had no way of implementing it, as their compliance team would not allow them to introduce new vendors into the system.

Then we looked at all the different players in the system to see what was holding it back at different levels and timeframes within the system. We were able to bring this corporate stakeholder to the table, along with many of the other stakeholders and industry leaders. Then we had a deep dive into the real issues holding them back from sourcing from these producers. If it's a set of standards for decentralized producers, then let's establish that together. Let's figure out what those standards are, as well as the assessments and remediation. Let's pilot it, refine it and get it out there.

Systems change takes time, but it is not a waiting patiently game; it's an action-oriented 'now' approach. Any steps forward is progress, but organizations cannot go in with the mindset that problems will just resolve themselves over time with minor or individualized interventions. When we asked the stakeholders to identify the most pressing obstacle for working with decentralized producers, they all agreed it was the many muddled layers of subcontracting that seemed too difficult, too messy and too sticky to touch.

However, in just three meetings with major brands, all the major stakeholders at the table and us as the intermediary who were in the right place of the system, were able to find the solution and it wasn't as hard as people said it would be. Systems change is possible, but takes eagerness. The dangerous piece of systems change is the waiting game and trying not to get lost in the timeframes. Without the drive to want to see systemic change, nonprofits can get lost in the gaps and stunt their own impact.

In asking all those established sector leaders to define these terms, it dawned on me that I was attempting to capture the difficulties in navigating the rough seas of jargon only from the perspective of those with enough experience to chart a viable path for their organizations. However, for many of the people who are nascent to engagement— the person who discovered an ingenious way to tackle poverty or inequality within a neglected community, to a donor much like myself when I arrived at my foundation with a desire to treat every dollar we give as a life-changer—this language can be an arduous detour from immediate action. And yet, much of it serves a purpose, which could delay the immediate action, but ensures that it is an effective action.

With that in mind, I wondered how these definitions would look through the eyes of those in this space with little to no experience with jargon: A donor and nonprofit leader, both with less than a year of experience in their current roles at the time of our conversations. As you can imagine, they struggled. And yet, their struggles are absolutely no indication of their work.

The donor is not just funding great work, but taking very forward approaches in strategic grant-making. The nonprofit contributor didn't bother waiting for funds to be raised before creating a clever and compelling plan to save lives. If judged by results alone—the thing we claim matters the most—we would all be in awe at their courage and success. Keep that in mind as you wade through their responses.

Sustainability

New Donor (US based domestic and international donor. Less than a year experience)

Ok, I need to think about it. How do I define it? (Sighs) We talk a lot about sustainability. (Long pause) I feel like I've been taught to ask 'how sustainable is your organization? What percentage of your budget is grants and what percentage is the initiatives that are meant to bring in money?' but we have never internally had a discussion for what we expect as a response. I guess sustainability is how much an organization can wean itself off of grants, but I am not sure how applicable that is to every type of nonprofit.

New Nonprofit (Latin American organization)

I think it refers to the ability for a person or a nation or an organization to find the means to be able to function properly without major waste. I would say it's a reasonable use of resources, especially financially or economically.

Impact

New Donor

(Sighs heavily) Yeah, that's a really hard word, actually, for me. Our foundation has been having a lot of conversations about that lately. The measure of... (long silence) doing something good. Impacting somebody's life. That can be directly or in indirectly. I'm sorry, I'm not being really good at this. (I reassure that there is nothing to worry about and to continue as seen fit or not.)

I think for us, as an organization, we want to know how we can create impact, but we don't always say it in that way. I mean, we think about the amount of money we have of course, but we also think about direct and outsourced mentorship, as well as our advice on any topic they bring to us without it affecting our grants to them. To me, that has an impact, but I am not sure it is the definition others use. As a donor, I think of impact as the impact of our actions on the organization more than just the grant.

And I mean that when we look at the impact of our actions—both good and bad—and more about how we are behaving as donors more than how they are working as implementers. There is that layer of how we examine the repercussions of our decision making on the organization and people they are meant to be helping out of poverty. We want to foster, not impede the big idea of ending poverty, so 'all in' has to mean 'equally in.'

New Nonprofit

An impact is a positive consequence on many levels that is foreseen in the making of an action or series of actions. It is a consequence that has been foreseen and has to be planned. There is a need for a protection for the future. An impact is not like a real consequence of something, but it has to be measured prior to the action that is going to be carried out.

When talking about impact, we need to think about the people or the specific area of expertise that we want to have an impact on. Basically, to sum it up, I would say it is a positive consequence on a not so short-term, more like a long-term thing. There is a dimension of planning and—what else did I say? It includes the area in which one is expecting his or her action to have an impact.

Capacity Building

New Donor

(Laughs) It's so interesting. We do use all these words all the time. In context, you think you have an idea what they mean, but on its own, it's tough. How would I define capacity building? (Long pause) Creating procedures and processes to enable people to have a larger impact. (Note: despite the brevity of the response in written form, the response took nearly two minutes in real time.)

New Nonprofit

(Long pause) Umm, I think it's the capacity—well, the ability—of a group to carry out its projects, according to the resources available to the person or the group.

Scale

New Donor

That's been one of these big words that we've been constantly hearing about. So how do you define the word I guess? (Long pause) Basically, gosh. Implementing the principles that work on an individual level to a... (Pause) to a society level, I guess. (Pause), I would say scaling something would be moving something from an idea to a full sentence. Then looking at the principle to see if it is possible. Scale is a way to see if it is an action that can function really well on its own or if it is just something that can function on a really large scale.

New Nonprofit

It's a unit...of measurement that is specific to an area of expertise. I mean there is no universal scale, I would say, but working in a specific field, there is a specific scale to measure...all kinds of things, but it could be like to measure the impact or measure the adequacy of the means according to the results. It is a unit of measure for people or organizations working in Human Rights. It's also a tool to be used to plan an action or series of actions in the future. It's a tool to adjust and adapt one's ideas and dreams to reality in order to maximize the impact that one is going to have.

Monitoring/Measuring and Evaluation

New Donor

(Long pause) Basically looking at the outcome of the results and measuring the impact. Also measuring the outcome of the process, measuring the success and evaluating what actually happens. I guess in the corporate world, it's about looking at the numbers and looking at what that data means. In the nonprofit world, it's looking at the financials, well not so much, but looking at the numbers outside the financials as it relates to the progress of programs.

It's interesting because you have to measure the impact and many times the impact is not necessarily measurable with numbers. I don't know. I'm so sorry. I feel like I'm not being helpful. Well, you wanna prove that no one knows what they're talking about so I'm helping you there.

New Nonprofit

Oh God. (long pause) I would say...I know it's a way of working in a professional way, but based on, in my opinion, what it shows about the person or organization, it shows consciousness and it shows the ability to not only act in the present, but the will to improve one's action for the future or improve one's philosophy or stuff. It also shows some kind of humility, because in order to conduct an evaluation of one's self or organization, one has to accept the possibility that his or her philosophy might be wrong. However, the evaluation is necessary in order to adapt and adjust the method.

Theory of Change

New Donor

(Long pause) Gosh, I'm struggling with this one. Give me a sec. (Another long pause) I guess a model on how a desired change is expected to happen? I guess that's really textbook, but it's just not something we are used to saying in our foundation. Not yet. I'm sorry. I'm really struggling with this one.

(I ask, 'Why as a donor, do you think you are struggling with this one?')

I think because we are looking for the big ideas to support, we feel as though the organizations that get us the most excited already include an explanation for how their model for success is going to work. Asking for a theory of change sounds kind of redundant, just another hoop to make nonprofits go through because we're bored.

New Nonprofit

(Long Pause) It corresponds to an idealistic view on the Human Rights issues. If means that if it is a theory then it has to be systematized. People who agree with this theory of change somehow have to be convinced the theory must have a systematic impact. This is not only a hypothesis, but it's a theory, so it must correspond to reality and its many dimensions. This is just talking about the theory part of the expressions.

I would say that theory of change is kind of a necessity. One comes to think that things are meant to change for the better and to make it a theory assumes that there has been thought put into it and a plan to prove that it is real. It creates a powerful incentive for action. As for the change part of the expression, I came to believe that small actions may not always have the positive impact I want, but in some ways, one small action can lead to a positive effect that can lead to another positive effect, and in the end, one can reach his or her goals. And it's a real motivation for me now.

Systems Change

New Donor

Basically, when I think of systems change, there are certain processes and procedures that were put in place that created all these problems that an organization or people want to change through their work. Let's say there is a school with these systems that has already been set in place around curriculum and scores. Then someone comes along with a radical idea and reworks the core curriculum with the hopes of changing scores and giving them more validity. This would be systems change for me, to create a different outcome on a larger level. I think of it as a radical change from the norm.

New Nonprofit

Shit. Is this the last one? (Pause) OK, a system includes a theory and a concrete means of action. Means of action includes collaboration and cooperation among people and organizations sharing the same goals and philosophies. A system is more of a global level that includes theory and means of action at a higher level. I would say it is a global philosophy, but it also has a social dimension because it creates a community. Within a system there is a community, for a system should be open and not closed within itself in order create an evolution or change.

So I would say systems change is a coherent gathering of theory, philosophy, community and means of action.

3

From the Horse's Mouth: The Dos and Don'ts of Fundraising from the Donor Perspective

This is what started it all. After I attended a session designed to help nonprofits maximize opportunities for funding, which left me and a number of other attendees diabetic from all the cotton candy advice, I reached out to a few dozen donor friends for more realistic feedback to offer nonprofits. I won't go into any specifics about that convening, mainly because few specifics were given. Kidding aside, I know as well as anyone that many, if not all such sessions are organized with the best of intentions.

The problem I have with anything that is meant to inform nonprofits about donor engagement is when there is a lack of respect given to the audience and the subject matter. Attendees from the nonprofit sector are all treated like potentially great fisherman who are just a few tips away from landing the big catch, while donors are spoken of as a school of homogenous big fish. Even the language used to describe donor engagement in these events sounds like fishing, such as 'hook' or 'catch' donors.

I still remember the first responses I received from donor participants of that original 'Hard Truths' document. This was the opportunity many of them had been waiting for: not to scold or teach or even comfort, although all of those played a part in their feedback. They wanted nonprofits to know that, whether they represented direct funding or were intermediaries to funding, they were human beings first. The anonymity allowed donors to choose how hard or, in some cases, brutal their truths could be. If you think donors are always brutally honest based on that one eccentric donor you know with no filter, then you couldn't be more wrong.

Many grant-seekers repeatedly reduce philanthropists to either obstacles or advantages to procuring funds. I've had plenty of moments that were honestly painful to endure, because the person met me with certain precepts instead of speaking organically. Whether or not there are set metrics and parameters around my foundation's funding, my personality and preferences are not divorced from how I work. And this is the same for all donors.

One of my closest friends in the donor space loves PowerPoint presentations. I hate them. We fund in the same areas, but approaching us in the same way would be a serious mistake. You don't have to consult a crystal ball to know the difference. When people request a meeting with me, I usually explain before we meet what materials I want prior and what you should be able to discuss during the in-person meeting. It surprises me how many people still turn up with a presentation, requesting to go through it even after I've expressly asked for a more informal meeting, and I've already told them that I've read through their presentation.

I also understand that nonprofits are humans, too. I understand some use the presentation as a way to calm nerves. However, if I feel an organization can only be discussed in technical terms or if questions I ask that the materials cannot address are not addressed by the representative, it looks suspicious to me.

My colleague is the complete opposite, who prefers to be guided through a presentation, as it illustrates how the organization captures its mission and provides the nonprofit representative with the opportunity of real time critique on the materials from a donor perspective. We may fund in the same areas, but our approaches are quite different. There is no template to approach us the same, except one: treat us like people. Listen, ask and seriously engage us as you would want to be engaged by others.

Now when I think of people giving advice, I think back to the members of my family who would always tell me how the only honest way to earn money was through hard work, right before they went to play the lottery. I say this to preface the following advice by other donors.

There is always a chance of, 'Do as I say and not as I do' in what donors proclaim.

Whatever has been said here by donors, it is still an individual opinion, whether or not it is a shared opinion. There may be dos and don'ts that conflict each other. This is not to confuse nonprofits, but to further illustrate that no matter how far removed donors may appear or how strong power dynamics may seem to reign, the human component to fundraising cannot be overlooked or sacrificed in order to template your work. And with that, on to the experts.

●●●

Do:

We know that it's hard for someone who started an NGO to now become a fundraiser, a successful fundraiser. If you fall into this category, one of the first things to do is find and create ambassadors for your organization who can speak to your work in a way that makes you comfortable. Another thing to do is to reach out to organizations who specialize not only in helping new organizations with direct funding, but in guidance on how to move forward. There are tools out there available to help those who have no fundraising skills gain them.

●

Correspondence needs to be tailored to the capacity of the foundation to which you're applying/approaching. Being the only person in a family foundation office, I don't have time to read a two-page letter that's trying to make me cry over some horrible problem. Long 'heartstrings' letters actually make me angry. Cut to the chase!

●

If you can't explain it to me like you would a 12 year-old, that means you're either hiding something or you're not clear. I rather hear it in a concise way instead of buzzwords, but I understand that buzzwords exist for a reason, so...

•

Be honest about your intent when asking for a meeting. If you want a thought partner on an idea or a new project, say so. But if you just want to ask for a donation, or ask to renew a gift, just say so. Donors are not stupid yet people continually make this assumption all the time (they must, otherwise they wouldn't tell such blatant lies).

People are constantly saying they want to meet with my donor to 'pick her brain' or 'provide an update on what we're doing' when all they want is a donation. Just say that. Some donors are just not that complicated. And the best way to negatively impact any relationship is to lie. Additionally, wasting a person's time also impacts a relationship in a negative way.

•

One major 'do' from our perspective is for the prospective grantee to start the conversation with the 'Why' of the organization rather than the more nuts-and-bolts 'What' and 'How.' We want to see the passion behind a brilliant idea and understand that an initiative is boldly committed to attacking a big, important problem. If you can't sell us on that then what you do and how you actually do the work is not likely to resonate.

•

Frame your proposal around the beneficiary and how they are being helped by what you aim to do, as opposed to framing it around the organization. This is key for people who are brought on to fundraise and are not the founders.

•

If you want to reach out directly to me, just send a short handwritten note to the point of what you are really looking for.

●

A good development director I think sees their role as a colleague who has an experience base that can and should, in little ways, coach the donor to see what it is like in the field. Paint the most accurate picture, especially for those who do not have capacity for site visits.

●

If you get a direct email address to a funder, treat that opportunity with the thoughtfulness it deserves. As every funder is different, there is no verbatim template. Some donors want more, some want less, but they all want to be treated with respect. Make it explicit why you chose to reach out to them specifically, not just for money.

●

If I decide to fund your work, do make me feel like a close partner with periodic little updates rather than newsletters and annual reports. When I invest in you and your organization, I care deeply about you and the work—not just once a year—and I want to know how things are going. When things go less well than projected and you tell me, I am far more likely to continue to fund your work.

●

For a first-time donor to an organization, I think it is important to show how other donations have changed things for the better, rather than highlighting the need itself.

●

Donors should be ambassadors for your work with no expectations of fundraising beyond the funds donated. Your board should be the ambassadors with full expectations of fundraising.

In describing the relevance of what you organization does, if applicable; remember to include how you plan to no longer be relevant in the future. More donors want an exit strategy, not just for themselves, but for the programs and charities they support.

•

When meeting with a funder, it is important to understand what the goals are in an honest way, because once that's out there, there is a better chance for a natural overlap. It doesn't have to be a perfect overlap, just an honest one and will make for stronger partnerships.

•

Treat funders not just as a person, but as a person who is in this for a reason.

•

Balance your testimonials or beneficiary stories with a clear plan of action. I find many nonprofits hide inadequacies in the inspirational story of one person when others are not benefitting the same way. Or worse, they present their story as if they are the savior of the story. That is not the look you want to portray in your first introduction.

•

Teach your donors how to be ambassadors, but also understand that your donors don't only fund you, so equip them with the most brief and succinct info for them to pass on to other possible donors.

•

An organization that has been successful in obtaining a donation from an individual or foundation should always 'thank' separate from 'asking.'

When a donor is shown results of his/her contribution immediately after and regularly, it is much easier to ask a second or third time, or on an ongoing basis.

•

Collaboration should not begin with donors or even other NGOs. It must begin with the board. Board members must possess the ability to exhibit working together well in order for an organization to fully prosper, irrespective of the cause or size.

•

Create an environment in your meeting where hearing a 'yes' or 'no' doesn't present itself. The best way to know if the person you're meeting with is a good fit for your organization is to let them tell you and listen. Come ready to have a conversation instead of a pitch. There is no guarantee that it will lead to funding, but it will be much more appreciated. Already have the information in a pitch committed to memory, just in case you encounter a funder who doesn't want to have a conversation and just wants the data.

•

In a meeting for thirty minutes or an hour, try to map out or outline how you want that meeting to flow. If you end up not leaving enough time to speak about the challenges of your work where you need resources or not enough time for the ask, you can't expect that we can go over the set time. Obviously, try to account for moments where natural conversation might take over, but make sure you get the points in that you really want me to know before we end.

•

Question donors about their philanthropic objectives. This can paint a clearer picture of whether engagement is even a possibility.

●

Master your introduction, especially in conference settings. Know how to be short and sweet when we have limited time. Know how to make me want to know more if we're meeting in passing and know how to be thorough without being too stodgy if we have the chance for a longer first time meeting.

●

Develop an individualized plan of engagement with each prospective donor. Figure out how they wish to be engaged (phone/email/in-person/etc.), what info resonates with them (heartstrings anecdotes; hard data & metrics), who is your liaison (donor directly, staff, board members, etc.), and their desire to participate in thought leadership of your work.

●

Be willing to brainstorm. Direct funding is not always a possibility, but if you're willing to have a lateral discussion, something much better can come of the meeting than a no.

●

Be up front. My mother used to tell me when I was young, 'you better tell me what happened before somebody else tells me.' It's the same for me now with my grantees. Don't let me find out from somebody else.

●

Be prepared to tell me how you found me. Although our organization accepts a certain level of unsolicited requests and I, myself, am quite open to introductions made from people I know, there is a limit. I will not entertain any requests from anyone who appears to have done a poor online search or even purchased my details from data firms.

•

Read the foundation's strategy before you initiate contact and indicate that your work is a good fit and exactly how. This is more important than a generic proposal to me.

•

When using statistical data to support the mission statement of the NGO, be sure the information is relevant. When there is a disconnect between the two, it immediately puts into question whether or not the data or the circumstances of the mission area are fully understood.

•

It's a sign of respect to donors who put a thorough amount of info on their website to acknowledge that you've done your homework and recognize a real fit. It is a sign of disrespect when that information is out there and organizations ignore it in the hopes that the lack of a true fit will just be ignored.

•

Bring in a program expert with you from your organization to join in on a call or initial engagement. We often get development people who take the initial meeting and want to nurture the relationship from the start, but sometimes it serves to include the technical person on the ground or the country director.

•

Yes, a one year grant is an audition grant, but it is also an acknowledgement grant. By all means, leverage it, maximize it prepare a plan to renew it, but also celebrate it and enjoy it. Multi-year grants are risky for foundations, but every grant is risky. While data and evidence make it easier to invest in your work, confidence and joy make it easier to invest in you.

•

You may have started a nonprofit that is doing great things or galvanized communities, but if you are pursuing global funds, you have to make sure the person who represents your organization is someone who can be an effective ambassador. As a private philanthropist who meets with a bunch of solicitors, I need to be able to clearly understand what you do, how you do it, why you need my help to do it and why you thought of me as a good fit besides my money. If you are not 100% able to accomplish all of these things, you need to hire someone who can do it for you or you will be in trouble.

•

Give donors a small dessert tray of options; come to the table already offering a good amount of delicious or appetizing ways to contribute to your organization, whether it be various funding opportunities or something else that could also be beneficial to your organization and the donor.

•

Revamp how you discuss general operating support. Don't make it about covering spending costs. Make it about keeping the energy and focus of the organization alive.

•

Donors want to be told, to some degree, 'This is how we do it. Here's what we can do and here's what we can't,' rather than, 'We want your money' in ways you think we won't be able to decipher.

•

You can't be all things to all people, but be the best thing for the people who count on your service.

•

One way to be sure your messaging is comprehensive and tight would be to have a person unfamiliar with the ins and outs of your organization review your elevator pitch and your one-pagers. This doesn't have to be a communications professional. Your savvy mom who has not paid much attention to what you've been up to lately, or your childhood friend who lives on the other side of the country would do just fine.

•

Do push back when donor requests are unreasonable.

•

Be honest and up front about potential challenges and risks in your proposals. No project is a guaranteed success. Tell us what could go wrong, why, and what factors could affect the likelihood of risk. Being upfront before you secure funding will lead to a stronger, more trusting relationship, and put you in a much better position if such a challenge does occur. Moreover, if/when something does go wrong, tell me as it is happening. Don't wait for the final or even interim report. If you are facing a challenge, your donors may be able to help, but only if you inform them in real-time and have the conversation about those potential challenges, before they occur.

•

Be innovative in how you present yourself in brief moments. A great idea by Human Rights Watch was to have business cards printed that also included concise, but important information about what the organization did and how it worked. This stays with a donor better than muscle memory of your encounter, especially if it is at a conference where you are one of possibly hundreds of people donors will encounter.

•

Ask one of your donors to offer you a list of conferences that they are invited to attend that might be possible for you to also attend. The chances of the conference being more relevant to your work are greater if someone who is supporting your work has been invited to join. But don't just take the list and run with it. Discuss with the donor which ones would best fit you and which ones might be worth missing.

•

One of the first qualities of leadership is self-awareness and knowing your limits. Build a plan for success for your organization based on what you can and cannot commit, from time and expertise to resources and connections.

•

When applicable, use your beneficiaries as a source for vetting questions that you might hear from donors. Tell them what you hope to do and ask what they think of it, how it addresses their needs and what needs are still left unmet.

•

Do a proper assessment of the leadership capacity of your organization, such as the Director and board members. It could be convenient to have a few friends be your initial board members, but the moment you are fully established as a nonprofit, everyone in a leadership role should know how to lead.

●

Conduct an Organizational Assessment (OD) to know the potential partners program, financial fund raising capacities before engaging potential foundations. The OD process will review the financial management systems, team building work, program development and monitoring. This indicates to donors if the organization has a strategic plan that shows vision, mission and strategic directions.

●

If it doesn't sound right, make sure it looks right. Make sure the work you are trying to do can speak for itself if it is seen, which can make up for any communication impediments you may have. Make sure that when you're able to put out that example to show people who are having a hard time understanding what it is you do, the reaction is, 'Oh, I totally get it now.'

You can't have a program that needs explaining and have poor communication skills.

●

Create clear and effective communications materials (both programmatic and financial materials). They tell your story when you aren't in the room to do so and they get saved in funder's archives and referred to in future years to understand organizational change over time. If they don't honestly and comprehensively capture the challenge you are working to address, your mission, how you work, and how you allocate funding toward the mission, then revise them to do so.

●

Present me with proof of your understanding as to why previous interventions fail. I need to know you are not planning to repeat the same mistakes.

●

Cross-check the programmatic information contained in your glossy communications materials with your organization's financials before sending them off to a potential funder. Discrepancies between what you say you are passionate about in your communications materials and what you are actually spending money on in your budget execution will undoubtedly raise questions among donors.

●

I go to a few conferences where I will have several interactions with NGOs seeking a funding partnership. My advice in those situations is more focused on the conversation before asking if there is a fit. More specifically, if you have to ask if there is a fit, there probably isn't one. Donors, especially Program Officers, are looking to make grants and when something of interest comes along, they will be proactive in asking for information and continuing the dialogue. The only time a grant-seeker should lead the conversation is after genuine interest in a funding relationship has been explicitly expressed.

If you think there is a fit, but the donor or foundation representative does not share the interest, prove your case to yourself first. Then ask some of your current or former donors who may know the foundation you are engaging if they believe there is a fit. If they say no, move on. If they say yes, ask them if they are willing to help you present your case in the most compelling way. It's better to return to a donor that has closed the door and knock with new information and purpose, instead of wedging your foot in the doorway, hoping to keep it ajar, but never fully open.

●

While I am sympathetic to an organization that spends excessive human resources on reports or updates or feedback, it does not negate my need for such things. When you approach a corporate foundation, do your best to make sure it aligns with your other top level donors that require regular reporting, unless a corporate or top level foundation reaches out first. This can reduce multiple reports for each donor.

●

Be graceful in defeat.

●

Who is the audience for your website? When a nonprofit directs me to its website and there are no financials, no impact data, no measuring and evaluation results, etc. I think they are only looking for groundswell donations from the public and they are not targeting institutional donors. For me, it is a problem when I see a 'Donate Now' button before I see a reason for making a donation.

●

I bet on the people. Your organization has to make me feel connected to the people. If all I hear about in your pitch is you and your organization, then I'm not betting on the people; I'm gambling on you.

●

Humanize the technical aspects of your work. I fully understand there are very intricate or technical themes around the world that are necessary, but they can sometimes go over my head. If you take as much care with explaining how your work will impact communities as you do explaining and developing your change model, I can feel more comfort in funding something more technical.

●

There are many differences between corporate and family foundations, some are fundamental and others are more complex. As you do your due diligence on a foundation, especially a family foundation, don't stop at what and where they fund, but look at how they fund. A larger foundation may have the ability to fund an organization or project regardless of funding needs, but smaller foundations can't afford the luxury of writing a grant where the money may not be needed, at least not in the short term.

•

Respect the process. What may seem like an arbitrary grant application procedure could be a thoroughly developed methodology for foundations. Those who are young to the space need to remember that larger foundations have staff that comprise of people with extensive nonprofit experience who are involved in how we create our curriculum.

•

Get out of your own way. Remember that you are privileged to meet with funders, because many vulnerable people stand to benefit from your successful fundraising efforts. If you are feeling shy or modest, lazy or whatever, remember that it would be irresponsible not to help caring donors connect their resources to causes that matter. Be direct. Be convincing. Be effective. The people who matter are depending on you.

•

I know this is about engagement, but it must be said to be careful in the process of reengagement after there has been funding request rejection. Before reengaging, you must first ensure that you have addressed every reason given for the original grant denial.

•

As donors, we all have different styles and ways of doing our job, so what approach works with one donor might not work with the next. The challenge for people approaching donors is to relate first and foremost as a human being who is in solidarity with the problems of the world and then as a person trying to raise money. As a donor, I enjoy the personal side of our philanthropy but as our foundation has grown, I have had to work to 'manage' the relational side of our work and keep it in balance.

More than anything, what keeps my heart and soul motivated to keep being an arc of justice in the world is being with and hearing the heart and soul of people's passion to create a better world. I personally consider myself, first and foremost, to be an activist, then a donor, so I personally enjoy 'grantee partners' who convey a spirit of solidarity across the donor/grantee line and a sense that we are all in this work together. I see my role as a 'donor activist,' a title that Helen LaKelly Hunt, a friend/mentor/founder of Women Moving Millions shared with me, which resonated greatly.

Our foundation has created a formal structure (i.e. an application process and granting priorities) to create boundaries around the relational aspect of our work. Even with this formal process, I would say that relations still are at the heart of how we do our grant-making. As a new philanthropist, I would say that some of the best teachers over the course of our foundation's first five years of operations have been some really awesome development professionals who somehow embodied just the perfect relational balance in the way they did their job. And let me say that I have great empathy across the donor/grantee divide.

It is much easier to give money away than to raise it! If I had to say what the 'secret sauce' is in the development directors I admire most it would be some combination of:

- likeability
- a passion for and knowledge about the cause they are raising money for, i.e. beyond just their own program, knowing when to be relational and when to be process-oriented, i.e.
- finding a healthy balance between the two
- not coming across as a 'marketer' but as an authentic voice trying to animate the mission and ethos of the organization, struggles and accomplishments alike.

●

Be genuine. Like grantees, donors vary immensely in what they are looking for and the way they want to interact with their grantees. It benefits both parties to be genuine from the outset to ensure that you will have a positive working relationship that potentially leads to long-term funding.

●●●

Don't:

Don't push a donor when resistance is shown. Step back and respect the reluctance. Then try again at a different time.

•

Don't underestimate the influence or power of a foundational staff person (ED, assistant, etc.). Don't try to go around the assistant or speak negatively about that staff person, unless you honestly believe something negative is afoot. Staff can be your greatest ally. People often have this fascination with meeting with the donor directly. Actually that's not always necessary or wise, for that matter. If most donors are like my donor, their attention spans don't even allow for that much time, which means they are not even getting half of your idea. A staff person can listen to a request and then breakdown the information in a way that can be more persuasive to the donor.

•

Whether you are a charity we support or one that has access to our personal information, please do not make an introduction to another charity without asking our permission first. It puts us in an untenable position and makes assumptions about our availability and our bandwidth.

•

One major don't: we're not fans of pre-packaged PowerPoint presentations. We find that they often 'institutionalize' the message and delivery, as well as the real passion and energy of the organization gets hidden behind a bunch of cool graphics on a page. We much prefer an engaging 1:1 dialogue which, even if it can be a bit scattered and unorganized, gives us a much better flavor for the organization and the people behind it. It also allows us to drill down to the questions we really want to have answered.

•

If a grantee or prospective grantee never disagrees with anything I say, it's a problem. I want to have a critical dialogue. The relationships are better when NGOs and grantees tell us when we're wrong. It's allowed. We want critical engagement and feedback as well.

•

While there is no guarantee that an unsolicited proposal will be read by a donor, contacting business associates of a donor or non-foundation relations as a conduit for your proposal is a guarantee that it will not be read, at least not by us. A number of NGOs have sent proposals or solicitations to our lawyers, our PR firm and even to our home addresses. This is seen only as an invasion of privacy and no matter how great your organization or pure your intentions, these methods can get you blacklisted.

•

Don't undervalue a telephone conversation; meeting in person isn't always productive. People always want to meet in person (I'm an introvert so maybe I just don't get it). But I have found that an in-person meeting takes a relationship to an entirely different level, and not always for the better. In my experience, agreeing to an in-person meeting gives some false hope on the nonprofit side that I'm more interested than I really might be.

Be open to a phone conversation first. I feel like the time of potential grantees is just as precious as mine, so I'm not eager to waste their time either until I know there is real synergy.

•

Don't bother sending any solicitation longer than four paragraphs that is not personalized. If you have the good fortune to reach me directly, it needs to be respectful of my time and of your mission.

•

Even if they are all underwritten, it is bad optics when your nonprofit hosts several events in exotic or luxurious locations. Foundations will struggle to understand your need. The worse thing for a nonprofit with budgeting gaps to do is appear as if they already have enough funding.

•

Please don't try to gain a meeting with me to hear about my work without being upfront about ultimately wanting me to hear much more about yours.

•

Treating donors as people whose only purpose is to give money and who don't have their own ideas or contributions to make besides the financial is a mistake. Donors don't like to be approached when the only reason that you are interested in anything they have to say is for money. Many of them can see through that.

•

Don't sugarcoat. Understand what the goals are in an honest way, because once that's out there, there's a better chance for a natural overlap that doesn't have to be a perfect overlap, just an honest one, which will make for stronger partnerships.

●

This may not be true for all funders, but my personal feeling is that lots of jargon is not helpful. Tons of buzzwords in a proposal make it hard to make out what it is your organization does. If you're not present to provide clarity, it could mean the difference between a proposal we consider, reconsider, or pass on.

●

I don't need gifts, I don't need anything as a thank you for taking a meeting or providing funding, especially if the gift is pricey. My gift is supporting your great work. Be happy with that.

●

Don't rely too much on our 990 forms. They don't always paint a full picture of a foundation or philanthropist. If you really care, ask us where our passions lie.

●

Don't ask every donor who funds you to join your board. If they offer to be on your board, create a set of expectations for both of you to agree upon.

●

If you feel comfortable in your relationship with a donor, don't be afraid to give them constructive criticism. Donors, more so than NGOs, often operate in silos, without learning how their peers operate. This

means that we are often unaware of better ways of giving or supporting our partners. We are capable of learning, so please help us improve!

●

Don't be afraid. At all. The worst a donor can say is no. So give that
donor a chance to say no to your best, instead of what you think wants
to be heard. It may not end up as a no.

●

Do not leave out your theory of change for the sake of brevity when
trying to make your mission statement more concise. Tell me about
what you do, but if it sounds like another organization or a few organizations, I won't push you to delineate. I will just move on.

●

Don't try to give me rose-colored glasses. Most donors have really
good BS-radar and know when something is missing or sounds too
good to be true. A good donor will press you when they sense this, but
even so, I've seen potential grantees stick to their guns rather than
admit a potential flaw or risk in the project. Presenting a funding opportunity as a guaranteed success sets you up for failure. It also sets
your donor up for disappointment.

So don't try to hide any challenges, risks, or issues in your project,
team, or organization. Talk about your challenges and talk through
your process of addressing them. How are you thinking about risk and
problem-solving? What are your contingency and risk mitigation
plans? I feel much more confident investing in a leader who states a
potential problem and shows they will be able to develop a solution,
than a leader who blindly tells me 'everything will be great.' Don't
pitch me when you have the opportunity to talk with me.

●

An idea and a plan are not the same thing. Don't pedal an idea alone as a full-fledged plan.

●

For me, the few negative experiences I've had with development professionals have been when the relationship feels too heavy on the marketing side. You don't have to sell a thirsty man on the benefits of water. Donors are also thirsty to support good work aligned with their support mission.

●

Don't hide your personal flaws. If you have an NGO and you know that you are not a good fundraiser, nor can you afford to fundraise, find one funder and be totally honest about your lack of ability to fundraise. If he or she believes in your work, that person should be willing to help you in ways beyond writing a check.

●

You don't need to go to a philanthropic consultant or business consultant to fine-tune your message. Go to someone you know who is a solid writer or editor.

●

Don't be condescending to funders. We actually read stuff, many of us have had lives involved in project implementation, and we aren't completely clueless about the sectors you are working in. In many cases, that's why we were hired as grant-makers.

●

Don't go crazy with the acronyms! I don't want to have to refer to an acronym guide to translate your annual report or grant proposal.

●

Do not use template language when you first contact a donor. I receive emails from people who say that they have reviewed our work and see alignments, but they are based in areas we have never funded or do work that we have never supported. You need to prove your case and be prepared to explain why in a non-combative way, while not sounding like you are grasping at straws.

●

'I want to tell you about our wonderful work...'

Get rid of that sentence. You want my money? Let me be the judge of how wonderful your work really is.

●

Don't reshape your peg just to fit into the shape a foundation has established.

●

Don't suggest a follow up to the follow up meeting. You get two meetings maximum to prove your case for alignment. Don't request another meeting if the donor doesn't initiate it. And don't mistake donors who agree to your additional requests for follow up meetings as interest. They are too polite or scared to tell you no. Five or six follow ups with no funding to show for it means you are willfully ignoring the writing on the wall.

●

Don't underestimate the power of a good story or the elements that go into a good story. Think about the last good book you read or movie you saw and what made the plot effective. You need to include the excitement, the humor, the right tempo, but ultimately you need to make sure your story is one the audience will care about.

•

How do you expect a donor to take any claims seriously of donors wasting the time of nonprofits when you are spamming us with emails? Unless there is a serious situation that needs constant updates, we don't need the weekly or sometimes daily emails that we get from some of these organizations.

•

I'm not going to connect you to someone when I don't know you or know enough about you. It is good to be proactive and ask for help beyond funding on behalf of your nonprofit, but don't overdo it. Gage the connection that you have with the donor in front of you. If the Program Officer is not as enthused about the work you're doing, it may not be the best idea to ask them to connect you directly to other funders in his or her network.

•

I respect NGOs that are not afraid to push back. Donors like to push, so don't be afraid to push back on donors when they are coming from an uninformed place.

•

Don't ever start an introduction with 'I know you fund' unless I or someone from our foundation has told you directly. Even if it is considered common knowledge, ask me what we fund or what interests us about your work and go from there. Funding priorities and strategies may shift or change over time.

•

How you engage a donor cannot be a copy and paste job. Bigger foundations will probably be more adept in handling the jargon surrounding your work, but that won't be as effective with small family foundations unfamiliar with your needs or terminology. Don't lose me before I get a chance to know you.

•

Don't come to an introductory meeting without bringing your financial summary with you. It's a cardinal sin. How can you ask me for money when you can't tell me exactly how much money you need based on current intake and budget forecasts?

•

Charity Navigator is great, but donors understand not every nonprofit can be effectively rated in such a way. Don't chase the star rating; chase the work and find a way to effectively bring donors along for the ride.

•

If we've had multiple meetings and I have not funded you, do not request another meeting unless you have something new to show me, especially if I have been clear about why I have not funded you in the past.

•

Don't waste the time you should be using to grow your donor base on trying to convince a foundation to renew a nonrenewable grant. Three to five years is a committed investment with plenty of time to find new growth partners. Whatever you think your best argument is for making an exception to the grant renewal policy, it will be difficult to counter the fact that you have not been able to grow enough to no longer need our direct financial support.

●

Even if you have a very charismatic Executive Director, don't make him or her the focus of why a grant should be made. If that person leaves, donors might worry that the direction of the relationship may go as well. Let that charisma pour into highlighting the mission goals.

●

Do not try to pass off faulty research and evaluations to us, especially when your existing donors are aware of it. This is a surefire way to kill your organization's name among major donors.

●

Don't underestimate the long game. It's rare for relationship building to happen overnight. Give us the time to get to know you, specifically if your focus point is relatively new or on the periphery of our current scope.

●

Don't let the size of the foundation sway the size of your grant. Understand our parameters, but come prepared to make a real pitch for giving at the top end of our comfort zone. If you come to donors saying every penny counts, you end up with pennies.

●

Don't mix up things in correspondence organizationally. I get worried about cohesiveness when I am engaged with multiple people within one organization and am getting differing views about the state of the organization.

•

Don't tell me that I have funded nonsense in the past or make me feel that way.

•

Before you engage a donor, do your best not to present yourself as a programmatic organization, but an organization that has a clear grasp of the problem and strong belief in the solution, where the solution is carried out in a multifaceted approach that includes, but is not limited to programs. Focusing too much on programs makes you look like a service provider instead of a progressive nonprofit.

•

I don't have to meet you. If you push for a meeting and then respond to any of my questions during the meeting with 'I don't know,' then I might hold that against you. Had I asked the same question via email, you would have been able to respond with the answer once you had it. Think about requesting a meeting after the question and answer phase of relationship building has occurred.

•

Do not think that a no is a total reflection on your organization. We have limited dollars and because something else resonates with us more does not mean you have to go through an entire organizational review.

•

Don't make assumptions when approaching funders associated with a famous last name, one you may see on plaques around your city or in the news. Maintain focus on why you are meeting with that particular person and not the other family members associated with that name. You don't know their family dynamics, so don't spoil a relationship before it starts by bringing up a relative. The name might be well-known, but you don't know the person well enough to navigate that conversation. In short, be tactful.

●

Don't be a statistics organization. Your pitch or materials and reports cannot have any real impact if all we see are statistics and data with no human context. Some organizations need to rely on statistics, but know how to rephrase a statistic to capture human impact.

●

On our website, don't stop at the grant application link. We provide many resources and took much effort to assure those resources are available to grant applicants. You could go through the entire process of filling out an application, but miss the section that says you can submit an already completed application from another foundation. You'd be surprised how often this happens.

●

Don't let nerves sabotage your entire pitch. It's OK to be nervous. We understand the magnitude of financial support just as you do. As long as you come prepared with the pertinent info, we don't expect everything else to be perfectly manicured.

●

Don't make your pitch sound like an infomercial. I don't want to be 'Sham-Wowed,' I want to feel like you are taking the situation seriously. I mentally disengage when it sounds like someone is offering me the end to abject poverty for just three easy payments of half a million dollars.

•

If you are the founder or the Executive Director of a charity, do not send new hires out to represent your organization until you feel like they also represent you. Coach them on the nuances of the how and why and not just regurgitate information.

•

Don't cross the line in your fundraising between being ahead of the curve and being disrespectful. I find it intrusive to receive meeting requests or proposals via Facebook or Twitter. I've even received requests to my private email address. It makes me wonder what other lines you will cross if you are willing to go that far.

•

Don't grow your budget based on one donor, even if it is a multi-year grant. Any foundation that has the capacity to increase your budget with one grant should also be able to help you identify other grant resources that can pick up where they will eventually leave off.

Definitely don't grow your budget with no guaranteed funding to fill the newly created gaps. When we receive end of year emails from organizations desperately seeking funding for gaps in a new budget that would not have existed in the previous year's budget, it points to too much ambition and a lack of foresight or preparation.

•

Don't rely too heavily on gimmicks to fundraise in an order to be sustainable. There are only so many Jeffersonian dinners a nonprofit can host before the novelty wears off.

•

Not every document you send me has to include your mission or pitch after we have agreed to fund you. A request for emergency funding or updates from the field on a program we support doesn't always have to start off with what the organization does. We're funding you; we already know what you do. Get to what you need or what you want to update.

•

Don't name drop. Just because you know a family member or friend of mine does not mean I should take a meeting with you, unless they vouch for you directly.

•

Don't overlook other implementing actors on your quest for funding. They can be a huge resource to your organization and to your mission.

•

Don't agree to anything with a donor that will alter your mission goals without talking to all the architects of that plan within the organization, especially if the community was instrumental in constructing the mission plan. Personally, as a small family donor, it disheartens me when an organization that convinced me to fund based on a solid direction does an about face when someone bigger comes along.

•

Don't lose the enthusiasm created from a good meeting in your written materials or proposal. Implement elements from our discussion into what you present, so we as program officers can show our board the ignition points and not just the entry points.

•

Don't forget that you are one of many organizations to contact us. Slow responses are most likely due to volume. The answer is not to inundate us with 'friendly reminders.'

•

I'm going to be honest. A lot of nonprofit people and even friends in the donor community say that we have to educate ourselves more to be better donors. That's great for institutionalized foundations with staff and resources, but not for philanthropists. I already have a job that takes away from quality time with my family. That job allows me to be in a position to be philanthropic, so when you tell me I have to dedicate more of my shrinking personal time to learn a bunch of crazy terminology just to be able to do some good in the world, I don't think so.

So if I have to make this a do or don't, I would say don't make me feel like I need to get another degree just to fund your organization and don't assume that philanthropists have the same time or learning resources that full foundations have.

•

There is a new trend in solicitation emails where people are introducing themselves in the first paragraph and then suggesting times to meet in the next paragraph. Some might call this ambitious, but I call it tacky and rude. The first step for a donor who has never heard of you is to vet you for alignment, not to meet with you based on one email alone. Don't ask for a call in your first correspondence. Definitely, don't suggest times for a call. Don't assume that because you think we are a perfect fit, donors will just take your word for it without due diligence.

•

Don't overpromise in your pitch, in your materials and, most importantly, to your beneficiaries. Working with humans and governments means that there is a level of unpredictability that cannot be accounted for 100%.

●

Funders understand that things go wrong, but if our usual point of contact is at the top, it's flat out wrong to have someone we've never met before deliver the bad news. Don't delegate the relationship to someone else when the going gets tough.

●

One pet peeve I have with nonprofits is the discussion around core funding. A lot is not said about it besides donors should fund it, which is said a lot. Nonprofits bear some responsibility for this, too. They pitch their missions through the lens of the programs created to achieve it and not through the core of the organization that created the programs. If you want core funding, don't leave your core out of your pitch. Explain the importance of staff to the organization. Explain the need for adaptable funding. Don't spend too much time on what you need and not enough on how you need it and why you need it that way.

●

Don't assume that having people of wealth on your board is a panacea. A friend and colleague had a number of hedge fund people on her board and they actually shut the organization down. They were having cash flow issues, something that every single nonprofit—and company for that matter—goes through at some point in time. Maybe not everyone, but it is not unusual at all. But when people don't know what to do, they do what they know, and that's not always what the organization needs. She went away on vacation and the chairman of the board, who worked at a hedge fund, decided it was better to just close the nonprofit. When she came back and found out what the board had done, she was like, 'What the hell happened?'

4

**The Nonprofit Toolkit – What Tools Donors Think
NGOs Should Have In Their Fundraising Toolbox**

If the previous chapter was about advice and intangibles that nonprofits should know from donors, then this is more about the concrete tangible that a nonprofit needs to have in its toolbox, especially those in their early stages or startup phase. To be quite frank, I think there is a lot of messaging to nonprofits that feels more like self-help than organizational help.

Yes, one should work on one's self before working on anything else, but after mastering breathing correctly, nonprofits would like to master keeping the lights on and not spending more time raising funds than implementing them. I wanted to push donors to dig deeper here and really point to tools, resources and/or operational behaviors that are musts for nonprofits to know and have.

There was a bit of a struggle for a few donor participants here and that was to be expected. The reason is simple. There is no way to guarantee funding to nonprofits. None. Reading and adapting the tools below may put an organization on better footing, but that same organization can still end up with budget deficits. Donors want to be clear that by saying, 'This is the best way to get funding,' it does not equate to 'This will get you funding,' at least not from them.

But this is not to say donors don't have sharp insight into the tools that nonprofits have access to and should utilize. Almost every response was given more than once, meaning these are tools that most contributing donors find essential to have.

Sometimes, though, donors are not the best resource in terms of knowing what should go into a toolbox for nonprofits. Some tools are straightforward, where donors could thrive in helping a nonprofit acquire. Other tools are more roundabout or strategic, where other nonprofits have found other approaches that work to their benefit. I reached out to dozens of successful nonprofits to see if they were willing to share some of their secrets and they luckily obliged. Whether from a donor or nonprofit, these tools highlight that resources don't always have to come in monetary forms.

From the donors:

There's a tool that Community Resource Exchange uses called, 'From Vision to Reality.' It touches on everything and breaks it all down for you. You get examples of budgets, resources, hiring skills. When you start a nonprofit, you have a million people talking in your ear, but this has been proven to work in having multiple tools laid on in a comprehensive way.

•

If at all possible, it's best to get some outside help, because it's very hard when you're in it to be objective, because it's your baby. If you can get someone to help you with the thoughtful planning and learning, it will help in the long run. It will cost money, but you can find ways around it. You can barter by providing a service for someone who can, in turn, offer you someone outside assistance or fresh thinking.

•

Nonprofits need to have their organizational structure in place. Many times, they have great ideas and an amazing heart, but there needs to be an internal plan and I don't mean one that explains how your organization will accomplish its goals. I mean the internal organizational structure. Whether a nonprofit has the staff in place or is looking to hire more staff later, nonprofits need to have a description of every staff person's role or contribution toward mission reach. This is also great in terms of highlighting the importance of administrative funding. When the staff can be tied to the mission in an integral way from the start, donors don't feel like their unrestricted grant has been thrown into an abyss.

•

Develop a handbook or database, since we are so digital now, of every tough question asked of the organization along with the answer that best represents the organization. Make it open for the entire organization to access. Development staff would obviously benefit from this, but all staff who finds themselves in a position to promote the organization should be able to reference the database and speak uniformly in their advocacy for the organization.

•

The devil is in the details, but so is the money. How did you get from the problem to the solution and how did you structure success to handle the many obstacles in your path? Plot out every detail of your projected journey. Have this in your toolbox if you're a new NGO.

•

A lot of companies look to grow, but don't have a Human Resources piece in place. Times will get rough for a nonprofit. How you treat your employees will determine if they are willing to go through thick and thin with you or leave at the first opportunity. HR is also responsible for the acquisition of new good hires, so don't underestimate its importance.

•

I'm always struck by how many people approach us not having done their homework on what's important to us as donors. This mistake comes down to staff capacity. An organization should have someone—even an intern—who can vet a list of prospective donors for true alignments, not forced ones. Staff capacity can help an organization understand that a grant proposal meant for our foundation and a different one may need to be adjusted for emphasis.

You might market in a different way or use different words, while not changing the focus of the work. A one or two man operation will just not have the capacity to complete this. I can't tell you how many people I talk to who are wasting their time and wasting our time by not doing their basic homework. So there are two pieces there: do the homework on all prospective donors, but invest in staff capacity, even at an early stage when there is no money to hire more staff.

One way to grow staff capacity for free is bringing in college interns or asking friends you know and trust to give labor donations instead of dollar donations. Ask them to donate 1-2 hours to your organization a week and task them with something you feel they could handle. Do it in a festive setting if that helps. Have food (probably not too much alcohol) and make it feel welcoming. Ask friends with teen-aged kids who either have free time or are out on a summer break to volunteer time and assign them with responsibilities you feel safe delegating.

•

Communications are key. Your messaging is the most important thing about your organization in terms of fundraising. Spend less time on the perfect name or logo. Spend more time to ensure your intro paragraph to what you do is concise, but not academic, so that it resonates with donors. When you're overloaded with requests all the time, you want something compelling to get your attention. It's almost a storytelling technique, how you can make what you're doing a human interest story. Learn to engage on a personal level, not just a technical level. You cannot forget the human lens.

●

Language is important. I know a lot of donors need grantees to show results, where our foundation cares less about that. We care about a commitment to learning, a humility and ability to be able to show their niche in a space where a lot is happening. We want to see how they fit in the ecosystem of everyone else in that space. That's the most critical for us, to see if the nonprofit is able to clearly define their niche to show they add value and not duplication. We look to see if they identify themselves as part of a community as opposed to just themselves. Are they a lone wolf or a collective player?

If they are a collective player, which we value a lot, they have to have the skills and the capacity to be able to develop and manage those relationships with their community. Collaborative work takes a different skillset, but also needs the capacity and time to be able to maintain the relationships in a prosperous way.

●

Money. You don't need your entire budget, but some money to implement the most important parts of your mission is really important to have. Crowd fund or beg everyone who will not disown you for startup capital.

●

Leadership skills should not just be seen at the Executive Directors level. I'm very surprised when I meet with the same person from an organization, but there is shared leadership across teams and we don't get to interact with them. Allowing us to interact with multiple levels of staff makes it easier for us to partner with you, because that shows us real cohesion and strength throughout the organization, not just at the top, especially when the ED can be poached by another organization. It is harder to maintain faith in the entire organization when our only interface was one person.

We are looking for viable, forward thinking organizations that can exhibit lots of different skillsets. More than anything, the presentation of leadership is a valuable tool that too often gets overlooked. We get proposals from organizations led by very dynamic persons and we immediately look at their secession plan. If that person plans to be there for twenty years, we see that as a problem and not an asset.

●

The number one thing you need to have when setting up is the confidence to wing it, because you don't have all the answers and you won't have all the resources when you're starting something. It really does come down to having the confidence to think, 'fuck it' and push forward through all the things that may hold you back and just see what happens.

If you have a tangible idea that you think can be implemented and successful, one that you think you can get funding for and you think will leave the sector significantly better with your intervention, rather than just the same or marginally better, then that will be what carries you through the tough times, and there will be plenty.

Everything else you will need will be byproducts of pushing ahead with confidence. The networks of support, talking to peers around you, having good friends and family who will stand by you, these are all necessary next steps, but mean nothing without confidence.

●

Google is your friend. It helps you out with so much. The key is knowing what to search for, how to search and how to harness all of the information in a productive way.

●

Drive doesn't sound like a tangible tool, but really it is. Drive is more than passion. Passion can fade when tough situations arrive, but drive can push you through. I can think of nonprofits who had the idea, but not the drive. When they faced adversity, they were very quick to go back to their Plan A lives and not realize that they had already made a commitment to people in communities of need or within their organizations or both. The minute things get tough, they return to their job in finance or join the family business or something like this.

Another 'non-tangible' tangible tool is to respect that commitment. This is why there is so much mistrust at the ground level, because so many organizations come and they get a good startup grant from someone who believes in them, but they don't know how to fundraise. The minute that grant is done, they don't know how to raise any more money, so they leave.

•

Use realism, not hyperbole in your pitch or your materials. It's a no-brainer, but many organizations come to me and promise everything. If I believe only half of what some of the nonprofits say who work in education that come to us for funding, they will have revolutionized the entire school system within the next five years and none of them have done it.

•

Having a website identity is crucial for the startup. Even if your organization is still in the processing phase, having a website and an email address that corresponds with it will help you look legitimate to the people you need to contact. It could even be a holding space that only features your mission statement until you are able to add more content. It will help you open so many more doors than going to people and saying, 'I have this great idea, can I meet with you?'

That presence online will allow you to go to seed funders, investors and people who you want to work alongside. It even gives you a place for family and friends to go to and refer others, since they will be your first network of support.

•

I think there are a lot of people who thrive in the operational side of the work, but are not capable of representing themselves and their personal motives for starting their nonprofit. To these people, I suggest that they create a personal CV of when they started to care about an issue, like they were applying for a job instead of a grant. What they did about it (bullet point their actions just like they were job tasks), for how long (document the timeline of those tasks), what special skills they have that are unique to the nonprofit space they are applying to, and their objective.

If someone has only one experience between being introduced to a problem and starting a nonprofit to address it, this allows me to point that out as a problem. That means they made no effort to see who was already working on the same problem or it wasn't significant enough to mention. It indicates a savior mentality that major donors usually tend to avoid.

●

Diversify the people who you choose as your first co-leaders. If you are all good at the same things, but still lack other leadership skills in key areas, you are bound to fail. Bringing in more peer partners later adds more cooks in an already crowded kitchen. You can't do it alone, but quality and strategy are better than quantity.

●

In addition to your assessment of your organization, prepare an assessment of the ecosystem of your focus area. Be able to provide something from an external relevant party that supports your added value.

●

Resilience. Understand that not everyone will like or support your ideas, but others will.

●

Have a strong board. By strong board, I mean people who have the time, willingness and the capacity to step in and really help the organization when needed. Members should be more hands-on, but not be obstructionists.

●

Nonprofit insight. Reach out to the nearest well established charity to discuss the many kinds of grants that are possible. Take a meeting to learn about the benefits of small grants and ways they leverage them, as well as which large grants to resist that are thrown at you that sound and look like a great opportunity, but can kill you as an organization.

●

Conflicts of interest. There is a difference between a connection to somebody at a foundation that is beneficial like a friendship and one that is not. If the connection to one of our staff is that of a former employer or a love interest, their recommendations of your work could put you both in a negative position.

●

Elevator pitch. Everything you think is important to know about your organization should be written down and with you at all times.

●

Understand the role technology will play in your work and the narrative you build around that. Don't forget the human element in the presentation and don't even suggest your technology will be the cure all. We've had this time when people thought technology would solve everything, but research continues to show that social interventions still have greater impacts than technology in many of the areas where we are based. Maybe this is just a European perspective. Perhaps someone from the US and in particular, the West Coast would give a different perspective, but I have stopped listening to people who tell me they will solve everything with technology alone.

●

Smart targets. Many startup nonprofits don't always know or understand that their missions are not the same as the targets they set to accomplish them. It's all or nothing. Create baseline metrics and set targets that show growth potential and directional cognizance among obstacles.

●

Mission priorities. Don't put the fifth step in front of the first.

●

A viable model that is going to advance the change that's desired.

●

Core leadership at the top. Sometimes the visionary founder has the idea and the passion, but then lacks some of the business acumen and the professional C-level skills that are essential to the functioning of the organization. I have worked with these kind of leaders of nonprofit organizations and the way they compensated for what they lacked was by sharing leadership with staff who could feel empowered when they represented the organization.

●

If you expect to receive multiple forms of funds (donations, fundraisers, social venture income), you need a strong financial team.

•

Professional communication materials beyond a website. Review materials from organizations you consider to be the gold standard in your field and see what makes them successful in messaging. I've worked with new and emerging organizations who have to make the case to donors, individuals and corporations who have not yet come to the table. Having professional materials that succinctly delineate what they want to achieve and what they have already achieved is one of the crucial nuts and bolts tools.

•

Develop a balance in messaging for fundraising. No matter how desperate your situation, do not beg and don't come off as begging. But don't sound like you don't really need our money and try to make me feel like it would be cool to partner. There are many other organizations that really need funding and know how to portray their situation effectively. We want to put our money where it is most needed, not where it looks the coolest.

•

In the end, money flows through not just impact, but through networks. In order to raise money for whatever idea or innovation there is, founders and the leadership of these new organizations really have to work hard and long at developing relationships with individual contributors, foundational donors—private, corporate and individual foundations—along with governments. I say government, because there are many government partners to consider, not just your home country.

This is done through moving around these circles, whether it is attending conferences or through peer referrals. Cold calls are the least effective way of building philanthropic partnerships. Demonstrating progress, entering network conferences and getting in front of donor agencies are some of the core tools needed at getting the most important resource your organization will need: sustained money.

•••

You must have a dedicated smartphone and if you do, then really familiarize yourself with the app store. There is probably an app that already exists that can help with the work you want to do, so search. The importance of a smartphone over a laptop or desktop is not just for the mobility. Apps that run on your traditional computing devices tend to cost money, a lot of money. Many of those same apps can be found in a free version on your phone and most work just as well. Phones also automatically save to an external cloud drive, so even if it's lost or compromised, the data is still saved and safe.

Also reimagine how to use everyday apps like Whatsapp and FaceTime. We use these apps to communicate with everyone, including internal communications. However, the reason we got on it was because so many of our partners and participants of our work were on one or both of these apps. It serves as a platform for communication and distribution of information and content.

●

Get accounting software. Do not try to do in-house bookkeeping on spreadsheets or something more informal. It will be something that comes back to haunt you year after year if you're not on the ball about that. There are many tools to choose from, including free options, and they tend to all run similarly enough to recommend one over another, so it's mostly about choosing an interface you're most comfortable with.

●

There is probably more emphasis on this in the Human Rights space, but software tools that combine project management with security is also very important across sectors because of hacking threats, which even nonprofits are seeing more of lately. Security based conference programs like SpiderOak offers complete anonymity for group calls. Even if law enforcement came to their headquarters, there would be no way to unencrypt it, so you can know that whatever is being said is completely secure. It has even been endorsed by Edward Snowden. It also has project management tools that a nonprofit would need.

Software tools are important, but tool adoption and integration is even more important. Don't just pick something that is the hot new thing; choose something that you know your entire team can use easily. It's frustrating to spend two weeks training your team on a software just to see enthusiasm or ease of use fizzle out. Or if software has to change, make sure the team is capable of handling those changes without loss of usage comprehension or morale. It's good to have a plan about how you intend to use the software and share with the staff to see if the vision is shared throughout.

Security might be a stronger issue for some nonprofits, while others might want more versatility on maintaining data from donations, as well as income social ventures. Salesforce is a great tool for corporate business and there is a free version for nonprofits that is geared for those types of nonprofits. I personally prefer Pipedrive more, but you can see what suits your nonprofit best. If you're worried about hacking threats, using an organization-wide password manager won't guarantee airtight security, but will put you light years ahead of everyone. These are all easy to find and not so difficult to use.

•

You need to be able to nurture each other as an organization. Hire staff that understand that it's a shared risk and a shared struggle, but will also be a shared joy. Someone who has spent less than six months at their last few jobs is not a good fit, unless they have a technical role.

•

Fellowships. Not everyone can be an Ashoka fellow, but they are not the only ones and many foundations are starting their own fellowship programs. If you're new to the nonprofit world, resist going for the grant when there's the opportunity to be a fellow: gain the knowledge, reap the benefits that come with it and build your network in a way that doesn't take away from your organizational commitments.

•

The tool is the way you frame your organization. You might come to the field thinking, 'I'm a maternal health organization,' but if you can think about yourself as a social entrepreneur, that opens up all sorts of new opportunities, not just to get funding, but to get training to better help you work from that ideology. If it is successful, you will also be less dependent on grants to keep the organization going.

It's the classic problem. You get into it because you're an activist or want to see a wrong made right or you have a certain expertise in one area, but it doesn't mean you will magically know how to run a sophisticated organization. Learning how to frame or reimagine how you plan to respond to the problems will also give you the skills you to better run your organization.

•

Organizational trust between colleagues can't be overstated. You will face highs and lows in the beginning. Working with or hiring a friend could help during the low periods, but if their only contribution to the organization is being a friend, then they could be responsible for some of the lows. Hiring people who look good on paper doesn't work either. It has to feel like a family.

When I think of how we were able to survive the early days, it really came down to that we liked each other. We trusted each other. We liked working with each other and were inspired by one another. That made establishing new processes, adding new policies, representing the organization individually to others so much easier with more efficiency.

•

Maintain strong financials, especially if your first grant is a government or large foundational grant. Financial integrity should be established before the money comes in. Make a plan for where the first places a grant should go, no matter the grant size.

•

Find a trusted referral. When you are too new to find donors, try to look for a complimentary nonprofit that is trusted in the field and have them look at your work. Their endorsement of you can be just as good as a donor's endorsement.

•

Luck. This sounds silly, but you don't get lucky sitting at home doing nothing. Put yourself in a position where a bit of luck can put your hard work in front of the right people.

•

Get good with creating and working with content. Record testimonials of your beneficiaries either discussing the problems they face that you help them with or how your interventions have changed their lives. This is your advocacy and your fundraising tools in the beginning. There is a fine line between advocacy and exploitation, so be careful.

•

Create your own philanthropic objectives. Refer to it when you create your strategic outreach plan to donors. Running to anyone you think will fund you can have you doing a lot of needless running.

•

There are opportunity assessment tools to help you gage which opportunities and partnerships you want to pursue and which ones are not the right fits. It may sound crazy to say there are opportunities that you would say no to in the beginning, but there are.

•

You are in it for the long haul, social change is a marathon, not a sprint—so plan the work accordingly. Make sure to build in time to evaluate your work within your plans and stop to assess and question your approach and what you are learning.

•

Listen, listen and listen. Don't ever assume that there is a 'need' for what you can contribute, but work closely alongside partners and communities to assess the needs and roles together, then find a place where you can contribute the most value.

•

If you are a Human Rights organization specifically, but true for all social change work, you must walk the walk on ensuring that you use technology ethically and safely, and not do harm (inadvertently or not) by sharing or using technologies that expose people to more risks.

•

Local expert knowledge in the physical area where you're working. If you work in a place where you are a foreign leader of that organization, you need local experts, not just staff who are local. But there should also be someone who is local and understands the interventions you are trying to implement for a deeper dimension. It's helpful to have both of those layers present.

•

Instead of trying to get everyone on your board who offers you money, create an incubation board. This is as opposed to an advisory board, which you should also consider. An incubation board can be where you put your biggest and brightest thinkers who have ideas that can innovate or improve how your organization works. Their decisions still need board approval, but they will still play a vital part in the organization.

An advisory board should be where you put larger donors who have the financial experience and bandwidth to improve fundraising and budgets, but may be too big a personality for the board or is simply not a good fit for that position. We have found that it is better to have multiple boards than to have too many people on one board. How you delegate who goes where can also reveal your delegation skills as a leader.

●

If you are working as an outsider in a foreign land, you must have either a command of the local language or have staff that speaks your language and the local language fluently. This is extremely important, because so much can be lost in translation, including information your beneficiaries need to understand completely or vice versa.

●

Plan B, Plan C and Plan D. Before you go to any donors, work out what your plan will be if your original plan of action fails or doesn't go as far as you had hoped.

●

Check out donor review sites such as GrantAdvisors.org. There are a few, but this one will help you know which foundations could look like a fit on paper, but will make you jump through too many hoops to bother.

●

Have a very clear sense of the boundaries of the mission. It's easy for a new organization to get pulled in a lot of different directions, because they are learning about what's happening on the ground and still forming the mission. It's important to incorporate all of that knowledge and adjust accordingly, but you don't want to start doing what every other organization is already doing. The whole point of being a startup is that there is a need for a new organization.

•

We send our top staff to the Management Institute. I hate most consultants. I think much of it is kind of bullshit, but the Management Institute has a two day crash course on nonprofit management. We have anyone who is supervising anyone go to the crash course. I know of a lot of other really good nonprofits who go there and they offer them all over the US. When you first start a nonprofit, no one comes into it knowing how to manage and it really does cover all functions of management.

•

Try to cultivate a network of mentors the same way you want to cultivate a network of donors. To some extent, that might be your board, but there are some people who are not good fits for your board for various reasons, but who could still lead or contribute in other ways. You should have a person you can call if you have an HR issue. That could be a question or a board issue or a content issue.

If you can't find mentors who can help you in such a way, pick nonprofits that you think are great and see if the ED will take a meeting with you, which they probably will because they'll be flattered and want to share the information they know. Then see if you can cultivate them as a resource to send questions when they pop up.

•

Always send 'Thank you' notes. For anything. Any meeting someone gives you, they get a thank you message the same day. Thank you notes are not just for donors; they are for anybody who gives you their time. They don't' have to be super long, just tell them thank you. It will go a long way.

•

As a leader, be yourself. It may not work with every donor, but it may not be worth having them as donors if you can't be yourself around them. A committed donor means you have a relationship and if it's someone you can't have an honest relationship with, it will be shitty for both of you.

•

Always keep in mind that there is no one size fits all. People who have done things a certain way that worked will tell you that's how things are supposed to be done and that is not true. When I began my non-profit, there were a lot of ways that other nonprofits were similarly run that I didn't love. I didn't know if that was going to be an inevitable destination for us, because that was the only way to do them or no one else had tried hard enough to do something different.

We decided to try a bunch of different things just to remain in our own comfort zone and they mostly worked. It takes tinkering. You're never going to get it perfectly from the beginning and you're never going to have it perfect at the end either. Look at a bunch of other models of how things are done and recognize that the right one for you will be some form of permutation of them all. Just remember it will most likely not go right on the first try.

5

The Good, The Bad and The Unbelievable: Donor Experiences With Nonprofit Engagement

What makes donors become the kind of ambassadors who find a way to mention their favorite grantee in every other sentence? And what makes a donor choose to take the stairs to the top floor if the alternative is sharing a lift with a certain NGO leader, or makes a donor do a Google search on the possibility of obtaining a restraining order on an entire nonprofit organization? Experiences. There are people in the nonprofit sector who get it, those who don't, and in some situations, those who have completely lost it.

While I continue to echo that there is no specific template for engaging donors or guaranteeing funding, there are definitely things that can be done and things that should be avoided at all costs throughout the process. Mistakes can happen of course, but there is a minor error in judgment (such as not having all necessary information prepared for a meeting) and then there is crossing the line professionally or ethically.

First impressions get all of the attention, but engagement doesn't end after initial contact. It can stretch well after the approval of a grant. For donors who don't get to experience the daily joys and frustrations of being on the frontlines, the only connection to what nonprofits do—

outside of site visits—is interaction with nonprofit staff. Amazing efforts that happen far from the eyes of donors can be lost in the actions of a representative who inadequately expresses their significance, or chooses ill-advised methods to get the attention of donors. A positive initial interaction with a charismatic individual who represents the organization can start an engagement off on the right foot, but at some point, people stop talking and the work has to speak for itself.

Every hiccup that develops along the way are only part of the engagement, if the nonprofit informs and involves donors. When donors discover organizational problems from a source other than the organization, it robs them of one of the main objectives in partnering: a relationship. Engagement is not the same as a relationship; it's relationship building.

If you're having difficulty differentiating between the two, consider dating as relationship building and deleting your dating app of choice to become 'exclusive' as being in a relationship. There is still continuous relationship building that happens, but there is also a level of trust and respect and even love that has been established on both ends. The engagement process continues until a nonprofit goes from a grant-seeker or a grantee to a full partner.

On the surface, donors sharing their memorable encounters with the nonprofit sector could be seen as a contextual expansion of the previous dos and don'ts chapter. While that is certainly true in part, this is also a glimpse into the experiences that have shaped the funding structures of donors or why they have them in place. If the dos and don'ts provided some humanity to donors, then these might serve to give perspective on donor behaviors and their giving guidelines.

The following experiences—told directly by donors in their own words—represent the actions that have touched them and turned them off.

●●●

The Good:

I was working on launching a grassroots initiative with a number of big NGO partners around adolescent girls. Early on, I spoke to one of the larger implementing partners about the direction of the project. They were a good example of an organization that had a clear focus in place. They didn't second-guess other smaller organizations and made sure their voice was represented to us as donors.

They were clear to say, 'give us money for this project and we're going to work it through our paradigm that we believe in,' and when we as a big corporate firm felt the focus was straying from what we had established as a whole, they were firm and honest in saying this is how we operate and how we see the best results. They did adapt themselves to work better with the other implementers, but I always respected that they were not afraid to stick to their guns about their objectives and approach, all in a professional manner.

●

From the get-go, I experienced incredibly clear, appropriate, wonderfully thoughtful communications. Once they realized I delegate a great deal to my staff, they meticulously created and adhered to a well-conceived timeline. They demonstrated superb appreciation of the fact that my availability is limited and I surround myself with gracious, top notch people who reflect my wishes/expectations and are trusted to do so.

We planned an event for the nonprofit. Info on the organization, bios of the key people and a proposed intro of me were provided substantially in advance. At the event, the organization's principals and staff helped me circulate, and fed me 'cliff notes' intros on the spot, making sure I was not waylaid by any overly zealous attendees. Very shortly after the evening, I received exceptionally heartfelt and beautifully written letters.

Gifts I do not expect and actually do not want, but they sent a gift that was so personal, special, offbeat and fun, and not costly to them. It was a little pink t-shirt with their logo. Its proud and grateful owner, Pupi Dupi, my 3lb poodle, uses it all the time. Mama Dupi finds herself often promoting conversation about this wonderful cause, which is joyfully, visually and uniquely much in our lives.

●

A good experience was meeting someone at a conference during a plenary. We sat next to each other and began a conversation. After the session ended, we continued to speak about the topic at hand and she did not try to work in her organization's mission into an already intriguing conversation. Only when I asked about her work did she quickly and clearly inform me. We exchanged information and when she reached out again, she reached out—not another one of her coworkers. She was clear and upfront about wanting to create a working relationship, possibly around our expressed common interests, but also wanted to maintain a relationship even if a working one could not be created. I never felt pressure.

•

We met with the understanding that I did not fund in the area, but was interested in what he was doing in that field. He came to the meeting with a clear-cut explanation of what he was doing and why it excited him to be working on such a cause, despite its heavy and dark nature. He answered my questions and provoked more questions and answers from me. His goal was to get me excited about the work, even if I never granted in the area and there was no expectation. After a series of other thoughtful meetings and emails, we found a way to work together that benefited us both.

•

Started with a fundraiser we attended. Thanked us very well, made us feel welcome. Kept us up to date with the progress on their program. Shared stories of how lives changed. Built a rapport and relationship, had us come tour the facility and see the people impacted. Had them tell us their stories. Provided solid financial information as to the costs of their programs as well as the impact. They not only told us of outputs, they shared outcomes and lessons learned.

They engaged our heads, our hearts and eventually our hands as volunteers. They did not make a specific dollar ask, which led us to give more than we normally would for a first time gift. We got back so much more than we gave. It is one of our favorite organizations, which we still support and have provided for in our will. The approach was gentle, like beginning a friendship, sharing our stories, asking about our passions, caring for us and what we were looking to do and finding a solution through what they do – they solved a need we hadn't quite verbalized and kept us engaged every step of the way.

•

One of the best experiences came from someone who attended a conference I also attended. We did not have a chance to meet there, but he obtained my details through the organizers. He wrote a very strong and concise two paragraph email. The first paragraph explained why he thought there could be synergies and not just that he thought there might be synergies.

The next paragraph felt like a movie trailer. He described his organization in a way that was succinct, but left me wanting to know more. A few strong lines spoke to the work, but with some energy. The rest said that if I had interest, he could tell me more in a format that best suited me. His email was mindful of my time and my philanthropic scope. It allowed me to customize the next engagement. The mistake many people make is using the first email as a bombardment of information. This was a rare moment of the opposite approach.

•

I had a fabulous interaction with a potential grantee that ended up withdrawing their application. We had been casually getting to know an NGO for several months and were very eager to support them. Given our narrow funding criteria, which we had gone over with them in detail, the NGO decided to wait on submitting an application until they felt they had the right scenario. After about four months, we finally received an application and began the formal process. Three quarters of the way through the process (and with all signs pointing to an approval for funding) something changed on the ground, which altered the context of the project.

The NGO informed us immediately. We discussed the situation and asked how we might still make the project work, but they pulled the application anyway. What was impressive is that they didn't pull the application because it was no longer needed or because they couldn't deliver on what they proposed, but rather because they had taken the time to get to know our criteria and mission so well that they didn't feel it was a good enough fit for us anymore. They didn't want to waste anyone's time or resources pursuing something that wasn't exactly right. The truth is we liked them so much we might have talked ourselves into making an exception and veering off strategy.

Their integrity and honesty helped us more than it helped them. As a result, not only are we more likely to give when the right opportunity does come along, we already feel like champions for their work, making us want to help them in any other way we can, whether it's making introductions to other donors, serving as a reference, or anything else they might need.

●

I had accepted a request to meet with the Executive Director of a nonprofit after a very trusted funding partner had vouched for them. After I confirmed, the ED asked if I wouldn't mind having the person who connected us join the initial meeting. At first, I had serious reservations. It felt like undue pressure to support an organization by having someone who I trusted push on its behalf. I agreed, but honestly entered with a sour taste.

However, I was pleasantly surprised by how it took form in the meeting. The ED explained that the presence of my friend was mostly to aid her in how she represented the organization and provide feedback post-meeting. After some light get-to-know-each-other conversation, it was like my colleague disappeared. The ED led with a short, but powerful story of why she started the charity. She spoke about other actors in the space, including ones our foundation supported, and how her work complemented theirs in a way that was necessary.

Towards the end of our meeting, the ED surprised both of us by asking my peer if there were any questions or potential issues with our work I should know that we failed to discuss. This could have been disastrous, but I appreciated her effort to get everything out of the meeting. I don't know if this could work for everyone, but I really enjoyed this approach.

●

I met a young representative of a nonprofit whom I was unfamiliar with during a luncheon for another charity. We spoke briefly before the program began and picked it up after it ended. She didn't push her organization at all. We were engrossed in the topic of the luncheon. I actually thought she was a donor and had to ask her to tell me about herself and the organization before learning she represented a non-profit. I'm often scared to ask a nonprofit rep to answer the 'what do you do' question, because I normally won't get to speak again for about ten minutes.

She was brief and connected it in a way that related to our conversation. We exchanged info and I looked forward to hearing from her, but was prepared that the next correspondence would be a more formal pitch. It never happened. The follow up email was a kind note thanking me for a great talk. She included a couple of articles that she referenced in our talk and the only link to her organization was in her signature. We shared several emails back and forth that were personal. The cynical part of me admired her long game, but I genuinely enjoyed our communications.

Then one day, she reached out to me with a proposition and not one that I expected. She said she planned to attend a one day forum and had been offered to host a discussion. It was on the same topic of our original conversation and she extended the offer for me to cohost. I was flattered and surprised. I accepted and it was a very rewarding experience. After the event, I finally asked why she didn't present a proposal for funding to our foundation. She said that when she reviewed our work online, she saw a possible fit, but not a comfortable fit. If the right moment came along, she would make the proposal.

She gained so much of my respect and I became the biggest fan of her and her nonprofit. We finally found a comfortable fit for funding later, but the relationship still exists and I am much more grateful for that.

●

A memorable experience was with one of our current grantees. Once the grant had been formally approved, they asked if they could have a meeting with us to discuss our other grantees in order to see if there were concrete areas for collaboration. This never came up during the proposal process and from prior experiences we were careful not to force collaboration between grantees. But the meeting was thorough and they took the lead to see where synergies were worth pursuing based on our descriptions.

They were not seeking additional funding for the collaborations, but looked to strengthen their own work and that of our other partners.

For us, we see this as a largely beneficial strategy and the results we continue to see validate it.

●

I notified our grantees that our foundation was undergoing an internal strategic review and to prepare for the likelihood that their grants would not be renewed. No organization likes to hear that and some fight unsuccessfully to see if they can be excepted if they fall outside the new funding guidelines. One of our grantees reached out to ask if we had any nonprofit participants in the strategic review, which we did not.

They suggested that we invite our best performing grantee to be a part of the process, so they could understand how we were coming to our decisions and better inform us. If we chose their organization, it would help them immensely to understand how foundations undertook strategic reviews, so they would be better prepared if this were to happen to them again.

Our board balked at this at first, but we came up with a compromise to share some information around the need for a strategic shift and what expected outcomes we were after. This inclusion made it clear to us that trying to create a strategic plan on funding without including the voices of implementers would continue to create unrealistic perspectives of outcomes. They made us question our methodology and look more closely at the examples of success from other foundations that we were hoping to mirror.

Although we found this approach to be an eye-opening experience, it is important to address the logic in why we excluded nonprofits from the strategic review process and the reaction of our board. Simply put, a wolf in sheep's clothing still looks like a sheep. We had great grantees, but we also found that too many grantees and prospective grantees were not engaged in best practices.

We encountered many examples of organizations inflating or manufacturing data, moving away from the original mission we bought into, and taking credit for the work of smaller Community Based Organizations (CBOs) without compensating them or doing so in an untimely manner. One or two bad apples is understandable, but we were seeing an epidemic and a strategic review was clearly necessary. If nonprofits were a main contributing factor to us having the strategic review, it made no sense in that moment to include them.

However, in our review, we were able to see that we were also at fault in how we recruited implementing partners and that was, in large part, due to the suggestion of that one grantee and their inclusion.

The Bad:

An organization I had not given to before came and asked for a significant gift. They apparently looked at some financial service data and the ask was in line with organizations we historically gave to. However, we had no relationship with them and they did not bother to establish one.

They never asked what we cared about or what we wanted to see changed. They just presented their pitch. Their pitch wasn't that good either, didn't really state what would have changed as a result of our gift or told a story of someone in the program. If they had tried to find out our interests and come in with a modest initial request, we might have reached the level of giving they sought. They just never connected with us as people vs. check-writers.

•

Sometimes when a good friend or colleague makes a strong introduction to nonprofit staff for a funding relationship, they tend to give the impression that a funding relationship is inevitable. My experiences have been unfortunate with some pushing for meetings and grant opportunities. I have had people call my cell phone looking for answers. The answer for anyone who calls me outside of work hours on my cell phone is always no. It doesn't matter who makes the introduction, there must always be a level of professionalism.

•

A few months ago, I hosted one of many events (approximately fifteen in 1st and 2nd quarter of that year) at my apartment where I provide nonprofits access with full underwriting (cocktails, hors d'oeuvres and/or buffet) for up to 65 people. These events can be friend-raising or fund-raising.

I found it rather ungrateful and downright insulting when, in the course of this event, the founder of the charity asked me to exceed or, at least match my prior year's donation, in support of their annual gala. If this wasn't distasteful enough, they showed no appreciation for my efforts towards devoting an evening to their work. Instead of taking advantage of the opportunities in the room, I was pressured in front of numerous guests! The evening was a true downer. While I will continue to support this organization, because I deeply care about their mission, my enthusiasm and endorsement is seriously dampened.

●

Shortly after I was divorced, I was invited to a presentation on a program by participants in an international environmental forum whose trip my former foundation with my ex-spouse had funded. After the presentation, I was cornered in a small conference room by the Developmental Director of the institution and the second-in-command. There, I was continuously pressed to express 'my interests' in supporting the institution. It was offensive on so many levels. I have not returned since, despite repeated invitations to similar events, nor have I given any further support.

●

I received a cold email from a group that had a project that could complement work we were doing with schools. My response was clear that we would not fund the project. However, we were willing to help them connect with schools to conduct their work. After having several in-person meetings that felt like they could have been accomplished through 30-minute phone calls, where I reiterated that we could provide some staff time and input but no funding, they sent me a detailed work plan that included us paying for their travel costs to conduct their work.

I understand the value in trying to develop relationships over time, but it is frustrating to give your time to try and help another organization accomplish their mission just to have everyone's time wasted by sneaking in a request for funding. Paying for travel expenses is a grant just as paying for your staff time, the materials or anything else.

•

I met someone doing some truly inspiring work in a region new to our small family foundation. The project was ambitious and they were honest about their struggles fundraising for completion. The largest grant we could have made would have only put a small dent into their deficit, so we met with the founder's Executive Director and brainstormed the possibility of a fundraiser. The Executive Director mentioned knowing many celebrities, including some who were closely connected to the founder. I should have been suspicious that if she knew so many celebrities, why was the work so hard to fund?

She promised many names and, for my part, I promised to underwrite the event to a certain amount and invite my own friends who I thought could make some donations. As I set about to obtain a space and send soft invitations to friends, I did not hear anything from the Executive Director regarding commitments, just questions about my progress. As the event began to solidify, I was met with many surprises and not the pleasant kind.

All sides decided that a fee based fundraiser would be the best idea, to guarantee some funds would be raised on the night of the event. Some of the bigger name celebrities she once had as confirmed guests were now coming, but did not expect to pay the entry donation. Other names that were presented as definite were downgraded to possible. Then I was told with no notice that the main celebrity guest, which we were most excited about having (who we were told had cared so much about the mission), would require an exorbitant appearance fee to be donated to the project.

This came as a shock to us and that fee took us way out of our budget for the fundraiser. The Exec. Director swore she had informed me, but no physical evidence existed that she had. This was now a total nightmare. Even though we had poured a lot into the event, the new costs, the lack of commitments for about half the guests we expected and the promise to my friends that those people would be there to justify the ticket price made it impossible to carry out the fundraiser.

When we notified the Executive Director of our decision as a foundation, she was very angry, beyond what would be understandable. She took no responsibility for her role in any of the failure. I sent an email a little later suggesting that we try something smaller since the project still appealed to us. I never heard back.

●

An ED of an NGO reached out with a very long email that had a very long proposal and a very long concept note attached. It took a few days for me to respond. The NGO was not in our scope, but that hasn't always stopped me from reaching out. I just happened to be really busy and couldn't see a partnership based on the info provided. So I replied to the ED and thanked him for reaching out, but explained that I did not see a fit and could not think of any ways I would be of help. I also mentioned how insanely busy I was, which I hoped explained my delay in replying. I told him that if something came to me that could be useful to his organization, I would be in contact.

He immediately wrote me back and asked me to send a list of some of my projects that I was working on so that he could have a better idea of what I supported. Even after I explicitly expressed that my time was precious and rarely free, he still tried to make a fit where I had explained there was not. It is not my job as a donor to help find a synergy. It's yours. I would have preferred if he asked that we reengage when I would be more available. He could have also just let it go.

Not every donor and NGO are a good fit. There is a good persistence and then there is a bad persistence.

●

We had a grantee who knew our five year grant was coming to a close and would not be renewed. We were willing to help in all ways to move them forward, but they focused their time on renewing a grant. We made introductions, but were told that they did not reach out until the grant cycle had closed. In the end, they had funding gaps that we could not address and they did not invest enough time in finding another donor to pick up where we planned to exit.

●

Four years ago, before I arrived at the foundation, we funded an emergency grant to a large organization to assist their work with a natural disaster. Our founder went to see some of the projects, but after that, nothing else happened between the organization and foundation. During this time, I worked for that organization and helped draft the proposal for that grant. Actually, I worked at an executive and consulting level for that same organization for fifteen years before I joined this foundation almost two years ago as the Executive Director.

Fast forward to this year. The new CEO of this organization wants to renew the relationship, so she sends an email requesting to meet with our founder. Of course, the assistant to the founder forwards the email to me. This was the first mistake she made. Unless you know the founder personally, you should go through the normal channels set up through the foundation.

So I call the CEO and ask her why she requested a meeting with the founder directly. She responds by 'informing' me that her organization received funding in the past, which I already knew, and that she wanted to provide an update on that funding. The reporting on this project had already been done, because I helped to complete it. This was the second mistake. Don't use a prior funding relationship to maneuver and manipulate your way into a new one. Even if she had spoken with another foundation staff member, they would have been aware of the reporting on this. It is a very small foundation.

I tell her that we already had the reporting done over two years ago, so she says, 'But we also have some other projects that we would like to present to you. And there is one particular program we have in mind.'

The program she goes on to describe is one that I was instrumental in building, but she had no clue who I was or my connection to the work she was trying to get us to fund. That was the third mistake. If she had done just a bit of research, she would have approached us in a way that wasn't rude, unprofessional or uninformed. These were junior mistakes for someone at a senior level.

●

I took a meeting with the founder of a multinational charity addressing poverty alleviation. When I asked how the organization was different from others working in the space, I was given a very template answer full of buzzwords like 'bottom up approach,' 'locally-led' and 'transparent' without real specifics. Based on that answer, I asked how the organization managed to work locally in so many different areas. The founder boasted of the partnerships with many local NGOs, but forgot to create a narrative of the organization's value-add to already existing mechanisms operating locally.

When I pointed that out, there was some stuttering and reaching for a better constructed answer, but I didn't feel like much of what was being said was genuine. If you are going to enter into a space that is already crowded, the most important messaging is not why your organization exists, but why it needs to exist. If I don't feel as if it needs to exist, there is no incentive to support it.

●

I'll never forget going to a conference that was supposed to highlight the intersection between social justice, social innovation and social investment. There was all this talk prior to the conference about solutions and for me, solutions means ending a problem. I realized at one of the final dinners that none of the people I met—none—were trying to work themselves out of a job. It was the last time I went to that conference. I know it wasn't a reflection of the conference, but a reflection of the sector.

I understand not every problem can be solved or solved in a short amount of time, but we as donors don't want to hear you focusing on building your presence more than you making yourself redundant. No foundation has enough money to fund all the issues. Foundations combined don't have enough money either, because it's not about the money; it's about public and political will. We need to feel like nonprofits are concentrating in those areas. I tell people that I want to support organizations that are looking to rent, not buy.

●

This happened to a donor colleague of mine who has allowed me to retell her story. She met with an NGO leader that had been courting her for a grant. Since she had no prior relationship with the work and it was not directly correlated to core passions, she said 'I've decided to give you a $40k grant this year.'

The NGO representative paused, and responded by saying that she was disappointed, as the organization was really counting on her to do something bigger. Shocked, my friend explained that this was what she had decided and as a first grant was all she could do. The leader continued to come back to needing a bigger grant—several times—with no appreciation for the initial gift.

After deliberating, the donor informed the NGO that she planned to withdraw her grant offer, entirely. They had no self-reflection as to why she made the choice to withdraw the original offer.

•

This is a negative experience that is not entirely the fault of the non-profit. I remember one of the very first grants I gave. I had found an organization who I thought was doing amazing work, so I contacted them and told them we were new to philanthropy and we're interested in funding if they were interested, which of course they were. We met and the leader was a super nice guy. He was very smart and the overall project was very good. So I told him to apply for a grant and he did.

The application was entirely different than what we had discussed because suddenly, he thought he had to comply with all of these rules that we never told him to follow, mostly around how he had to present the organization and what they do. He ended up giving us this super NGO-ized proposal, where I didn't even see traces of what the organization was all about. They were these super advocates that were campaign oriented before the proposal and suddenly they had this training approach like every other typical NGO.

So I called the guy and asked him, 'What are you doing? What happened between our conversation and the application? Why did you submit something so different?'

He said, 'Oh I thought for the application I had to make it more official—'

And I stopped him and told him, 'No. That's not the stuff we want to fund. We want to fund your protests and your advocacy. We don't want to fund your training that you organized just because you thought you had to. I can't blame them completely. It has been really hard for me to learn that even though I feel like I'm good at building relationships and have tried not to come across as the 'big funder,' there is still a massive power difference and nonprofits still feel they have to do needless stuff even when I tell them no.

•

I had a horrible phone call with a small NGO that wouldn't take no for an answer. Their founder had unexpectedly passed away about six months earlier and they needed to hire new staff as the founder had been doing the job of 2-3 people for virtually no compensation for years. The participants on the call were the new ED (promoted internally) and a board member (the founder's daughter). The board member quickly usurped the conversation and while I was certainly sympathetic to her personal loss, it was clear in the first fifteen minutes that it wasn't going to be a good fit.

After thirty minutes of listening (and not being able to get a word-in edgewise), I shared my candid feedback that it wasn't a good fit, but offered to quickly review our criteria with them in case there was a better fit down the line. After reviewing each criterion, I explained why their situation didn't qualify or meet those terms.

The board member challenged me on every point. At this point, (nearly fifty minutes in to the call), I let them know that I had a hard stop at the end of the hour and reiterated my feedback that it wasn't a fit. The board member continued to talk, arguing why she thought her organization did fit our criteria and how she felt a duty to her family's legacy. I finally hung up after an hour and fifteen minutes, and needless to say I would never entertain a proposal from that organization again.

•

This is not necessarily one experience, but as a private donor, I hear many grantees tell me that they want to get together more during the course of the grant to discuss the work, but also grow as friends. I always welcome this. I feel it brings me closer to the work and makes me feel more like a partner than a money giver.

I also care very much about the friendships that come from those in-person meetings. My good experiences have been when I meet with grantees and a good portion of the time is spent on updates and the rest of the time is more about us talking about ourselves or our favorite new books. It feels like a friendship and often times it becomes a friendship.

The bad experiences have been when the grantees say they want to catch up and get to know me better as a person, but we spend the entire time talking about the organization and when I try to steer it to a more personal path, it gets quickly redirected to work. The worst experiences are when each informal meeting is an attempt to get more funding instead of showing me the appreciation of the current grant.

●

A charity contacted me requesting a meeting. The person who emailed me sent comprehensive materials to review and asked for a quick fifteen minute meeting to follow up once I had time to review in order to discuss opportunities for alignment. I reviewed the work and did a bit of extra due diligence before I replied and agreed to a quick meeting. I liked what I read about them and thought I could use the fifteen minutes to get to know the person who reached out and answer a few questions before proposing a more comprehensive meeting. I asked if he thought he would need more than fifteen minutes and he said no, that would be enough. I budgeted 30 minutes just in case and scheduled it during a busy day. The communications between the staff person and I were very good. He was light-hearted but professional, so I was looking forward to our call.

The meeting was meant to be just us, but days before the call, he asked if his Executive Director could sit in on the call. I didn't see a problem with it. Then, about five minutes before the meeting, I got an email asking if one of the in-country staff could join the call. I told him that it was only meant to be a quick intro meeting and that we could have longer meetings later, but if he felt the need to include other staff, I wouldn't object. The ED replied to my email that she felt the staff person's inclusion would be highly valuable.

I joined the call, but they were not ready. They were trying to add the country staffer, but were experiencing technical difficulties. After five minutes, I mentioned I had a limited time. They pushed to add the staffer. They finally added the staffer twelve minutes into a fifteen minute meeting. Then they pushed for more time, even when I suggested postponing the meeting. Since I had fifteen more minutes budgeted, I let the meeting continue. The entire time, the Executive Director and the staffer spoke, mostly to repeat information I had already taken the time to read. The person who originally emailed me said about five words. I didn't say much more. I had to force them to stop speaking after the budgeted thirty minutes had passed and there was no time left for me to provide feedback or comments.

I was very disappointed in this meeting and all my good feelings about a possible relationship were deflated in just thirty minutes. The ED immediately emailed me and was clear she would be taking the lead on communications. I wanted to tell them that their eagerness ruined my excitement in working with them, but I just delayed responses in correspondences until I felt better about recommending the work for funding. The ED failed to recreate that excitement and didn't trust her staff member enough to grow the relationship, which was a strong enough indicator for me to finally pass on the recommendation. Sometimes less really is more.

●

I received an email from a person I never remembered meeting from an organization that I could not remember hearing about. However, the body of the text heavily implied that we had met during a conference and discussed possible alignments. I knew I had been to that conference so this was entirely possible, but it bothered me that I could not recall any correspondence. I put the email to the side with a note to look into the organization the next day.

The next day, actually while I was reviewing their website, I received another email from the same person. This time, instead of being addressed to me, the salutation read, 'Dear <<name>>' and where our foundation name once was, it now read, <<company>>. From the looks of their website, this clearly was an organization and not some scam. I checked the conference participation list and saw the organization listed. I'm pretty sure they looked at the same participation list. I understand that part of the benefit of attending donor integrated conferences is access to this kind of information, but this is the worst way to treat it.

Had the organization honestly said that they did not have a chance to meet with me during the conference, but felt there could be alignments based on real investigatory work on their end that they cited, then getting a duplicate email with the same errors could have been forgivable as a hastily sent email. What I received amounts to fraud and I would never entertain any dialog with them or any organization I feel is taking a similar route to relationship building.

The Unbelievable:

We had a grantee who my donor gave a huge, multi-year grant. Personally, I had problems with the organization because they were constantly (I mean every year) asking for an early disbursement of their donation because they were having 'cash flow issues.' Despite my reservations (and sharing this with the donor) I would often respond to the early request for funds. But one year, we were tremendously backed up in the office and could not honor an accelerated request. So the grantee tried to go around me and email my donor directly. Not only that, he spoke very negatively about me.

My donor knows me and she knows my work ethic, and didn't believe it for a minute. She immediately forwarded me the email. I was too mad! I'm extremely pro-grantee, so for someone to even suggest that I might withhold a grantee's money or I was not doing my job, made me very angry. I immediately wrote back to the grantee, openly copied the donor on the email, and read him like an open book. I'm the person that made sure he received all those previous donations not only on time but early, so I felt betrayed and angry, as did my boss.

●

During a time when I was dealing with serious personal matters, I had a charity contact me that I had given a grant to the year before. The contact at the organization was looking for another grant as part of a time sensitive matching challenge. Given our relationship, I explained that despite my interest in wanting to help, I was going through something in my private life that demanded my full attention and as soon as I had the opportunity, I would reconnect. The response from the contact was unbelievably inappropriate on several levels.

He continued to push a phone meeting and the challenge, despite my response. He then compared the importance of the organization's opportunity to the importance of my personal matter, without even knowing specifics of what I was going through. I found that completely unacceptable. I was so horrified that I could not respond. A year-long relationship was soured with one email.

•

I sat on a roundtable panel on philanthropy for children from a domestic and global lens. Afterwards, I sat in on another session that one of my co-panelists led on philanthropic best practices. A guy representing an NGO asked a great question that I felt I had a good answer for, but couldn't answer at that moment as an audience member. After the session, I went to the man and offered my advice (without wearing my affiliation badge). I was more casually dressed than some of the others at the conference. He looked me up and down and couldn't have been less interested in what I had to say. He nodded without saying more than OK and walked away towards my colleague from the panel, who he knew was a donor.

The colleague pointed to me, apparently to indicate that I funded in his area. Then he walked over to me, smiling as if nothing had happened. He said, 'I'm sorry, I didn't properly introduce—'

I stopped him there and said, 'You have a good day,' before I walked away. Your organization can only be as good as the people representing it. These are the people who give charities a bad name.

•

There was a devastating flood in the heart of Georgia's capital, Tbilisi. It claimed the lives of at least twenty people (mostly women), leaving dozens of families without housing, and killing most of the animals in Tbilisi Zoo and the city dog shelter, leaving the rest loose in the city without food or homes. In order to reply to the disaster, our foundation launched an Emergency Grants Program to provide support to the survivors of the flood.

In total, we provided a number of small grants for women's initiatives that supported the post-flooding processes of rehabilitation. One of the grants given was to an organization whose project included providing support for women and girls residing in areas affected by the flood. Before we provided them with a grant, a representative of that organization came to our office and shared with us the problems women in the affected area faced, and later applied to the call for proposal. We never supported that organization before, but we found the representative to be convincing and thought that it was crucial to support the survivors of the flooding through the methods they outlined.

A month after the first meeting, the same representative from that organization visited our office. Only she was not there to provide an update on the grant we gave her a month ago; she was there seeking another funding opportunity from the same emergency program… disguised as someone else. Giving an excuse that she had the flu, she gave us a different name with a changed voice. The woman was wearing a face mask covering half of her face, dark sunglasses covering her eyes and a huge hat covering the other half of her face. Our staff members, perplexed and confused by the outfit, started an investigation to find out who was this woman really.

After trying to track her down on social media with the two names she had given, we were able to determine that the woman with the flu was indeed the same woman from the organization that we had already funded. Our Grants Manager and M&E Manager went in the field to monitor the implementation of the project. At the site, they met the 'beneficiaries' who had no idea about either project, had not received any legal or psychological support and when our staff members told them about the Fund and the program they were supposed to be receiving, they became very enthusiastic, saying that they would like to apply for this grant, which they should have already received.

Later, our foundation had several in-person and telephone conversations with the mysterious woman, who denied everything and tried to convince us we were wrong. In order to not call the police, we requested an interim report, as well as the final report from her organization. It was presented to us with no flaws at all. They were very good in faking the documents as well, but not actually doing any of the work.

●

We were engaged with a nonprofit whose work be loved. We also loved the founder, but felt she wasn't always the best at communicating to us, as well as communicating the strengths of the mission and work to others. She had made a gaffe in the past that we were trying to overlook in order to support the mission my boss and I loved. We really loved the work. She had submitted a formal multi-year proposal at my urging, but by the time we had received it, the foundation hit a busy patch. What would have been a quick approval was delayed and I relayed this on to the founder, but assured her that we would provide a response as soon as possible.

Around this time, she finally hired a Director of Development, which we were all happy to finally see happen. Without knowing the new hire, we had confidence this would resolve some of our own issues with the founder's communication shortcomings. I asked the founder to connect me to the new Director as soon as possible and we would be happy to help her in any way we could. She connected us via email and I replied to both women that I would be willing to schedule a phone call as early as possible to get the ball rolling on ways to help. Again, we loved this organization.

The new hire replied and we scheduled a meeting for the following week. Then the founder sent an email to her new Director saying that before she took a meeting with me, they should have a discussion first. She proceeded to write very disparaging things about me and about my boss. She also claimed that the proposal she submitted less than a month before was actually an outstanding grant that we had yet to fulfill. Well, she meant to send it to the Director, but she accidentally sent it to me.

The email made me almost question her sanity. Why would she lie to her incoming staff about a proposed grant that was not yet approved? The comments about my boss and I were out of line and showed a complete lack of respect for us. Reading the email was painful since, once again, we loved this organization. I was reluctant to share the email with my boss, since she had made a personal investment in the organization and a grant from us was pretty much guaranteed to happen. I gave her until the end of the week to realize her error and see what contrition she would exhibit. She never referenced the email, as it became clearer to me that she was unaware of what she had done.

I notified my boss of the incident. As expected, it was decided to cut all ties with the organization immediately. I respectfully cancelled the meeting with the Director and sent an email officially declining the proposal. Still no clue about her error, the founder was shocked at the decision and pushed to speak to my boss directly, which I strongly advised against for her own benefit. She made a number of attempts to make us reconsider. Neither my boss nor I ever told her about her email, but politely made sure she understood we would not support her work.

The biggest shame in all of this is that we loved the work. We still love the work. The founder made it impossible for us to ever support that organization in any way, even as an ambassador to other potential donors.

●

After an unforgettable experience working with an implementer in a country that was previously uncharted for us, I asked other donor partners if they had any recommendations for other possible opportunities for us to work in the region. One organization popped up a couple times, so I looked into their work from their website and based on the endorsements, decided to reach out. As I waited for them to respond to my meeting request, I thought to ask the opinion of my grantee, to see if he had any feedback on the group.

He told me that he had been offered a position there a few years ago, when his own nonprofit was struggling. He considered it and became closer with its leader. Running a similar nonprofit, he was curious about how their budget was high when his own budget was so much smaller but was still able to buy many of the same materials. The founder told him in confidence that they had found a way to inflate the budget to more than twice as much as needed, while they pocketed the rest. They realized they could run all the programs they had for a fraction of the budget assessments and created a scheme to steal money.

All the top level staff was aware. The accountant was the one who helped fix the books. Vendors would create fake receipts and once they were paid, they would give the organization the difference back in cash, with a cut for themselves. Since all the projects were completed, they did not feel like they were cheating anyone in the community. They justified their behaviors to my grantee as some contrived protest to anti-colonialism.

The salary my grantee was offered would have been enough to cover many of the expenses at his own nonprofit and not be reliant upon international donors as much, but he said he couldn't take the job and have a clear conscience. I believed my grantee and asked him if he could provide me with an invoice from a vendor that he shared with this other organization, which he did. When the other organization finally replied to my email, I asked if they could provide me with a receipt for costs, so I could better base my grant. They did so with no hesitation. The receipt indeed showed a price point of nearly 1,000% more than the one from my grantee.

With the reluctant blessing of my grantee, I sent the information to the donors who referred this organization to me, but asked for discretion, so I did not put my grantee or his organization in harm's way. That also meant that unfortunately, we did not report this to local authorities. I would not have shared this story had my grantee not left that area, although his work remains. I still struggle with whether this is the fault of donors for poor oversight or the fault of greed rationalizing obvious wrongs into something acceptable.

•

Early in my philanthropy, I gave many unrestricted grants to organizations without demanding reporting on how the grants were spent. Annual reports were good enough. My lawyers then pushed me to be more diligent in this reporting. I notified all current grantees, including one organization I particularly enjoyed funding, for a report on how the funds for my last two grants had been spent. I would have honestly been happy if they sent me a report saying staff had been hired to grow their capacity.

Instead, they stalled on the reporting. Being busy, I didn't push until the lawyers pushed me. They said they were working on it and after months of waiting, even I was annoyed at how long it took. I finally contacted the CEO directly and asked for the report. What I received was a list of travel expenses, not in and out of the field of work, but to luxury hotels and locations nowhere near the scope of the mission. These were explained as expenses for attending vital conferences, but they were not clear on which conferences. I can't begin to describe how much that hurt and how betrayed I felt. I have no doubt in my mind that the work of this organization is still vital, but I can no longer support it the way I had in the past.

●

One of our grantees approached us to support a new project that they saw great merit in implementing as soon as possible. After I reviewed the proposal, we decided to approve a grant. We understood that they wanted to implement quickly and since our next cycle of grants was not until the end of the year, we moved up their grant by one month, which they had confirmed would be enough time.

However, a few weeks after grant approval, the grantee asked if we would be able to move up the grant a lot sooner, like now. Unfortunately, the person who could approve that kind of expedition was on leave due to a private issue. We conveyed this to the grantee in a very candid manner. We also pressed the grantee to determine the seriousness of the situation that made the grant so urgent. The response was that nothing serious had changed too much, but circumstances on the ground were constantly changing. We did not think this warranted disturbing our colleague and asked them to wait a week, when the leave was supposed to end.

Throughout the week, however, we received a 'friendly reminder' every other day about the grant. At the end of the requested time that basically went ignored, our colleague had not yet returned from leave. We notified the grantee and they asked if someone else could approve it, which was not really possible. We were reluctant to reach out when there was no indication that the grant was desperately needed.

Then there was an email stating that the grant was desperately needed. Without giving any specifics, we were told circumstances had become more immediate and the grantee needed the funds at once to implement ideally. We felt terrible for both the grantee, who we trusted and knew that if they said the situation was serious, it must have been, and we felt bad for potentially interrupting our colleague during a very difficult time. We asked for the weekend before reaching out since it was the end of the week, just to give the colleague more time and they agreed.

On the following Monday, we received a message that the grantee had planned to take out a loan to cover the size of the grant. We didn't want that, especially if it meant incurring fees and interest. We finally reached out to our colleague, who did not immediately respond. It was very uncomfortable, but we pushed for a response the next day until we got one. Our colleague reviewed and approved the request. The grant was sent to the grantee the next day. We knew it would take a few days to a week to be received. We sent an email to the grantee to notify them that the grant was disbursed and to please confirm upon receipt.

What happened next felt like something out of the Twilight Zone. The grantee confirmed receipt, but also wrote that the grant was no longer needed, because another donor had stepped in to cover the costs of the program. The program, set to last six months to a year, had suddenly concluded, apparently finishing much sooner than they had anticipated. Since we had already sent our grant, they suggested that the money be put in their core budget or used for an upcoming fundraising event.

None of it made any sense. Their last email indicated they were forced to take out a loan, less than a week ago. There was no mention that the program would be or could be downsized or completed sooner. There was no mention of another donor. While we could understand not wanting to discuss an unconfirmed donor, the only thing that was familiar was the event, which we had already declined to support. We obviously asked them to try to explain all of this, hoping—while doubtful—that they could offer anything satisfactory or even plausible.

It took quite a while to get a response from the grantee, to the point where we were about to call them right before an email came in. They blamed much of what happened on an unsent email, which was impossible to believe with all the ones they were able to send when we asked for time. It's true that this could have all been a misunderstanding, but it felt much more suspicious than that, and from one of our trusted grantees of all organizations. We seriously considered asking for the funds to be returned, but agreed to make that our last grant to them. The worst part is that we forced someone back to work who should have only been focused on personal matters. The funniest part is that the grantee didn't understand why we chose to end the relationship when the reasons were too many to count.

●

While on a site visit to a potential grantee, I was introduced to a number of young girls who were not able to attend school, for varying reasons. After one brave girl tearfully spoke of her desire to go to school and caused every other young girl to tear up, I asked the nonprofit representative for an estimate of costs to send one girl to school. I was quoted a very low number and I asked the rep how confident she was in the costs. She assured me that the ceiling rate was a very small amount. I ran the numbers and based on her estimates, I felt I could make a small personal contribution to pay the tuition for at least 2-3 girls to complete secondary school, with a buffer for those who may have needed to attend primary school first.

After double and triple checking the numbers with the staff, I felt confident enough to tell the girl who bravely spoke out that I would personally make sure she would have the opportunity to go to school. She was thrilled, as was everyone else. All in all, I committed $5,000 USD for sending the girls to school for at least two years. I never make promises unless I know I can deliver, so given the relatively low costs, I felt this was one I would keep. That was until I received the first budget from their office.

The previous costs for primary and secondary had doubled and tripled, respectively. New undiscussed expenses were added and the total budget offered per girl was double my total intended donation. I wrote back, perplexed by the budget. I also had done some homework to verify the costs for inflation. The numbers I found were more in line with what I was originally quoted, so I emphasized in my reply that this was not from our foundation, but something I wanted to do from my very limited personal finances. There was no room for bartering on my end.

The response was a curious one. There was an acknowledgment that the numbers I found were correct, but they felt the best school for the girls was one that costs considerably more than the average schools. There was also a revised budget. Instead of having reduced costs, the total budget had increased...by over 400%. I thought I had made a mistake with currency conversions and reran the numbers only to find myself back at a budget that was more than four times larger than the maximum amount I clearly stated I could do.

I requested a call to discuss this directly. The disconnect befuddled me. It felt like the organization did not believe that this endeavor was purely mine and thought I somehow had access to foundational funds to cover costs outlined in their budget. There was no way that this budget was created for someone with a middle-income willing to make a goodwill gesture. I mean, the budget included a place for paying staff and administrative costs, as if this were a formal grant.

The call did not resolve anything. The staff maintained that they were not comfortable sending any of the girls to the local schools which was sold as the original option, and that the only viable option was the very expensive private one, despite admitting that the school was presently overbooked, so the chance of the girls gaining entrance was nearly impossible. I saw the promise I made to this young girl slip completely away.

I did well to hide my anger, disappointment and the confusion that I still have about it to this day. However, this experience has left the bitterest taste in all of my time in philanthropy. I take responsibility for making a promise before having all the information in front of me, but I could never have imagined that I would not have been able to even send to school the inspiration for the pledge. This is easily the most discouraging moment for me trying to work with a nonprofit.

●

When I told one of our stronger grantee partners that I was looking for more grassroots organizations to add to our portfolio, they recommended a group that was fairly new to formal institutional work. After a few meetings, the foundation agreed that they would be a good local partner. Because of their inexperience, I stressed that we would walk them through any of the steps of the granting procedure that confused or troubled them, including reporting.

The small group had never received a grant from an organization that required more standardized reports. I took this into consideration and did not expect anything too fancy from the first report, but it was necessary for my foundation to have this to encourage my board that there were benefits to funding smaller grassroots groups. I offered help in writing the report and improved data collection and analysis. They politely declined. As the time approached for the initial report, I sent reminders and more soft offers for assistance, but they said they were fine and the report would arrive on time, so I didn't push.

The report arrived about a day late, but I didn't mind. Reading the report, I was really impressed for the first few pages. The work sounded familiar to what they were meant to be doing, but not exactly what the grant covered or what I knew they had been working on. Nonetheless, it was very well written overall, which surprised me, given their difficulties with the spoken command of the language. As I read on, there were mentions of programs that we knew nothing about and did not seem to be in their capacity to complete. A page later, I noticed an error: where the group's name should have appeared, the name of the recommending partner was written instead. I found it odd, but since they worked together in some ways, it was an acceptable mistake. It was the only grammatical error I identified. Continuing on, it happened again. This time, I felt like what I read made more sense with the name of our bigger grantee than the smaller, newer grantee.

I pulled up the most recent reports from the bigger grantee to see if this was a case of plagiarism. The reports didn't match this new one, but something was going on. I contacted the first organization to let them know my suspicions and see if they had insights into what could be wrong. My contact there said he didn't have any information to share. I had no choice but to bring my concerns to the smaller grassroots group.

Once the Director was confronted with my suspicions, he admitted that he had been given a very old copy of the bigger organization's report and advised to 'borrow heavily' from it, due to similarities in the work. I couldn't believe our bigger grantee had been complicit in promoting plagiarism. When we confronted them again, they denied it initially, but finally admitted to it. This was terribly disappointing that they would do this and then lie about it instead of at least attempting to explain the logic behind such a move. That was the end of the relationship. This was supposed to be the launch of our foray into grassroots funding and it started off with us losing two grantees at once.

●

I was invited to sit on a panel on a topic that was the focus of our philanthropic scope. One of the other speakers was the head of an organization that had recently sought philanthropic support from us, but we narrowly decided to move forward that year with another partner. I hoped sharing the panel together would give me something to take back and show in their favor for the next round of grants.

He was curt with me before we began the panel. During the panel, he personally attacked our foundation for not being progressive. The irony was that the organization that we chose in favor of his was chosen because of their more progressive approach. I was shocked at the way he behaved and when I looked into the audience, he wasn't winning himself any friends. The moderator deftly navigated away from the tension and I just maintained my composure. I was more embarrassed for him, to be honest.

After the panel, the organization leader came up to me. He sensed from the mood of the room that he behaved inappropriately. He said no hard feelings and I remained composed and respectful until I was able to excuse myself. When I returned to work, I let my staff know about his performance. That killed any chance of us taking them on as a partner.

6

Addressing Donor Misconceptions

As just illustrated, donor experiences account for a large part of the donor perception of the engagement space, but not for all of it. The experiences in the previous chapter belong to individuals, not donors as a whole. Many donors have never had these experiences, good or bad (and hopefully unbelievable). They enter philanthropy with only perceptions of nonprofits and, to a greater extent, misperceptions.

I know I certainly entered philanthropy with misperceptions, though mostly positive. I thought smaller nonprofits, for the most part, were altruistic and all necessary in their own way. I had different views on larger nonprofits and international NGOs, where I wasn't all that sure if they were completely necessary. As a member of a few local charitable efforts before joining philanthropy, I only saw the good. I also saw the easy. I wasn't privy to fundraising structures or struggles.

Those experiences contributed to the misperceptions I carried into early opportunities of choosing which organizations were worthy of funding and which ones were not. Positive or not, they did not accurately paint the picture of nonprofit needs, both generally and specifically, and both large and small.

There are other donors whose perceptions of nonprofits come from a similar place to my early days in philanthropy, or are based on reading articles that focus more on efficiency than reality. I remember being advised by donors to read such articles to help our foundation improve its philanthropic giving. Among the helpful suggestions, I also saw numbers and guidelines that didn't address the human factor, unless it called out the unscrupulous side. There were no references to handling constructive failure or why the percentage of a budget dedicated to general operating or salaries was rigidly set at no higher than 10% to 15%. I couldn't shake the feeling that we were legitimizing the arbitrary.

As important as it is for nonprofits to understand from donors—more so than third parties—what donors expect when being approached for fundraising, it is no less important that donors understand the realistic conditions in which nonprofits operate. The only thing worse than funding a bad organization is funding a good organization badly. The following chapters are meant to help better inform the donor with as much effort as has been put in informing the nonprofit sector. It begins with addressing some of those misconceptions donors have of nonprofits, as told by nonprofits.

I reached out to hundreds of nonprofits of various sizes that work globally in several different fields and asked them to answer these three questions:

1. What are the biggest misconceptions about your field or general focus of work you believe donors have?
2. Without revealing yourself, what are the biggest misconceptions about your specific work and/or your organization that you believe donors have?
3. If you were able to speak frankly to a donor about these misconceptions without fear of repercussion, what would you say?

Just as I had done with the donors, I asked nonprofit contributors to keep it personal and not miss the teachable moments. I did not want them to speak about their opinions on existing misconceptions, but about the ones they knew existed based on first-hand experiences. The goal was to cover a wide range of nonprofits across the spectrum. The net cast was also spread over my own grantees, where there would be no anonymity.

I tried my hardest to assure that there would be no retaliation if the criticism bore any resemblance to the author of this book. Thick skin and selective memory would work in their favor, so I commend the ones who were willing to take aim in my direction. I did notice that responses from most of my grantees were more polite than from other nonprofits with whom I had no formal or informal relationship.

I know, as a donor, I am far from perfect. I took stock of these responses as much as I hope other donors will, for a more informed donor is a more informed advocate, as well as a more informed change-agent and change-supporter.

●●●

What are the biggest misconceptions about your field or general focus of work you believe donors have?

We receive government funding for our direct service work, but the law requires private matching funds. It can be very difficult to raise these matching funds, yet we cannot fulfill the requirements of the government contract without private money. Foundations often are not interested in funding direct service work, especially when the perception is the government funding takes care of all of our needs.

●

We can do this work without philanthropic funding. It feels like donors are shocked that we haven't figured out a way to charge children to use a toilet or have access to clean water when in school that is equitable. All our work is done with 50% input from the local community. Our funding via US youth engagement makes the work possible. I see organizations that say that they are doing sustainable work that is income generating, but it has come at a high cost, and is still dependent, in large part, on philanthropy. We value our philanthropic donors and work hard to be sure every penny is well spent. The focus on return on investment works in some fields, but not for schools in the traditional way. The return on investment for schools is educating the force that will truly change communities long-term.

I met a man who told me how his organization's work in Congo became sustainable. They figured out a supply train for a community that all grew potatoes. Through buying trucks and expanding the market they could sell the potatoes. They then brought in container health centers and charged fees for services—due to the increased income, people could pay—they then built water kiosks that sold water and employed a few people to run them. He felt we could do a similar model.

I asked him, 'How did you buy the trucks and the health containers?'

He said, 'Oh, we had $1.5 million dollar funding from USAID.'

I asked him if they had to pay it back and he said no. So is it really a sustainable model? That remains to be seen, but the USAID money is no more than a fancy grant. There is an enormous need for philanthropy that can help organizations do amazing work, but thinking innovation alone will lead to sustainability is a silly misperception that donors continue to have.

•

Child protection or child rights is not a standalone field and therefore should be not dealt with as such. I am lucky to work with a small number of donors who truly understand and support child protection as a standalone field. However, there are many donors who focus solely on supporting children, but who are not willing to give child protection the individual attention it needs. Their perception is that violence against children is a byproduct of other factors in a child's life that, if treated, will assuage the need to protect children. This makes our job as fundraisers in the sector much more difficult, as the reference points are much further away from the reality of our work.

Working with national Community Service Organization (CSO) members further complicates my points, as many donors are focused on supporting direct service delivery, instead of on strengthening local grassroots organizations to do this work better themselves. I have noticed that there is a shift away from this thinking, but it has been a slow shift thus far.

•

Funding Human Rights should yield faster results. In the world of Human Rights, change happens slowly. It can takes years to research and document Human Rights violations, and achieve the regulations and legislation to create sustainable change. An annual impact framework will show only incremental progress towards these long-term goals; it's the longer term vision we need you to invest in.

●

The biggest misconception is that one hat fits all. The nonprofit leader should be able to perform every function needed to run an effective organization and the donor can do the job of the nonprofit founder just through funding. Many donors think that because they supported a school in Malawi, they are now experts on how schools are run in Africa.

I feel like the course of my meetings with donors starts with them asking me about my work and ends with them trying to alter our approach based on projects they have funded in the past. They are not asking themselves about the things those organizations did to get those results that they didn't tell the donors about or if those results have not been exaggerated to satisfy an impatient donor.

●

Global mental health is incurable or just too big to deal with, that it is all about people sitting around in their own piss without hope. Mental health is not perceived well in the West, so their points of reference are the failed or underperforming mental health systems that exist there. They assume that if the West is not doing well enough in their view, then there is no chance for less developed regions. The truth is actually the opposite, because the approach is different and can be sustained in ways that don't fit western approaches.

●

The thing I used to find most frustrating was the rather naive donor view on collaboration among NGOs. Many people assumed that all NGOs compete with each other in a not very productive way. In fact, everything we have done involved collaboration. Given that we were advocating for changes in policy, we wouldn't have achieved anything other than through coalitions. But these coalitions didn't always include the organizations that donors thought they should include.

People were always asking me why we didn't collaborate with a range of women's organizations. However, their goals were often only broadly compatible with ours. And, for successful advocacy, you need a really clear, sharp focus. So virtually none of the organizations with which we collaborated would have had 'women' in the title.

●

Nothing new, but the continued obsession with low overhead is counterproductive. Not that organizations shouldn't be frugal, just that the race for the bottom on overhead sometimes makes it difficult to afford essential things that improve quality, like training and research.

●

Working with vulnerable populations presents many challenges. Most strong nonprofits work to understand their beneficiaries, designing projects, indicators and goals with overall impact of this population in mind. Oftentimes, challenges or surprises arise within these populations that can cause a nonprofit to change direction or make program updates in order to truly respond to the needs of those they are serving. The misperception is that we should account for the unknown in our strategic plans and that these surprises are more of a reflection of nonprofit's lack of preparedness.

Strong donors understand that flexibility is a reality of the work, and value transparency over a rigid adherence to initial objectives that may no longer be relevant. However, oftentimes if a nonprofit must respond to needs and go outside the parameters of the proposed project, issues with the donor arise, which may not encourage full transparency. It is better for donors to always encourage and support a collaborative and transparent communication, where the grantee may approach the donor at all times with relevant changing needs and updates.

●

Anti-human trafficking is too complicated an issue. Donors often want to focus on massive impact and scalability, which can be achieved in our programs, but the path to freedom is a difficult one. We need shelters, advocates and a greater community to provide support to women and children who have been abused. Sometimes that is not necessarily scalable, especially with the cost of operations in cities like New York City or even now Bangkok, where prices are going up.

•

Donors, at times, over-focus on one organization's goals and activities without taking into account the networked approaches and collaborations that happen 'behind' or in conjunction with the work that is facilitated by their grant. When our organization engaged on the issue of systemic state abuse (police brutality) in Brazil, it did so in conjunction with a diverse set of actors, from media collectives in the favelas to Brazilian NGOs, as well as lawyers, journalists, and others.

There are informal and formal ways by which the landscape gets mapped, the tactics sequenced, and information shared. Funders, by and large, are excluded from these dynamics, and not always through any fault of their own. As a result, their infrastructures tend to not be set up to facilitate this type of 'ecosystem' approach. While we will be accountable for its outcomes and indicators, the larger picture of the progress that is made in the field across the different participants is less focused.

•

Many think the country we operate in is a corrupt country with an arguably illegal government and any donations will be stolen by that government. Many people ask me why we chose that place when the fact is that for all the political issues, the government works well to establish good relationships with the nonprofit community, especially when it comes to children.

•

The misperception we face most is that climate change or environmental protection is an all or nothing field. Getting one region to do the right thing environmentally means almost nothing if its neighbors are not compliant. We have been told by donors that they would prefer total buy in from all target parties before they would commit to funding, but they are not willing to support the scaling of our organization to accomplish that.

We cite the example of deforestation in Haiti vs. the environmental protection efforts in place in the Dominican Republic. Both share the same small island, but the impact of tropical storms and natural disasters are disproportionately more severe in Haiti due to the lack of implementation for reforestation and other recommended environmental measures. The work done in the Dominican Republic has not suffered without Haiti's buy in.

This also speaks to the other misperception of donors. Because we work in climate change, they think we won't be able to show the tangible results usually seen in humanitarian work. In fact, there are many tangible results we can point to that indicate climate change is real and supporting nonprofit work can show marked improvements in people's lives. It may not be packaged in the same heartwarming format for mass consumption, but the impact is undeniable.

●

The Human Rights field is expanding as new actors are able to participate, the enhanced movement includes disparate and unexpected participants, from social movements to NGOs, from citizen witnesses to lawyers. The value comes from sequencing and coordinating tactics among these actors, and building strong connections, sharing information. This is a currency that is hard to translate to funders.

●

Funders have rightfully addressed the issue of more funding flowing to Global North organizations and less to organizations that have less access. However, the misperception is that the same monitoring and evaluation tools co-created by nonprofits in the Global North can be equally applied without adaptation to the grassroots nonprofits and

Community Based Organizations (CBOs). The collected data will not match what donors have come to expect. This data is sometimes used in a simplified way that undermines effective partnerships and collaborations.

In our experience, what works best to create concrete impact is coordinating between groups and networks who are experts on the issues, embedded into the local culture, political dynamics etc. and then create linkages to other groups to complete or help build the skills, influence, networks, levers needed to successfully create change. That could be linking to a regional network, it could be partnering with a large international NGO, or it could be partnering with a group that is an expert or has a methodology. It depends on the needs and the issue.

In my experience, there is a clear need for intermediary actors who have the capacity to assess what the needs/learnings are in each territory. Use the bird's eye view to know that what a group is doing in one country or community or on one issue that can easily be adapted for another country or advocates who are deeply focused locally, but working on a similar issue.

•

Service-learning and the skills that come from youth engagement are not viewed as important to educational outcomes. While we need to educate students to have adequate skills in maths, reading and science, we also need people who can work in teams, are leaders, are creative and are willing to take risks. Gathering statistical data that shows that our program changes academic scores is not easily done, but the stories and feedback from both teachers and the youth are powerful. Our program changes the way students view the world, and will lead to a generation that cares about more than themselves.

•

The only way to operate internationally is through international NGOs. The reality is that many if not all of the known INGOs that exist in our sector delegate most of the work to smaller NGOs like us anyway.

I was invited to a conference and had a chance to meet with a funder. We spoke and I asked her about what her foundation funded and if there was a possibility for a partnership. She said she preferred to work through a particular INGO, because of the possibility for greater impact. I didn't push and we continued to speak about some of the specific projects. She began to tout one of her favorite projects of the INGO and halfway through, the work sounded familiar. It sounded familiar, because it was our work. We had 'partnered' with this INGO, which meant we had done the work and received less than the promised funding almost a year later than it was promised.

I told this funder that we were the actual implementing organization and provided other details of the project. She was surprised that she had not heard of our organization. I don't think INGOs are bad or redundant, but I believe many funders have the misconception that INGOs play the biggest and sometimes only role in nonprofit interventions.

What are the biggest misconceptions about your specific work and/or your organization that you believe donors have?

Work that cannot be measured by metrics is not important or worth funding. Most of the work that my organization does is very difficult to quantify and measure. Even if we do manage to measure, it is so unique that it is impossible to compare to other organizations. At times, the pressure to measure and show impact is overwhelming and can lead to a feeling of 'we have to show something,' which muddies the waters unnecessarily.

•

The only way we are able to yield results in our country of focus is to pay bribes to the government or local officials. Every dollar we receive is accounted for and the government—the local authorities most especially—understand the importance of the work we are trying to accomplish. We use a local-led approach so if local officials tried to take money that the entire community knows is meant to eradicate hunger and abject poverty, they would have to answer for it. Still, people perceive the country as hopeless and corrupt, so corruption is the only way we can have success.

•

We are perceived as a government agency even though only 20% of our funding comes from the government. This misconception can halt a relationship before we even begin to engage.

•

The issues we focus on are international in scope. Right now many unaccompanied children are fleeing Syria and Afghanistan for Europe at the same time that Central American children are seeking safety in the U.S. Certainly governments and their enforcement agencies consult with each other to learn and borrow ideas. We are doing the same—consulting with civil society in other countries to learn and exchange ideas—yet funders see our organization as purely U.S. focused and decide we do not fall within the scope of their international projects.

•

The work we did acting as a negotiator between governments on critical policy issues was viewed by most donors as autopilot diplomacy. They thought that governments naturally talked about tough issues with each other. Donors, particularly individuals, didn't understand that these dialogues didn't 'just happen' and that they wouldn't happen without a third party (usually non-profit) intermediary.

•

Many donors seem to have the misconception we will have a steady stream of core support funding to pay our salary costs. For a Human Rights organization of our size, the payroll comprises around 60% of our annual budget. Yet funding to support the people who will be conceiving our strategies, project managing our research, and delivering our advocacy is typically capped at 7-10%. Core funding is like gold dust for a small NGO. As a small specialist organization, our main asset is our skilled staff team. We need to recover salary costs from project specific-funding, and without this, it's a constant battle to establish job security for our people.

•

For my organization, the biggest misconception is that we are not capable of providing everything we have diagnosed that our community needs from us or that we cannot do it right. Many donors and even some board members (who are also donors) have said that we have mission creep. They insist that we cannot provide education, basic healthcare, shelter, food, and employment. However, when you serve in a remote area of a country like mine and you are the only organization, you must come up with unique ways of addressing needs in order to save lives. This is not mission creep; it is a holistic approach, and the results in our communities have shown it works and works effectively.

•

Because we have earned revenue, a small percentage of donors feel that we should be fully sustainable. They sometimes forget that we are a workforce training and development agency that serves survivors and the most vulnerable women around the world. With that, we will never be fully sustainable, for our products are a means to an end, but not the end.

•

Donors don't always understand that we do both direct service and policy work, and that our policy work is driven by the issues we see in doing direct service work, serving as an advocate for individual unaccompanied children. It is so important that policies be informed by individual people who are directly impacted by the issue at hand.

•

The field, including donors—with a few exceptions—does not yet understand the crucial influence that information and communication technologies (ICTs) have on every single issue around the world, especially as it pertains to the effectiveness and security of activists. While there is a growing understanding on certain issues like digital security and the increased threats and risks to those who engage in activism or speak out, the tendency is to see these threats still in a narrow light, e.g. can we keep the identity of a Human Rights defender concealed. The impact of ICT's is much broader than this.

Perpetrators of abuse and other bad actors actively use these technologies to repress, do harm, marginalize, prevent organizing, conduct surveillance of movements like Black Lives Matter, create damaging counter narratives (e.g. in the LGBTIQ sphere), to dissuade and threaten anyone who engages, from the 'moral supporters' like people who share on Facebook to activists in repressive regimes who get targeted.

This undermines and—at best—neutralizes many of the investments that funders make, in any sector. E.g. a group that works on women's education in Pakistan or women's political participation in southern Africa, will be much less effective or put many of their members at risk without being thoroughly versed in and briefed on the safe and effective use of ICTs. The flip side of this is the enormous potential in the use of ICTs to advance causes when used well and create the networks needed to achieve progress.

•

I think donors see our work as only impacting developing world schools through funding implementation of water, sanitation and hygiene education, when a whole other part of our work is to educate youth to become empathetic global citizens who realize that their actions have impact that is changing the world. It is not only 'nice' that we are engaging youth on an enormous global issue; it is essential and important work. We need to educate the next generation to care about others, and reach out to make the world a better place for everyone. I feel donors look to make a decision about whether an organization fits before understanding the mission.

•

My challenge is less with professional donor staff at foundations than individual donors. Since we do tech and raise money from donors that have made money in tech, their misconception is that all problems have a market-based solution. And then they push us hard on why we're not proposing a highly profitable project and what's wrong with it through that lens. I have to keep explaining that we are not doing tech enterprise badly, but philanthropy—with tech—fabulously well. It's just difficult to overcome a career's worth of hard-fought lessons about what ventures won't make money. Lessons that work great in business won't always work with nonprofits.

●

We receive government funding for our direct service work, but the law requires private matching funds. It can be very difficult to raise these matching funds, yet we cannot fulfill the requirements of the government contract without private money. Foundations often are not interested in funding direct service work and assume government funding covers this. At this point, all private sector donors should know that governments are not covering operational costs.

●

We've met donors who don't even know where the country we work in is located who are not willing to work with the unfamiliar.

●

We work in diagnosis and treatment only, when, in fact, we are responsible for one of the most disruptive models that has been developed in the last few years in healthcare. The lack of the razzle-dazzle shows that nonprofits are often expected to put on doesn't make it appear as radical to donors as it really is.

●

We work internationally, yet the perception of what we do is that it is only U.S. focused. We work with civil society in the children's countries of origin, with both direct work and research/policy organizations.

•

Appearing at conferences where a donor may have sponsored us or we were invited to speak means we have 'arrived' financially. I've had a donor come up to me and remark that he's seen me at many of the same conferences, so he assumed organizers were funding us or we were able to pitch our message to many donors. It's frustrating, but also scary to hear that when you are still struggling to make a budget and you're not even allowed to pitch at many of these conferences.

If you were able to speak frankly to a donor about these misconceptions without fear of repercussion, what would you say?

I would ask donors to pursue a relationship focused on partnership and joint collaboration. I understand there are internal pressures (Boards, etc) to ensure the money has the highest impact or return on investment. However, this is not always possible, and comparing malaria tablets with reintegrating children with their families or building the capacity of local CSOs to advocate for national or regional change is not a useful pursuit. It can mean that good work is overlooked.

•

If this was a great business opportunity, somebody would be doing it as a business. It's not: the market is actually going to fail to meet this need for the foreseeable future. So, you need to take off your business hat and put on your philanthropy hat. Now let's talk about the best way to solve this through a nonprofit approach.

•

We travel regularly to the country and ensure that projects are legitimate and donations are spent appropriately. The Trustees take nothing from the Trust and pay all of their own expenses. However, where is the reality in expecting us to be the face of our organization to donors based in the West and still be hands-on at the ground level? This can only be done with operational budgets you want us to cap at unrealistic levels. Overhead is necessary for long-term stability or even growth of a non-profit, but time management is also key.

●

Form respectable partnerships with the organizations you support. Treat your grantees the way you expect us to treat our beneficiaries. Stop being condescending or disrespectful to people just because they are born in a different country or in a different economic make up. Because we don't always call you on it doesn't mean we don't notice. Money does not make you an expert in all areas of life. If you cannot treat people you support with dignity, it is better that you take your money and leave.

●

There is a push for more data and I completely agree with it, but creating more of something that already exists is much easier than creating new data in an area where there is little to none available. One of the toughest problems in creating groundwork data is combatting the assumptions that were in place to make up for the lack of data, and it often comes from donors. There is a donor mythology that creates a narrative about the issue—its cause, its severity and its solution—that is based on many factors, none that include hard evidence.

When some donors are presented with data that contradicts the mythology, they are not shy about showing their skepticism. This kind of thinking is dangerous, because it can pollute the evidence gathering process. Nonprofits who are afraid of what will happen if their data doesn't match what donors want to hear will try to force an agreement between the data and the mythology. Donors have to stop bullying the data collection process and create a safe space for refutation.

•

Spend some time in our region of India with us before you make rec-ommendations based on what the social-economic landscape is like in the United States or Europe. We value your insight, but please do your homework first. The best thing is to spend some time on the ground if you are serious about large scale impact.

•

Stop making ill-judged and very poorly assessed assumptions about mental illness. There are many ways to manage and remedy mental illness which are very effective and also cheap. These must include whole life models. With mental illness costing $6 trillion USD a year to the global economy, don't you think it is about time to support men-tally ill people so that they can realize their full potential as citizens, whether it is going back to work, school or family life?

•

If donors can also begin to adopt standard approaches to grant pro-posals and reporting, that would also be a great idea.

•

A request for salary support is not an attempt to profiteer; we simply want to deliver the program without a creating a loss for our organi-zation. We never fail to deliver on your own compliance requirements, despite the workload that this creates for an already overstretched team. So please trust us!

•

Our work in the U.S. has an impact on work in other countries. We've exchanged ideas with civil society in Europe and Australia. Funders should recognize that even though a program is located in the U.S. the work can have an international impact.

•

It is critical to fund direct services since policy work should be informed by the people who are directly impacted. There is always a need for organizations that only do policy work, and they should certainly consult with NGOs doing direct service work. However, the work on the ground, and the people affected must have a voice.

One of the comments I've heard is 'we don't fund soup kitchens,' meaning the funder wants to give grants to organizations that do research and policy in order to bring about systemic change. Systemic change is what we all want, yet the soup kitchens must inform the research and advocacy in order to bring about that change.

•

There is a need for capacity and space to jointly speak about and map the landscape and the needs for a project, an issue, a campaign, in order to come up with shared plans for strategies and solutions before we enter into a donor dynamic. It is extremely valuable to have conversations about the landscape that are not interpreted as covert funding asks.

•

Human Rights change is incremental. We are in it together for a lifetime.

•

Once you vetted us and have seen our work, and if you trust us and our expertise, and that our leadership can devise effective strategies and make the right decisions, that we are good and ethical partners who will be nimble when the landscapes changes, then provide us with multi-year grants that are core support. Don't call us your part-ner until you are willing to treat us like an equal partner. The key ele-ment of every relationship is trust.

•

Decide: are you funding your dream, funding someone else's dream or funding to change someone's reality?

•

We are grateful for multiyear grants, but if you have made it clear that the grant is nonrenewable, please manage the requests you make for our time. We already have to spend less time focused on mission than we really want and more time fundraising. The detailed updates and field visits and in-person meetings when you are already familiar with our work and have already made it clear you will stop supporting in the near future really doesn't make much sense. Of course we are happy to show you what your grants have enabled us to do, but there are ways to do it that are less time consuming.

•

I am going to be honest, I don't understand the popularity of donors who say they only support evidence-based work. Evidence of what, that our mission is correct? We can only find this out through trial and error. Evidence usually means something tangible, something objec-tive. In this space, evidence is completely subjective. I can say that since we entered a community, there are fewer children suffering from malnutrition, but if I fail to mention the government instituted a program to treat malnourished youth and donors don't have access to that information, the evidence of our success looks solid to the donor, but is nothing but serendipity.

There are too many variables to claim that there is absolute evidence to prove one approach works, especially when there are constant changes in the landscape. This makes less sense when placed against the backdrop of phrases like theory of change. By definition, a theory is an idea we hope to prove without having all the evidence yet. If we had the evidence, it wouldn't be a theory, because we would already have the answers.

Most nonprofits are implementing plans we hope will work and then wait for the results to see if they do work. If they don't work, we change strategies to find a better solution. We don't know if they will work before implementation, we hope. We need donors to help us prove that our theories work and not just come in after the hard work was done with no money or support. I wish donors would say what they really mean when they talk about supporting evidenced-based work. What they mean is, 'I want evidence that your work will have the impact I think it should have, and not what the community or the nonprofit leaders believe it should have.'

●

Donors talk a lot about offering resources other than funding, but they seem to leave this up to NGOs to figure out what that means, which creates a guessing game. When I have asked donors to give examples of the resources they offer, the normal response is advice or something that sounds a lot like advice. For all the talk of innovation that donors want to see from NGOs, this is an area ripe with donors to improve their own innovation.

The opportunities are there. Private donors funding education can create internships or entry level positions within their businesses or even at their foundations for the most outstanding students who still find access to opportunities difficult after finishing school. Donors funding Human Rights can help get stories from their grantees out in the international media. Institutional donors have similar capabilities, but we—as NGOs—cannot tell donors what these resources should be. I would say to donors to internally define exactly what resources you can and are willing to offer, and then share them honestly with your grantees.

●●●

The year before I hosted the session that ultimately led to this book, I cohosted another session on collaboration without borders. I'm big on interactive role play during my sessions, as I believe it gives real-life application to the thoughts and opinions that we try to express.

Consisting of an almost equal amount of donors and nonprofit reps, we gave the attendees several scenarios around very real issues with which many in the room could identify. For example, we took the topic of severe poverty and asked a group of five participants to focus their attention on poverty as reflected in a random inner city in the United States. Two of the five were meant to take on the role of donors focused on poverty alleviation, two would be nonprofits tackling the same issue in any way they felt made sense and the fifth person had the role of beneficiary, also to be portrayed in any relevant way to the topic. We gave the groups time to see how they would form their mission, how they would engage each other and how to incorporate the beneficiary into their plan of action.

As with all first time exercises, I hoped for the best, but tried to prepare for the worst. My primary goal was to offer the attendees a glimpse into the various working parts of social problem-solving and offer them a chance to see the problem through different eyes. My secret goal was to give nonprofits a platform to really show donors how things are done. I was keen to see how the nonprofit participants would fare as donors, but was more excited to see them as beneficiaries, since my own perception was that donors would have a higher propensity to be more out of touch with beneficiaries and viewed them more as outcomes. I could not have been more wrong.

Donors who played the role of beneficiary expressed incredible introspection into the humanity of the situation. Some even gave their characters names and backstories to provide more authenticity. They were able to separate themselves from their actual donor roles and immerse themselves into the needs and expectations of the fictitious beneficiaries. For every scenario with a donor playing a beneficiary, whether it was a child wanting quality education or a pregnant mother newly diagnosed with HIV, the entire process was well informed from the ground up and the exercise was a huge success.

How can I best describe the way nonprofits performed in the beneficiary role? Two words: Oy vey. Through the various stumbling blocks on display, one problematic theme was evident: The nonprofits struggled with how to separate themselves from their work, at least not enough to adequately assume the beneficiary perspective. Some non-profit participants were from grassroots organizations, while others were based in the West and yet, the results did not vary much. One 'beneficiary' kept trying to fit the model of her nonprofit into her character, disregarding the clear differences between the two. Another actually mentioned her organization in her character's role, despite the two having nothing to do with each other. In some cases, the rest of the group minimized the role of the beneficiary in order to create solutions for the beneficiaries. There are so many tangents I can ramble on about that, but will resist.

Other beneficiaries played by nonprofits struggled with the concept of creating a beneficiary role in the first place. They expressed that the beneficiary character was redundant since the nonprofit was already represented. Lacking a relevant narrative and directive from these participants, the other members of these groups created their own beneficiary narrative. Upon reflection, that session seems worthy of its own book as well.

The nonprofit performances were as surprising as they were disappointing. Whether they didn't want to miss an opportunity to plug their work in front of potential donors or they misunderstood en masse that they were meant to create a beneficiary character based on the scenario and not the mission of their organization, this exercise reinforced the very false stereotype that nonprofits cannot see past their mission's focus or interests. It was also one of the first hard lessons I learned about my own misperceptions.

So what does that story have to do with this chapter? As much as I am grateful to all of the people who contributed to this chapter, the process of collecting feedback brought me back to that experience. The feedback here required a certain bit of nuance and care. Asking nonprofits to air frustrations specific to their work in a way that has to be more about the issues than the work, while maintaining some level of anonymity is no easy task.

Still, I felt the people I reached out to for their contributions were up to that task. I thought I was clear that the format was for utmost anonymity. I warned that the use of any specific names would be removed, so focus on the misperceptions instead of highlighting their programs. I also assured those who expressed concerns that anything received that might be too specific as to compromise their identities would be edited accordingly.

Although I received the brilliant responses featured here, as well as others that I did not use, more than half of the responses I received focused only on the organization and plugged themselves by name instead of speaking to the space in which they operated. The majority were actually so org-centric that they were unusable. There were mentions of organizational initiatives that were being launched or currently in place that failed to address the questions asked. They were basically one-pagers that didn't even offer any misperceptions, but rather confirmed one.

That was discouraging to say the least, because I know many of those who submitted the unusable feedback and know they have wonderful experiences to impart. In fact, I had discussed some of the misperceptions that inspired this chapter with some of these same people in earlier settings, which is why I had sought their participation. I even asked a few people to resubmit with a clearer message to the questions and, with some of the results, it got worse. This and the session experience speak to a lack of nonprofit adaptability when out of their comfort zone.

During the session, nonprofits had no problems when in the role of donor. Conversely, when asked to contribute to the more straightforward parts of this book to follow, nonprofit leaders flourished. This is not me chastising nonprofits, but using this as a possible teachable moment. I have already planned to discuss this further with many of those who submitted the unusable feedback to work through the matter of detachment and adaptability. And as my own experiences have shown, we all have misperceptions and issues to suss out.

7

Questions & Answers: Burning questions from the nonprofit sector
...and responses from donors

When I was first asked to write a book based on the 'Hard Truths' PDF, I refused. I had no interest in creating a full-length finger-pointing at nonprofits, as if donors were infallible. I wanted to focus on creating something that mirrored the entire Hard Truths session. I wanted to have a conversation, both virtually and literally. This is where the virtual effort begins.

Yet another continuation of the misperception theme, when I put out a call to nonprofits to offer burning questions they had for donors, I expected to receive one hundred variations of the same five questions. When the dust settled, there were over seventy unique questions, including a few I would have never have thought to ask. Luckily for me, the myriad of donors who stepped up to take on these questions were much better equipped to do so.

There are a number of foundations that already offer questions and answers on their websites, such as the Ford Foundation, which would be a great resource for grantees seeking additional answers. However, when I asked nonprofit participants if they knew of these existing forums, the vast majority were unaware. What should be a widely regarded resource for nonprofits becomes another bubbled success of foundations trying to be more than just a direct financial source, even when that bubble is pretty significant in size. Sometimes our efforts to uncomplicate philanthropy are like trees falling in the forest and nonprofits are too far away to hear.

One effort I did strive for in this chapter was not just getting all of the selected questions answered, but to have at least two responses to these questions. I wanted to provide perspective from different voices within philanthropy. This goes back to my earlier point that no two people in philanthropy are the same or think exactly the same. What works for one may not work for the other, further proving that it may be best to rip up any template you have for donor engagement. Don't rip up the plan; just the way you decide to implement it. And with that, the questions. And answers.

Question:

Why do funders focus on innovation so much? The work charities have been delivering for years is no less important than recently innovative work.

Answer:

Everyone likes the idea of the 'hot new thing.' The psychology behind this is probably related to the same reason we buy new clothes each year, even when the ones from last year still function just fine. Some of that psychology we will never be able to overcome and is just part of the business.

In other cases, I think that some funders are explicitly or subliminally trying to find a silver bullet. Even if a program works 'good enough,' if you believe in such a thing as the 'perfect' model, then you will always be on the lookout for the new program that fits that bill. In this case, 'innovation' is often substituted for 'effectiveness,' and we gravitate to the former, even though we are actually seeking the latter.

A third reason is legacy, credit, and ego. When a funder puts their name on a shiny new product, brand or service, it is a special kind of ego-boost that is greater than adding your name to a long list of other supporters. While not tied to results, this does matter to some private funders and that's OK. As long as they are honest with themselves and their grantees about their motivations.

Answer:

Philanthropy must maintain a certain level of diplomacy, which is not always easy. Donors tend to speak in code, or they hide behind the aspirational language. I find that when I am speaking to other donors and the word 'innovation' comes up, we are talking about long established NGOs—often ones we have already funded who make it very difficult to separate from, and not because of the caliber of the results, but because of the aggressive style of the development team.

The question says the work is no less important, but is it relevant? Innovation is not about reinventing the wheel; it is about moving the existing wheel closer to where it needs to go and done in a meaningful way. Sometimes when donors cite innovation, this is our diplomatic way of saying we don't believe your organization has significantly moved the wheel.

Question:

How do we inspire potential supporters to follow through on the introductions to their board or other individuals?

Answer:

First, is that introduction something that you proposed or the foundation Program Officer proposed? If it's the former, they may not be as comfortable making such an intro yet. At our foundation, there are two levels of decision-making between me and the board, so that is not something I can honestly promise. Also, if you make a request to meet with a board member, take into account that Program staff often gets requests like this.

You should have a clear reason why you think there is a connection to you, your work and a specific member. If I am the one to suggest a meeting with one of my board members, I would normally have one in mind, so if I have not yet made the introduction, I would say one thing to do is to send me information that is geared to an intro to that person as a reminder. If you do not receive a response from me, it could be for many reasons, few which should have you worried.

Board members—or anyone I try to connect to you—also have to confirm the introduction. That is a timetable I cannot control and these are most likely very busy individuals who may receive similar requests all the time. The key is patience.

Answer:

I think it's wonderful that you used the word inspire. Donors want to be inspired, so the organizational goals and programs should inspire. Inspiration comes in story form, not analytically. Give us the stories to share with our network. Even better, help us create our own stories to share.

Our board members trust us enough to know that we have looked over the facts and figures. If they see our joy in supporting a particular grantee, they are more receptive to learn more about that organization. Introductions can never be guaranteed, but it helps if I am excited enough to get them excited about what your organization does.

Question:

What makes you decide to stop giving to an organization? There has to be a better way for organizations to not be taken by surprise at unexpected diminished funding or nonrenewal of a grant.

Answer:

At our foundation, we create mutually-agreed upon milestones with our partners at the start of every new grant. Meeting these milestones is an expectation of the grant and we monitor the progress of achieving them over the course of the grant period. If a partner is not meeting the milestones we may decide to scale down their funding over multiple years or if there are any red flags we may stop funding at the expiration of a grant.

To make sure our partners are not taken by surprise, we do hard renewals at least three months prior to the expiration of a grant. This gives our partners a three-month buffer to plan for any changes in funding. Additionally, six months before the grant ends, we look for any major red flags—poor performance, failure to reach milestones, dramatic shift in fit or major fraud—that would stop funding at the end of the grant. We inform partners with red flags as soon as possible, typically before the three-month buffer, if we decide to stop funding their organization.

We believe it's important for our partners to know the intention of the grant from the start. We are clear at the beginning about whether it is a one-time grant or if the partner can expect continuous support from us.

Answer:

Overpromising and under-delivering. Lack of the right kind of communication. Discovering problems via third party or on our own. If we feel there is mission drift and have pointed it out with no significant change, we won't renew a grant. More importantly, how could anyone be taken by surprise that a grant has not been renewed? Unless a multiyear grant is halted prior to the final year, there are no expectations for a donor to renew a grant, at least from the donor side.

Question:

Why do you request a cold LOI or proposal as a first contact step, but decline to take an email inquiry to see if our mission meets your interests? We have frequently come across an organization that says they do not take inquiries, don't provide contact information, etc, but then when we are able to get in touch, they are happy to share information and learn more about us, or at a minimum tell us if/why we would not be a fit for their giving. It feels like 'no inquiries' or 'LOI only' is put up as a false barrier when, in fact, if you can find a way to connect with someone, they're usually willing to speak. Just not sure of the rationale there, writing an LOI that gets to the foundation out of context just means more work for them to review when a two paragraph email could be enough for a yea or nay.

Answer:

My email is listed, but I can understand why others do it this way. First, before contacting an organization, you should know that your mission meets their interests. If they are funders who do not list a lot of information about what they do, they likely only want to identify grantees by finding the organizations themselves or through references from others they trust, so you would be wasting both their time and yours by emailing.

Second, I think you are correct that the LOI is creating a barrier. It means that only organizations who have researched you and demonstrate they have identified you in particular as a partner and funder can reach you. Yes, if you manage to get an email address or a direct introduction, we will be willing to speak, but your finding that way to connect means that you put time into tracking someone down, which you would only do if your mission really is aligned with the funder. Unfortunately, there are many grant-seekers who do not filter who they contact, so funders need to put up some barriers to protect their valuable time.

Answer:

This question makes light of the volume of interest a foundation receives. What a nonprofit sees as a lack of openness can very well be a lack of capacity. When you go to the movies, you first see if there is available space and if so, you buy a ticket and get in line and wait to present your ticket. You have to show proof that you belong in that arena. That is all we—and other donors—are doing, creating a system that lets you prove our arena is right for you without us stretching ourselves too thin.

Our current focus is on health. Even though we make it known that we don't take unsolicited requests, we still receive many on a regular basis. What if you're a nonprofit working in the field of health and a foundation that is designed to help you reach your goals is impeded in connecting to you because it is inundated with requests from other nonprofits that are not even in scope. Nonprofits know the difference between receiving necessary funds sooner than later. The LOI and non-solicitation policies allow us to reach the nonprofits which we want to align with in a more efficient manner.

Question:

There are a slew of movements happening in America now that are gaining momentum, but are not resulting in wholesale change. Occupy Wall Street, Black Lives Matter and immigration have brought millions together, but the problems still exist. How can philanthropists get behind these initiatives better? Is it only about funding? How would these movements be funded in a way to affect change?

Answer:

This is a great question, one that many donors including myself have struggled with. Some of the movements that are referenced don't always have a well-known representative and the ones you encounter may have much more local needs than a national agenda. I think one thing we can do as philanthropists is create more spaces for the leaders of these groups to be identified and given a larger platform. Donor-led town halls instead of or in addition to the traditional political town halls.

There is a great organization I love called Good Pitch that brings movers and shakers across philanthropy and the arts to support the completion of inspirational documentaries. I would love to see something like this created in the social justice space for the purpose of unification and advocacy. Traditional methods of funding just won't work with advancing these movements.

Answer:

Well that's the problem. These groups have never been funded. I don't know about Occupy Wall Street, but Black Lives Matter has never been funded at a level of significance. Google gave money to some organizations run by BLM members, but you have to remember that something like Black Lives Matter is a coalition. But no one is funding coalitions because they are not set up for the structure of being nickel-and-dimed to death that many nonprofits can survive on.

The problem with philanthropy's involvement with these issues is that we see these issues as race and class, but not as a mindset that has to change, including our own. You have black folks in philanthropy who act as though they don't understand what the movement is about. Then, of course, white folks in philanthropy go to them to seek their counsel on entry points and are stonewalled or worse, dissuaded from offering financial support.

If donors want to support causes like Black Lives Matter or immigration, the first thing to do is track down and identify the leaders. If they can't identify the leaders or see that those leaders are not using their potential, then that is their first entry point: fund leadership development. It takes operational support to fund the unpredictable and no one is funding that. And if they are, the amounts never rise above just enough to get by.

I know this for a fact, because I have a good friend who has been trying to help BLM and the amount of money they are able to raise is staggeringly low from the philanthropic world. The problem she identifies is youth. People do not shy away from the racial or political aspects, but because of the lack of trust in youth. Instead of dismissing them for their inexperience, we should see their youth as an asset and improve their leadership skills. That is the magic recipe. To be honest, donors just have to reach out to these groups and ask them what they need directly. It's really not that complicated for someone who wants to get involved.

Question:

After the award has been granted, how much communication is too much? We have monthly newsletters, stories from the field, reports, but I can imagine it will be overwhelming to donors who have multiple partners if they are receiving such a high level of correspondence.

Answer:

You are correct. Nonprofits can go overboard with updates, but the best thing to do is ask your donors what level of feedback they prefer. The most important communication is success stories. Even an overwhelmed donor will appreciate knowing that their support of your organization is working. Everything else should be an agreement between you and the donor.

Answer:

Make it aware to the donor before the grant is finalized who your current donors are that require reports and ask them if they would like to receive the same reports. Ask them if it is possible to reduce redundancy in reporting and, during that conversation, have them define how much communication is too much. I think communications are important and NGOs need to do them for donors and for themselves more importantly. However, communications need to be speaking to broader constituencies and not just to donor demands.

There are many NGOs who have internal communications teams that are focused only on communicating to their donors and not on building, and mobilizing public support that is a whole other framing for the communication. It is not too much if it is speaking to a broader audience and the NGO has to speak up to make donors aware of the power a communication can have when it is not put in a silo.

Question:

What advice would you give to a fundraiser or grantee who is working for a new organization that is yet to deliver on metrics/impact or its theory of change, because it is such early days?

Answer:

That's such a loaded question, because if I were a nonprofit, my question to donors would be, 'do you need all of that?'

Funders need to understand that not every project is going to have metrics or impact. If you can't understand what it means to be a startup, why fund them? It's about funders taking risks and being OK with that. Still, you have to convince funders that you are going to deliver when the time is right or you're gonna get somewhere that will take us forward as partners.

I personally would come at that question so differently in terms of what funders need to do to support groups that don't have the impact and metrics yet. Otherwise, we will be stuck with organizations that are not innovating. We will have a field that will get stale and we will be stuck supporting all the same stuff, if that is all donors look for in grantees, which means those big organizations. We don't' need more of that, so push back on donors who tell you those things are necessary for an initial grant.

Answer:

Make sure you come across as a strong leader who can compete in the field. If you don't have a track record, maybe show your track record from other work you've done. In making the case, donors like to see planning that seems well thought out, but also feels flexible, so they can trust that you can respond to potential problems you may face as a relative newcomer.

Considerations on the donor side are more about whether it fits in our portfolio and will it offer us a place where we can create added value. It is less about presenting metrics when you are obviously a startup. If you are trying to connect with a donor who does not traditionally fund startups, it may be best to move on. However, if there is a shared synergy in the field of work, the best representative to that kind of donor is to have one of your original seed donors speak on your behalf. As a startup, you may not know how to answer certain questions that an experienced donor can on your behalf. They are also better positioned to assess the risk in funding your work.

If this is about finding that seed funding or initial grant, show that you are prepared. Know who your competitors are and give an honest account—truly honest account—of why you think your particular startup is needed. When you start a company, you usually give a portrait of your assessment of where you fit alongside your competitors. This isn't much different in the nonprofit world. It is possible that the donors you contact already have a relationship or at least an opinion about the other nonprofits who are working in your area, and judge how you judge them. This is something we certainly do when a startup presents a landscape assessment that includes other actors.

So, look for common ground and very much try and look through the eyes of the funders, in terms of what they need to know. Usually that is concrete information and, if they are unfamiliar with your work, a simple analysis of why you should be a part of their portfolio. If you think a funder is a good fit, but they are making you go through a number of hoops to prove it, you can also move on. Be picky. I know it's hard to take that stance when you are struggling for resources, but saying no now doesn't mean saying no forever. You can always reengage that funder when you have the metrics or information they require.

Within our own foundation, when a startup comes to us for funding, we may give a soft no or a partial no. A partial no means that the connection point has not been established yet, but we believe in time it can be found. We still have questions about the theory of change. We judge how much we are willing to risk based on that and may provide far less funding than requested, but this can increase once the relationship continues. When you get a partial no, go for it. Run with it and build for the future relationship, even if it's much less money.

When I have to say no or give much less than people are asking, it is frustrating for me as well. I think it's important for nonprofits to know that. I always seek partnerships shoulder-to-shoulder with any grantee, be it project funding or core funding. Core funding—of course—even more, because that means we are making a long-term relationship. As a partner, there is a sense that I will get real constructive critical feedback and involvement from that organization, beyond the usual updates. Partial funding, to a degree, means partial partnership and I cannot expect more from an NGO partner than I am able to put in.

To move from a partial partnership to a full partner, I need to get the impression that this organization or the founder knows what he/she is doing. I need to know how strong the commitment is to the cause, how well they have assessed the risks, what I think the reaction will be to failure, both organizationally and individually at the founder level. Then I can determine whether or not we can enter these risks together as full partners.

Question:

Why do certain funders refrain from simply saying that their organization will make decisions based on what it unilaterally and subjectively feels is the best way to support a situation? One of the most refreshing conversations I recently had was with a foundation funder during a group discussion about funder-fundee dynamics in the context of competitions for grant money.

People were arguing that competitions are not fair, because the applicants spend too much of their efforts and resources trying to win a grant. The funder was empathetic, but unapologetic in simply stating that a decision to grant money and create a partnership is inherently not based on a fairness principle; the funder chooses selectively and based on their objectives who to grant money to. In my experience, that was a simple but uncommon explanation about how decision-making works.

Answer:

The answer should be because donors don't really feel that way, but I'm not so naïve. However, while a fraction of donors may function from this kind of ideology, this is not a winning strategy, especially if this is an institutional donor and not an individual. Perhaps this donor was speaking only to the subject of competitions, where his comments would have more merit, but there are too many competitions to be lumped together under the same criticism.

There was a competition co-created by Chase and Facebook that awarded grants to charities based on how many likes they garnered during a specific period of time. This would not take up many resources for a charity, but since the winners were based on popularity, it justifies questions of fairness. There are other competitions that only require a written essay and recommendations.

Grants through competitions are not a smart way for any good charity to create and maintain sustainability. The foundations I know that host competitions also provide grants using guidelines and metrics. These contests are not a major part of their portfolio and they shouldn't be the major part of any charity's funding portfolio. What sense does it make to spend so much in energy and resources for a one time gift that can't be renewed?

I can't defend a donor I never met, but although donors can rightfully choose which causes they wish to support, we try to establish the fairest possible model to find those who are best positioned to create evidence-based solutions. Program Officers have to present to our trustees. We don't have any unilateral power. Our trustees make the final decisions and choose from a group of charities that have been heavily vetted. The job of finding grantees is not a simple one and we try to position ourselves to find the best organizations to support. Although I don't necessarily agree with this donor, it says more to me that he attended a multilateral meeting to provide insight to charities. A unilaterally selective donor probably wouldn't join in this kind of forum.

Answer:

Interesting question. Our foundation actually started off that way. It was being run as an open competition. Any organization could apply, come into the mix and be evaluated. In that model, it was just getting ridiculous. I think we were receiving thousands of applicants and were stressed to try to compare apples against oranges. We would have these really strong organizations from countries that had established very strong civil societies, such as Uganda, Tanzania, Kenya, India, and so on.

Basically, applicants from these countries kept winning the award year after year. It was obvious that the award was unintentionally weighted towards their success. It was a case of awarding on the strength of the organization, but not the strength of the organization's mission goal or potential impact. Unfortunately, the countries that had stronger civil societies were winning, even when we saw that programs were sometimes stronger in other regions where the standardized version of how we expect a nonprofit to look wasn't always followed.

Upon some serious reflection, we decided as a foundation to shift the model towards a more closed process. We decided to pick specific regions and made sure we rotated after a certain period to make sure we recognized the lesser supported areas. We moved to a referral process so once we identified what the needs are in those countries we would go into, we would have a preset list of partners to support until we were more established on the ground. We also wanted the process to be as transparent as possible.

We created a stage process where we reviewed the referrals and sent out independent consultants to help with the assessments and inform our first set of cuts. From there, we then ran independent panels to remove any air of favoritism or preferential selections. Now I think we have a model we feel most comfortable with. As funders, we have gone through a journey to discover how to make what we do a bit more transparent and more accountable, and with less waste of the organization's time. Because we were getting thousands of applications, but only awarding a couple dozen, the rate by which organizations were getting through was so minute. We wanted to be mindful of the time organizations were putting in to apply.

There's something about how donors will go through the process internally to change and shift that is lost in communications. The way they will communicate it is the usual, 'We have gone through consultations and are making changes for more efficiency and we want to be more transparent,' but they won't be more open about exactly what prompted them to make a change. One of the things I don't think foundations are doing enough of, which I'm proud to say we do, is more of a participatory grant-making approach, to involve beneficiaries and other implementing organizations.

Within our grant awards, the panels are made up of independent experts in the regions, but also previous awardees who, I would argue, have been somewhat better at making the decisions because they really do understand the context on the ground more so than even a regional expert would. I think many donors are trying to move away from that unilateral approach while others are still lagging behind. The first thing is that it has a lot to do with donors being more honest about what they are learning and why with organizations on the other end.

The second thing is that we as donors spend a lot of time speaking to each other about what our grantees or awardees are telling us about what the situation is on the ground, but we don't spend enough time amplifying or bringing their direct voices into our conversations. We should be doing that more and that's something we are trying to do more of in our foundation. The third thing is to involve more participatory models of grant-making, so that decisions are held more with the people they are going to benefit more, who understand the context more than we do.

Philanthropy comes from an inherent place predicated on an unfair or unequal balance. Philanthropy is created from vast wealth and that power dynamic seems to translate into a lot of the ways that foundations choose to operate. Some of the ways that true partnership happens is when there is dialogue between donors and NGOs, recipients, winners, partners or whatever you want to call them. Then there needs to be real openness from donors about what they are learning and the mistakes they are making. And don't just share it with other donors, but share it with their grantees or whatever shape the ground level partners take.

We should have much more of their voices within donor forums and they should be working with us to inform our funding decisions or wholly making the decisions for us where we have no real expertise. Many foundations are shit at doing this, but steps can be taken to re-balance the unevenness within the sector.

Question:

My organization reached out to a prospective donor for funding. After a few correspondence, the donor notified us that the grant request was declined, but encouraged us to reach out in about a year or so to see if there was a chance for a future partnership. This was a promising response that we took at face value. In that year, we also felt that enough had changed and grown within our organization to merit reaching out.

When we sent an email to see if anything had changed on their end to justify reapplying for a grant, the donor strongly lashed out. We were accused of harassment and badgering the donor into support, which was not the case at all. We didn't even send our usual updates so that we respected the request to wait a year. My first question is, how should we have responded to that response? And short of reading minds, is there a way to avoid a situation like that ever occurring again?

Answer:

One of the best things to do in that situation is to politely apologize and blame some kind of misunderstanding in the last correspondence. Also, acknowledge that there will be no further correspondence unless the donor reaches out. Resist the temptation to defend your organization or set the donor straight. It is very likely that this has nothing to do with you or your organization. I think this was about that individual donor, who could have had a bad moment or was dealing with something else and your email came at the wrong time.

To answer the second question, when a donor declines to fund but offers you to try again or reach out at a later date, there is no real way to prevent what happened to you from happening again. This won't be a popular answer, but you might have to put the onus of reengagement back on the donor. Tell them you will wait for them to initiate or ask them how or if they would like to be informed of your work between the rejection and the time they specified for reengagement. The best advice I can give here is don't take it personal and remain civil.

Answer:

It's difficult to say. The first thing I would want to find out is whether there had been a change in staff or personnel or if simply someone else received that message and the person you wanted to contact is either in a different role or no longer with the foundation. If that was the case, then I would try to get in contact with that person to clarify the situation. Very often, you write to a central email address, so maybe you were dealing with multiple people.

There could have also been a significant shift in strategy. If you haven't already looked at that, it could be another option. If it is the donor and they act in such a hostile way and that is the person you would have to work with, then it is probably going to be very difficult to continue or try to have a successful working relationship with that person. I know very few people who would act this way. That is very unlikely to happen in the foundation world. Most people are actually decent and nice people.

How can you avoid it from happening again? The only thing you can try to do is try to explain. Try not to be too defensive. Explain that there was a misunderstanding and you're sorry it has created this situation. Nobody in the foundation world would do this on purpose. Nobody. I have been working in this field for fifteen years and I don't know a single person who would do that on purpose.

Question:

How do you think about your responsibilities to organizations applying to your foundation? Have you considered providing feedback for rejected orgs so they might understand and potentially improve their presentation or their work?

Answer:

Definitely. I would think that's extremely important. Every time that we receive and application or somebody's applying for a grant, we always try to make sure we give a reason of why we arrived at yes, no or not right now. We want them to know what could be done better and what's being done really well. That's one of the main things that we do now, always looking at what we can help improve, even if there is no money associated with it.

Answer:

Just to clarify, this is about providing feedback to organizations that have gone through many rounds of vetting for a grant. If it is not, then I don't think foundations have the capacity to respond to every solicitation, whether or not solicitations are welcome. If this is about the vetted organizations, then I think the first responsibility a foundation has to an organization it is seriously considering for a grant is transparency.

Explain at the beginning of the process why there was interest in forming a partnership, what the possible roadblocks could be in forming that partnership and the expectations both sides would have of the partnership. This keeps the nonprofit organization aware of what could help or hinder the prospects of a grant.

I personally feel that a potential grantee should only be contacted three times:

- to be told that they are in consideration for a grant,
- to be asked for necessary documentation for the vetting process (and this should be done once, not habitually, where it can take time and resources away from an organization),
- to be told whether or not a grant has been approved.

This is the policy we follow in our grant-making. Foundations have to be respectful of a nonprofit's capacity or else we risk coming off as hypocrites. In all honesty though, foundations must have more responsibility to the organizations that were not rejected. The introductory feedback on roadblocks to a grant should suffice. We don't have the capacity to fix everything that is wrong with nonprofits. I listen when nonprofits complain about the unnecessary exploitations of their capacity by donors, so I don't think the answer is misusing the capacity of foundations.

Once we find grantees with whom we want to partner, our focus should be to help them to the fullest of our capacity. Sometimes it is not about something an organization has done wrong or could improve. It could just be about one organization being a better fit than another. There isn't much feedback to deliver other than that.

Question:

How do you learn about small/new orgs that aren't in your networks or haven't built up a reputation yet, especially those in contexts far from your base of operations? Do you worry that you are favoring those groups more visible to you, at the expense of others?

Answer:

We perform site visits. When we visit current grantees, we also plan scoping visits. We post requests for proposals in an effort to reach people who are not in our network, but there is only so much we can do. It also comes down to how effective we find our current grantees and grant-making strategies. If we are satisfied with the work of our grantees, which we are, it doesn't make much sense to change the manner of how we found them.

I get this question a lot. Whenever I hear it, I think of someone saying to me, 'I know you're happily married, but there's a hidden island of beautiful women you should try to find and explore.'

We don't pick grantees because they are linked to our network. They still have to pass a vigorous selection process and present a strong case that they represent the beneficiaries in a way that we can be proud of as a foundation. We cannot be all things to all people and we shouldn't be ashamed to say we are happy enough with who we already have, especially when the results favor our approach.

Answer:

Absolutely yes. Everybody gets very lazy, relying either on the contacts they already have or through word of mouth. I've seen that work very well, by asking organizations that donors are funding to recommend partner organizations or somebody they think it's important for donors to speak to, but, at the same time, that has an inherent flaw, which is a limited chain. If donors want to work very locally, that's great and this is less of a problem. If they want to expand their base of operations and impact, this approach is no good.

The solution comes down to governance. If donors have a board that is open to very active philanthropy and active funding, then that means that a huge part of the job for the donors—in this case, program staff—is actually going to be finding and actively searching for new partners. This entails desk reviews, calling up people, scouring the internet, constantly reading good newsletters, reading publications like The Chronicle of Philanthropy and Stanford Social Innovation Review that's going to be reviewing nonprofits in and out of your field, and then following up on all of this.

It may mean capitalizing on opportunities, like connecting a scoping trip with a conference set in a place of interest. This requires a lot of dedication on the part of the donor. Without a very explicit mandate or benchmarks to reach in terms of the organization, donors are always going to be limited.

Targeted open calls are another good way to get people to find donors. It helps if there is a theme that they want to broaden their base in, but not just for funding; for identifying new experts in the field that can play a pivotal role when the time comes to expand the base of grantees. The donors reading these open calls may not have the knowledge base to assess all of the proposals received on an open call. It's also so much easier to communicate with other donors and evaluators now, so this really shouldn't be an obstacle. The only real obstacle is a lack of will.

Question:

Why do you think your opinion as a non-expert should drive our strategy? I have worked with a major donor who has very strong ideas about what a good way to go about doing our work would be—specifically, this person wants to move the dial on the issue we work on in one state. Our organization has spent a good number of years bringing the states along to an acceptable baseline response to the issue we work on and now we wouldn't prioritize 'going hard' in one state, given the dramatic improvement in most states, the competing federal strategies we work on, and the limited capacity and resources within the org.

Unfortunately, if we can't satisfy this donor's desire for a specific state strategy, we will lose out on a potential major gift in the $20k to $30k range, which is a big gift for us. We wish we could persuade the donor that we think the strategy we've set and choices we've made will lead to, in our expert opinion, the best result.

Answer:

At our foundation, we aim to provide expertise in areas where we have it. Our partners know what is best for advancing their organization. When we think their technical strategy may need rethinking we will offer advice, but more importantly we try to link the organization to similar organizations that we fund. We believe the technical advice is most useful from a partner NGO who has dealt with similar issues.

We do find that many of our grassroots NGO partners have limited time and resources to focus on administrative matters such as fundraising, organizational capacity and communications. From being exposed to so many organizations and hearing similar concerns with administrative issues, we feel that we can provide expertise and advice in these areas. Through our capacity support program, we use a participatory method to analyze our partner organization's capacity and together we look at how we can strengthen their staff and systems.

We also believe that technical advice is not so black and white. Technical advice from a non-expert can help bring a new perspective into the organization's strategy. Sometimes having someone from outside the organization provide a 30,000 foot view of the organization can bring in a new perspective of their strategy. A funder's technical expertise, even as a non-expert, can help formulate strategy, but we believe that it should be in a more advisory role and not tied directly to the grant.

Answer:

It begins with identifying the commonalities between partners and what we want to do strategically. If it doesn't fit, then it doesn't fit. We're not hunting after changing your narrative, as we hope you are not hunting after money. It is not necessarily about changing the opinion of the donor, but is more of a collaborative environment.

I would try to explain using the expertise you gather in the field that the proposed strategy may not be the right one. And if donors are still convinced that they want to do it in certain ways, they have to find someone else to work with. It's a simple answer.

Some donors will look for wiggle room when a partner offers it. Make your strategy so concise that a donor understands before he asks that the strategy was expertly crafted and that it has to be implemented your way. Also, before you use terms like non-expert, make sure you can prove why you are an expert and make sure you know for certain that the donor critique is not from an expert point of view. He could have consulted with other actors before making his suggestion without giving you that detail. Don't just assume.

Question:

Monitoring the impacts of any project is essential to understanding whether or not an organization is really making a difference. Everything definitely can be measured, but should it be measured every time? Impact monitoring is often expensive and time consuming. For organizations that either already have impact data of their own or impact data from similar programs that can be used to estimate a program's impact, why do many funders still insist on conducting and paying for (or not paying for) project-specific impact monitoring when it may be just a waste of time and money?

Answer:

Yes! Absolutely. That's exactly how I feel. Some evaluation needs to happen. I don't know how that looks, but we spend way too much time and money on it and it just sucks the life out of the field and it shouldn't.

Answer:

I understand this argument both ways. On the one hand, if you know it works, why test it again? However, if we aren't testing it then how do we know if it is still working, or working in this slightly different context? There are enough examples in our sector where we falsely assumed that a successful project in context A would work in context B to justify not constantly monitoring. I do think that projects should be measured every time – but the degree of measurement should fit the bill. You get an annual medical check-up and to skip that just because you were healthy last year would be dangerous. But likewise, when you go to that annual check-up, you don't get a colonoscopy every time.

Also, if a funder wants M&E that is not already part of the NGO's process, they should pay for it. Period.

Question:

Why have donors become so obsessed with scale, even at the expense of quality? In Africa, we scale organically, but often we feel pressure to scale like a business. Local solutions offer real and tangible outcomes, and the potential for transferability to other similar sites. Why is this not considered impact, compared to inch deep, mile wide programs?

Answer:

We fund both types of programs because there is a need for holistic NGOs offering community-led solutions along with larger NGOs focused on scaling up their programs. From our experience, we find that local solutions have difficulty showing their impact compared to the mile wide programs. The effects of the local solutions or community-led solutions need to be better quantified. Local organizations need to show funders that their very mile deep, inch wide solution is a worthwhile comparison with the inch deep, mile wide programs.

Compared to mile wide programs, local organizations typically have thinner expertise, but they work across many different sectors. Additionally, they have tremendous expertise in localized knowledge and invaluable trust from the community. From a sustainability point of view, local organizations can have a much longer impact on the local community, but this additional value of localized expertise and trust needs to be communicated to the funders.

Community-led organizations need to bundle their programs to show the impact they have on multiple aspects of the community such as health, education and the environment. Funders need to see that it is a cost-effective program with long-term impact that is best suited for the community. We believe that there is a major need to improve M&E systems across local organizations to show the impact of multiple interventions.

Answer:

There are different types of donors, obviously. From what I've heard at my foundation and beyond at other foundations, there is a concern for making changes at a systemic level. It means that something changes that is permanent or as permanent as things can be. To do that, there is very often the belief that a small project can change only the lives of a few people in a community setting, but if it is not taken up and expanded, then you run the risk of whatever good it did disappearing. This is why some donors are obsessed with scale.

Another reason is the increasing concern about metrics in general and measuring things. Scale then falls into that current trend of trying to measure everything. The outcome of metrics is scale. You mention organically and I think we are far from that. I think the sector has shifted. Not everyone and again, there is a huge variation of donors. Overall, the obsession with scale has to do with the drive to do things that have a sense of permanency, where if it is taken up by the government or by any kind of entity that can use it in a broader scale, it can reach many more. The other is that the obsession with scale is basically an obsession with metrics. At the end of it all, donors are trying to understand if what they are doing or what they fund is making a difference.

Question:

How do you know how much weight to place on overhead/ management excellence vs. programmatic effectiveness? Do you expect groups to have strong central organization/management even if you don't fund it? We run a very standard overhead percentage (generally 15% or so). We recently applied for a grant with a foundation, but were made aware during the process that we needed to keep our admin costs at 7%, even though one of the main criteria for the grant was organizational excellence, along dimensions that would require reasonable investment in administration, not just 7%.

Similarly, we recently had an existing donor revise down the maximum allowable administrative costs, with no change in expectations for the project or the administration to support it. In these situations we are thus faced with tough options: applying for a grant knowing we have to raise significant additional funds, not applying at all, or somehow trying to 'reclassify' costs to make ends meet. We have gone with the first choice in both instances, but we would love to know from any donors that set admin or overhead costs at a certain level: what are they using to understand how 16% is bad or 14% is good? Have they seen impact metrics connected to this, predictably?

Answer:

We have a 15% operational limit, but we will often be flexible. We do support some flexibility on that, but we do try to stick to the 15% cap. It's tough, this question of overhead. Very honestly, I think there is a case to be made by nonprofits to talk about why they need more overhead. Maybe they could have a one or two-pager to outline exactly why that is and where that goes and how it links to sustainability.

It is sort of a rule of thumb to cut admin costs at 15%, so why did our foundation choose that cut off? I have no idea. Are they tracking the impact of 15% vs. 7%? No, I don't think so, but if you're working with foundations who listen to their partners and what they have to say, then you have to communicate the importance to them.

For example, we fund an organization that has a higher overhead, but they talk about that in their business model. So if the organization asking this question had some sort of one pager or dedicated space to why overhead needs to be higher and how does it link to some organizational management, donors might look at that and either say, 'That's great, but we can't do it. That's just the way it is.' Or you have a foundation that's open to reconsidering. Maybe they could work with you internally to help you better define it for other donors, something I like to call creative budgeting. I think what some people put in overhead and what others put in programming is sometimes quite creative. Sometimes those things are clearly defined and sometimes they are more open.

It's about telling a story around overhead. You will have some foundations that will be set in their ways. They want to set a precedent that's set in some logic, but you have to talk to the admin people about why those numbers have been calculated. I think there's some deep tradition behind it that I don't even know. I don't know if someone has looked at that question so carefully. Maybe someone has. Google it. There has to be some good papers in support of those numbers for them to exist so broadly.

American universities, for example, charge very high overhead. Why do they do that? From my understanding, it's because the US government used that as a way to supplement their research funding and give them some way to bolster the institutions. It was intentionally built in there as a way to transfer support for some of the core costs around research. The US government's funding practices around that totally skewed the market, so when we get our proposals from some of the biggest Ivy League universities, they want 50% overhead. Forget it. We have paid 20% overhead before, because there was some rationale behind that, such as the staff were going to be dispatched to represent the cause, so we could justify the costs that way. I can't add more to that other than to find a way to build a story around your need for higher overhead.

Answer:

I should have expected this question. As (EJ) knows, I am a staunch believer in keeping overhead low, generally between 10%-15%. Listen, like I've said many times before, everything in life related to numbers is arbitrary. Why can we drive at 16, but vote at 18 and wait three years after that to legally drink? The speed limit is sometimes 60mph and other times it's higher or lower. All these numbers are arbitrary, but we accept these parameters and operate inside them for the most part.

The constant question around overhead gets on my nerves because I didn't force you to start your nonprofit. I definitely didn't force you to come and solicit me for funding. You chose to approach me, even when my guidelines are clear on what I give and how I give it. Think of someone asking to come into your home to use the bathroom and then complains that the toilet paper isn't soft enough. It sounds crass, but it's true. I'm not going to feel bad because I won't write you a blank check for something that's not proven or doesn't have a plan to not need my funding or anyone's funding in five to ten years.

Reclassifying funds is really the smartest thing to do. Take a page out of the book of larger organizations that have been able to exist with mostly government funding, where the restrictions are the toughest. They understand the art and science of tying some admin costs to the programs they run. It makes total sense to say, 'We need to hire these people to execute these directives from an untested plan,' instead of expecting donors to guess how much money should be left totally in your care without a clear distinction or link to how it will create results.

Everything in a nonprofit is a program. Performing advocacy is a program. Hiring new staff is a program. You can call it hiring new staff and be rejected or call it capacity escalation or increased field deployment and have it approved. It isn't lying; it is giving a name to where my funds are going. Larger nonprofits understand this more. While you're complaining about the speed limit, they are getting where they need to go and a lot faster.

I think nonprofits misunderstand the concept of the 15% or 10% cap on administrative costs, at least from my perspective. You are asking for a considerable amount of money for something you hope works. We can talk about a proven model versus a startup, but it is still hope that you are asking us to bank on. Within a grant I give, 85% of it goes to the mission as laid out in the implementation of that plan. That implementation will be in the form of programs. Those programs can be labor intensive and require more staff be built. As long as I understand the process, it is all a part of the 85% portion of my grant. 15% is the part I give you that has no plan. Core funding doesn't tell me anything about where my money will really go.

My advice would be to improve how core costs get integrated into the programs and structure of your organization and repackage what core costs mean to donors.

Question:

I frequently find that whilst our core values and approach might be completely in line with a foundation's vision, mission and guiding principles, it is often difficult to see how we fit into a foundation's priority areas. How common is it for a foundation to fund a 'special project' within a nonprofit? Does this kind of funding even exist?

Answer:

Every rule in the world has an exception – or two, or three. Special projects fall into that category, so yes that kind of funding exists. In fact, I don't know any funder who has never funded something outside of their stated priority areas, but frequency varies. Personally, I've found that special projects tend to be more common in privately funded entities where decisions are based on personal choices rather than a rigorous and uniform process.

The other thing to recognize is that vision, mission and guiding principles are distinctly separate from priority areas and it's completely appropriate to fit the first, but not the second, and therefore be ineligible for a grant. Think of it in programmatic terms. Your vision is a world without hunger, your mission is to provide nutritious school lunches to those in need, and your guiding principle is based on the belief that everyone has a right to healthy food.

Well, hungry kids in South Africa would meet your vision, mission, and principles. But if you've defined your 'priority area' as kids in Detroit, then you aren't going to start sending lunches to Johannesburg, and that's OK. You have your reasons for focus, and so do good funders.

Answer:

This kind of question is all too commonly asked and I hear it all the time, which just goes to show that motivated people who are doing excellent work continue to outnumber the resources available to them. There is a limited amount of funding. I'm hearing so often, 'Funding is available. There's plenty of funding around.'

There isn't. There simply is not. There are a lot of specialized areas and not so specialized areas that merit, in my personal opinion, a lot of funding support that aren't getting a lot of funding support. Advocacy, in general, is one of those things. It is easier for a shelter for abused women to find funding than it is for a women's coop or NGO that focuses on systemically changing the conditions that create and foster that abuse. Long-term solutions to a problem are just not as attractive as something that tangibly treats the repercussions of a problem.

This is something inherent in the divide that goes between mission and final objectives and the impact that is being sought. The impact being sought out is so often really basic, simple digestible metrics that people can relate to without having to consult a dictionary. As soon as it gets a little bit more complex—we're talking about systems, advocacy, qualitatively assessable things—it could be much more aligned to a mission, but it's not going to read as well in an annual report or it's not even going to be understood by a board because they need to know the people inside out who are doing the work on the ground.

So this is a tough one. It means you may have to knock on a lot of doors and sometimes modify your proposal, which is the worst thing, but you have to sometimes reframe what you're doing in order to get funding so that you are splitting between what attracts donors and the real objective that's doing the more unappealing things that are still more pivotal to creating systemic change.

The people who actually work with the boards, the Program Officers or the advisors, need to be the allies, in my opinion, with the NGOs. There is usually more of a predisposition for them to work with the NGOs that they know so much better than the boards, which they see—sometimes, not all the times—as more isolated, living in their ivory towers, that don't bother connecting with the NGOs on the ground. This is so much better than placing your difficult to explain, but necessary work into the category of special project, where it loses significance for both you and the donors.

Questions:

While some donors are interested in early stage organizations (first three years), very few have a focus in supporting 'adolescent' organizations (between five to nine years old). Why not focus support on organizations that have proven some impact, but need funding to get to the next level? Starting an organization is not the hard thing, building and sustaining one is.

Answer:

The fact of the matter is that donors have their own interests. Many choose to fund early stage organizations because their funds have more of an impact and they are able to have more input on the organization's strategy and growth.

We don't agree or disagree with this strategy. At our foundation, we mix our portfolio of partners to focus on grassroots NGOs, comprised of early stage and 'adolescent' organizations, and innovators, comprised of larger NGOs and for-profit social ventures. Our goal is to find the right mix of organizations that allows us to influence the field through leveraged funds and partnerships allowing us to have the biggest impact we can with $10 million a year.

A donor's prerogative can be hard for a NGO to understand, and we know it's often not clear or consistent. What's important for NGOs to understand is the 'value chain' of donors. There are many different types of donors out there from small family foundations like us to institutional funders like the Clinton Foundation. The size of the funder typically influences its focus, whether it be on small-scale organizations or bilateral organizations. It's important for organizations to do their donor research to find funders who support organizations like theirs. Similarly, donors should build relationships up and down the 'value chain' to learn about new organizations and potential opportunities.

Answer:

Imagine if this question was presented to the donors who supported your organization four or five years ago, when you were early stage. Not to be rude, but even as I see some validity in the question, it still sounds like you just want the money to follow your organization, which is understandable, just don't hide behind it. There has been a concerted push for donors to assume more risk in their giving, to create a space for new methods to be realized, instead of taking the safe bet of international NGOs or 'proven' implementers.

At some point, you were the beneficiary of early stage funding. Why would you deny another organization the same kind of support that has the potential to change people's lives? I could counter your question by asking why we should fund an organization that has only shown some impact when we can fund the traditional actors in the space who have decades of proven impact.

Don't get me wrong, I think bridge or capacity growth funding is crucial. As a donor to both early stage and mid-level organizations, I see the need for bringing in more donors to spread the reach of a proven model. Donors are not always so easy to convince to give more at a more sustained pace, even when there are results, but honestly, I think a bandwagon donor is much easier to find than a courageous donor who is willing to take a chance on a concept.

Capacity growth and sustainability may not get the kind of funding it needs, but as someone who spent several years working at nonprofits at all levels, it troubles me to think that someone from that sector could describe the process of creating a startup that can make it to the three year-old mark as not hard. It's all hard.

Question:

It appears donors are now moving from funding nonprofit work to creating in house programs that are self-implemented. Why? And where does the nonprofit who has proven itself at ground zero go if all funding goes this way?

Answer:

Our foundation is a family foundation. One that has invested in numerous projects and organizations, but saw few desired results. The founders were frustrated with the lack of deliverables being promised and not delivered. This led them to take a more direct approach. This may appear narrow to some people, but they could have also changed the focus to something easier to fund or left philanthropy entirely.

We do not work alone and still work with nonprofits, but not with direct funding as much as we have in the past. The conundrum we faced was when the evidence revealed inefficiencies with the implementer's model or the results were not equal to what we invested.

We would have been criticized for asking the organizations to change their models if it meant shifting from their mission. The decision was not made lightly. There were several rounds of surveying the field to create our new strategy before we made the change. We work in an area with multiple donors funding in this area, so the trustees did not feel we were creating a gap in the funding landscape.

I don't know the focus area of the person asking the question, but my own thought is that you don't have much to worry about. Not all donors are in position to do what our foundation does, nor do they want to be. I would dispute that donors are moving to this model. They are, however, moving towards funding more evidence-based work, so if your model is proven with evidence, then the focus should be finding the right donors. If you find potential donors are instead creating their own ground level programs, there is still nothing stopping you from partnering with them collaboratively as implementers. They can turn out to be strong ambassadors to other donors on your organization's behalf.

Answer:

That's a really hard one. I agree there are a lot of organizations who are moving in this direction, obviously including us. It's so founder-driven why this has happened. I would say from our perspective, we wanted to create something where we saw a need that would not compete with other nonprofits. Our founder wanted to do something around tech for NGOs and he wanted to be a co-founder of something in Silicon Valley around tech. It literally goes down to that. It's so arbitrary.

It doesn't matter that the rest of us—the people who work for him and advise him—are saying something different. It's his money and that's a risk that comes with private philanthropy. At the end of the day, the thing you end up saying to the rest of your staff who would say, 'this is so unfair,' is that it is still his money. He can do whatever he wants with it and if that means at any point in time, he doesn't want to fund what we have been working on anymore, you just have to live with it.

It's unfortunate and if it sucks for us, I can only imagine how it could affect our grantees. We're all susceptible to the funder shift. Unless you are an endowed foundation that's indefinitely endowed or have billions in the purse, you're still at the beck and call of a founder as much as a grantee is to their grantor.

In terms of starting programs, our flagship program is a collection of donors and is a donor led program. We knew that if we were able to bring donors to this niche issue, it would be best served as a donor partnership where donors could see the results for themselves and not feel like there was any pressure on the grantee side to embellish for the sake of their livelihoods. We also could share more information and open more doors together in philanthropy and change more hearts and minds rather than if our funding was going into an existing body.

What we have done is work really closely with organizations and funded them to do the programmatic side and deliverables. We've funded them to do the capacity building, which has so far been a win-win. What I think organizations should think about is having a business model sufficient enough where you are relying on only one or two donors in a space. If you are only funded by a few donors and one of them decides to set up an in-house program similar to what you are also doing, then you need to figure out either how you are going to compete with that or figure out a way to compliment it or collaborate with it.

The point is to make yourself invaluable even if someone else starts up something similar, whether it is another nonprofit or a donor. The best thing to do is to establish yourself as a knowledge base in the area, so donors will still feel a need to at least consult with you before making any steps on the ground.

I do see this as a big problem and to speak about why this is happening, it has a lot to do with the closing civil society space in areas like Latin America and in India, where big donors are withdrawing philanthropic support because of rules and regulations that make it harder for them to support. This creates the problem you described in your question. The smaller domestic donors take a very autocratic approach. In Latin America, many of these kinds of donors just fund their own programs. They won't fund with anybody. They won't fund anything that is not within their programs.

The same can be seen in India, with the new Corporate Social Responsibility (CSR) legislation that mandates businesses to put money into social development. All these companies are saying instead of giving up 2% of our profits, let's just start a foundation in our own name and just pile that money in there. But they don't create foundations with the intent of helping existing actors; it is about shaping social development in their own, often uninformed views, because they felt forced into it, not because they see a humane benefit.

Question:

What most turns you off in an organization? What are the main reasons you might decide not to give to an organization, other than it doesn't align with your areas of focus?

Answer:

Poor communication. I want to know that I am not just giving you money, but that we are going to work together to ensure the greatest amount of impact possible. This means that I need to trust that you will communicate when changes occur in the programming or issues arise during the grant period once they happen. I want to see at the beginning of the relationship that there is honest and timely communication so I can feel confident it will continue during the entire grant relationship.

Answer:

We are not unique in this way, but we have a strategy beyond area of focus. It has to align with our strategy. If we already have an 'equivalent' organization fulfilling the role that this other organization would do within the strategy or the specific objective we have, then we are not going to fund two organizations to do the same thing. But to think about something that puts me off is organizations that oversell themselves. Organizations that do not have a degree of self-reflection also turn me off. Well maybe I should apply that to myself, too.

Question:

What do we say to a donor who is willing to pay for implementation and M&E of a new approach to our mission, without providing any funding to strengthen or evaluate our current model, which is still underfunded?

Answer:

Wow. I'm assuming this happens because someone asked the question, but it is a little bit of a shock to imagine a donor would pay for both the implementation and the M&E of a new program, but not put anything towards the core mission. First, I would want to know if this new model is something that you presented as something that was possible without identifying to the donor that the current mission still needs to be funded.

What I would say—or what I would do, I guess—to let the donor know that the mission needs to be funded is include in the M&E how the organization benefits or suffers from not having the core mission funded. If the new model is shown to be better than the current one, then there won't be any need to continue funding that anyway, but you would want to get assurances that there would be continued support for the new model while you shared the M&E with existing donors and had their buy in for the new model. Donors who are willing to fund a mission shift should be aware of what that could do to an organization. If not, that's your job to explain it to them.

Answer:

The case to make in order to ask them to fund beyond just the new innovative, which a lot of people are trying to document, is to show how that new innovative is embedded in a core function of the original mission. Talk about how you need the foundation of the organization to be funded before you can reach toward the new innovative. Highlight that if they want to do this new work and support a new model and fund the M&E, which is critical, that you're struggling with your core operational pieces. Ask them openly if they would be willing to support some of those core operational pieces to be able to have the space and ability to do the new and innovative.

We listen to our partners. Just recently we funded an organization that suddenly had budget constraints due to a change in government. We planned to fund a very specific project, but the Executive Director came to us and told us how these cuts to the budget would affect their ability to carry out the programs that we agreed upon. Instead of the ED trying to build in all the core costs around the secretariat that wasn't really about their time or our funded work, we understood that they needed additional support just to maintain, and provided it.

That came out of discussions because she articulated to us what the challenges were to successfully implement the new piece when their basic functions and the core functions and core mission were stretched. So to this question, I would say to just try to articulate the costs around the basic that remain while trying to implement the new and innovative. That's what would work on our side.

Question:

Do you fund based on mission alignment or charisma/leadership of the respective NGO leader? Recently, I heard a donor say that if I don't like you, I will not fund you. Just wondering, how much do funders really look at impact vs. the personae or personality of respective NGO leaders?

Answer:

I hope that every funder would say that they at least intend to fund on mission alignment! What's the point otherwise?!?

We are results-driven and our funding decisions are based on mission alignment. That said, personality biases are part of human nature and will thus always have some influence, for better or worse. This is why process and rigor are so important in decision-making. We run every applicant through the same information collection and decision making process. We use a qualitative and quantitative matrix that each member of the grant committee must complete for each and every project. The matrix compares each proposal against our specific, pre-determined, pre-defined, pre-prioritized, internal criteria. This forces us to draw the line between 'I really liked him/her' and 'yes, this meets our pre-defined criteria for X, Y, and Z.' It also means we compare applicants to our internal standards rather than pit them against each other where personality differences can have more influence. If you want to be impact driven, you have to apply the same rigor to yourself that you apply to your grantees.

I also wonder what the donor you quoted saying 'I don't like you' really means? If it means that you wouldn't want to hang out with that person on the weekend, that's an irrelevant fact and would not factor into our decision-making process. But it may also mean 'I didn't trust them; they didn't strike me as having the necessary qualities for sound leadership; I'm not sure they have the charisma needed to line up other people behind their mission; etc.' Those are legitimate concerns and would factor into our mitigating criteria.

Answer:

Charisma is definitely important and is something that is undervalued by many smaller grassroots organizations. Leaders of these types of organizations mistakenly believe or are erroneously taught that the facts will speak for themselves. That is not true. Someone needs to be the voice of the facts and it helps if that voice belongs to someone donors can understand and, yes, likes.

But this is not an either/or situation. If you cannot communicate our mission alignment from a position of leadership or with some minimum amount of charisma or passion, it won't work. If what you say is all charisma and no substance, donors can sense that you are wasting their time. An organization that already has impact doesn't need to say it with charisma, just confidence. Be proud of the impact and the pride can be a strong substitute for not being more extroverted or charismatic.

Question:

If you decide to support an NGO based on an introduction by a friend or family member who is on staff, but later leaves the organization, how can the organization best ensure that your relationship with the NGO doesn't leave when that person leaves?

Answer:

We have actually changed our funding structure from multiyear grants to more short-term grants. We are more careful because of the frequent change in relationships. We usually work with individuals. Our support is of their ingenuity. If they leave, it is difficult to know if those ideas can still be generated within the organization that is left behind or if we should follow the people who have proven to create and/or implement solutions. It is difficult for these organizations to always remain in our focus, because we provide small grassroots support to build capacity.

Usually when people leave—since we deal with early stage organizations—it's usually the founders who leave. So it's even more relevant, because we have built relationships with founders, not just the first hires on the development side. If the founders move on, we're usually more interested in their new endeavors. It depends on why they moved on, definitely, as well as the success they left behind. It isn't a black and white decision, where we immediately stop funding the organization. It also can be a matter of outgrowing our own capacity to support the organization. Because our focus is in early incubation, we tend to move with the active founders, the serial NGO entrepreneurs. For us, it's a good thing to be able to shift to new innovative initiatives.

For us, when the person who represents the project is not representing the project anymore, but having legally bound obligations to their existing organizations—even when you see shifting opinions happening as a result—that is very difficult to handle. We moved away from general support grants because of that. We found that if we hand people a bucket of money, they don't necessarily further the cause of the larger community around the project.

Since we do help organizations with structuring and capacity building, as well as the governance and legal framework, we will stay in touch with the old organization up to a point where our focus objectives have been met. That makes it less of a conflict and more of a mutual agreement that they've outgrown our relationship.

Answer:

We fund based on results, not on sympathy grants. Those connections to organization staff cannot compensate for solid results. If an organization secures a grant or even just a meeting through family ties or other close relations, the job of that organization from day one is to show donors that there is more to it than the one person they know. Let the face of the organization be the organization and not a friend or family member.

In terms of what steps to take, don't let that person be the only point of contact or even the main point of contact to the donor. But at the end of the day, you have to trust the work. Unless it is a two-person operation, no sensible donor is going to leave an organization they have enjoyed supporting because a friend or family member has moved on. Of course it matters why they left. If they come to us and tell us to end the relationship or show evidence of misdoings, then the relationship is over. If not, you should have until the end of the grant cycle to maintain the relationship. If it cannot be renewed, then either something in your outcomes or communication is weak or the donor was not seriously invested and doesn't need to be part of your onward journey.

Question:

How do you balance wanting to stay in line with strategic priorities, but also wanting to fund innovative projects that might come up outside of planning cycles?

Answer:

We have no grant cycles and accept applications on a rolling basis, so luckily for us, the timeline part of the question doesn't apply. However, the question of sticking to the mission versus veering off of strategy is one that funders deal with constantly. It's our version of mission creep. To put it in analogous terms, an off-strategy, innovative project can be as tantalizing to us as a donor offering large sums of money to veer off mission is to you. How do we balance it? By coupling set rigor with built-in flexibility.

This coupling is achieved by starting with a very clear and articulate strategy that is coupled by a uniform, systematic, and rigorous decision-making process. But notice I said 'clear and articulate' versus strict; 'rigorous' versus rigid. Building flexibility within an established system is where you can get the best of both worlds.

But just like your rigor is structural, you have to make your flexibility structural too. If your standard process is to have the board meet once a year, then create a 'rapid response' subcommittee that can also meet once a quarter, as needed, to review these off-cycle opportunities. Saying you want to be flexible is rarely enough. You have to build it in. Once you do that, you can create a system for case-by-case analysis allowing you to fully consider those 'off strategy' requests without losing your priorities or the opportunities they may bring along.

Answer:

I'm a third generation philanthropist at a family foundation. Family foundations have always had institutions to carry out their work. That teaches you humility, because the needs don't change that much and you feel like part of the solution. As you grow older, you see how concepts revisit. Our strategic priorities don't change much, but are we talking about innovation that comes out of the blue or changes that are proposed after reviewing the M&E to find a more effective approach?

The first is impossible to plan, because it does not occur so often. The other sounds more like funding a new theory of change for the same goal, which can be problematic. If, through M&E, the data suggests a new approach, which is stronger and still leads to the ultimate goal, that is great and we can find a way to work together. If the M&E shows that the theory of change was not working, and now there is 'innovation' to come up with a new theory, then that is much harder to support.

However, I really feel like we need to take a stronger look at how we interpret innovation. The term innovation implies something new, but when you have the luxury of a longer view, you see that people focus on the technological more than the social aspect of it. The research has shown us that technological fixes are more of a problem than a solution. There's always a social side to what we want to achieve and we will not learn it from the technical side. Technical solutions, we know since the development of nuclear power, comes with advantages and it comes with risks.

When we have a technological breakthrough, everyone is super excited and enamored with this new thing. Only afterwards do they take a real look to see what's missing or what needs to develop. On the other hand, social development is more long-term, more structural and needs investment, but it is always new. It sounds like the same old story, but it's always new people, new generations, the excitement of youth and new experiences. The themes remain more or less the same, but the social innovation comes from the space we create for the new members of a community to present their solutions instead of being bound to outdated methods. There are always people coming up who are cleverer than we are. We acknowledge that problems adapt and change. The solutions must do the same. This is innovation to me or the kind of innovation I look to support.

Question:

Do you recommend that nonprofits reach out to board members or would that be crossing the line of solicitation?

Answer:

In our case, we don't accept outside proposals. We are active and have a team that scans the scene for interesting developments. We are depending on our board members. They are the ones who perform the scouting. In a sense, we encourage that kind of relationship building, because we are interested more in an individual relationship, not a group organizational one. Usually, when people solicit our board members, it will have very little effectiveness in creating a relationship.

Answer:

Absolutely not! Especially if it is a formally structured foundation, it will be seen as skirting all the steps that were put in place for nonprofits to engage. It will be perceived as arrogance, especially by the program staff. To meet a board member in a neutral setting, it is completely acceptable to engage, but to directly solicit a member or to make contact after already engaging with program officers is going too far. Follow protocol even if it doesn't guarantee the desired results.

Question:

Honestly, how important is recognition? I have heard donors say that they don't care for recognition, but in one instance, a donor was really upset when I forgot to include her name in the program book.

Answer:

The answer will vary depending on the donor, but if you make an offer to provide name recognition, it is up to you to deliver. It isn't the donor's fault that you forgot to include her name. Remember that donors often have no personal insight into how your nonprofit is run. Not including a name in a program book may seem minor, but it could also be the only proof a donor has of your delegating and multitasking skills.

Another thing to take into account is reciprocity. Some donors want to see that you are just as proud to be associated with them as much as they are proud to be associated with you.

Answer:

It really does depend on where the organization is coming from. From my view, because we give actual awards in addition to our funding, our donor loves to see the award displayed prominently on site visits. The rest of us couldn't care less about that or how they choose to acknowledge us, but I think the recognition should be matched by the contribution and not just financially. If the donor has made site visits and been an ambassador for your work, it is only right to recognize them when appropriate.

Question:

Why are more funders not open to standardized program reporting? For example, our organization develops quarterly reports that cover updates on all of our programs as well as the organization's progress overall. For a group of our donors this has worked very well, but others still require more customized progress reports specific to their grants, even when the progress of their projects is covered in the larger quarterly report. Reporting is certainly necessary, but it also often consumes a lot of time and resources for the NGO. Streamlining the process would save time and money. Could there be an effective way to address this with funders?

Answer:

In our organization, we have different reporting formats within the different departments. I'm a research funder and since we fund research, I'm more interested in specific information than my colleagues who run our Africa work. They have to look more at diligence and financial reports. Whereas in our case, we require more of the intricacies and data. We have our own key performance indicators (KPI). We have our systems to monitor our performance.

Very often, as is the case here, the results of the programs flow into a performance measurement system that a foundation has established or the donor in general has. This is the case, in particular, for larger foundations. Because of this, the reporting must be standardized in a way that fits into our system. We do not just use the reports as a confirmation that the nonprofit organization is doing something. We are dissecting it and creating additional reporting for research purposes.

You also have to understand that the foundations are not always working in the same countries where you are working so different reporting requirements are in place to accommodate the differences of operating in these different areas. Here in Switzerland, we do need different information than foundations in the US. That said, our policy is to minimize reporting requirements. We've really boiled it down to very few numbers. I hope that no partner of ours spends more than half a day writing the annual report that he or she has to submit to the foundation. I do know that this is not the case in other places.

One thing I've noticed is when multiple donors fund a project together, they have trouble agreeing on a common reporting format. That makes it tough for the nonprofit. If you run a project that has eight donors and each donor has a different deadline for reporting and different formats, then a nonprofit would spend half of its work life writing these reports. I think we have a way to go here, but I must say we do need different reports in order to justify what we do to the authorities that demand it, but as Program Officers and Program Directors, we need that information to be transparent for our board. We need this information in a similar reporting format from all our project partners. Otherwise you're just moving the burden of reporting from the nonprofit to the foundation staff. Either way, someone has to do it.

Answer:

In my foundation, my team definitely requests customized reporting. That was necessary for the budgeting aspects (trying to follow the trail of resources and how they were allocated over time) and I think that it will be difficult to convince donors to have that kind of in-depth customized reporting on budgeting go away, unless they are offering unrestricted funds. To the extent that they are restricted, I don't see much flexibility on that.

The pressure that donor organizations are under, in terms of their audits, is to be sure that they are complying with all the IRS regulations. I think it would be impossible to suggest that foundations change their reporting structure. Budgeting reports could conceivably be done away with, even if you have similar programs that are working on a particular issue area. However, for the narrative reports, I don't know how we could reconceive the information that donors need to report back to their trustees about the impact of the programs. When it becomes mixed in with funding from other organizations that may have contributed to the same project, it would be too difficult, in my opinion, to tease out what each institution's particular role was to the success or failure of a program.

I think generally what I'm saying is that each donor agency in the end is responsible to a corporate board, a US or congressional board (if located in the states) or a very economically successful board of trustees. The people who are behind those decisions really want to see the extent to which their resources contributed to the social change that they were intended for. For those reasons, I feel like it's going to be a hard sell to ask these entities to reduce the accountability that their grantees will be providing them, both narratively and financially.

Question:

What should American nonprofits know about European foundations? My feeling is dealing with foundations is different than dealing with European governments, where core funding is low and red tape is high.

Answer:

European foundations sometimes come from a very long history and you will be dealing with that history, which won't change very fast. With proper foundations, you usually have very rigid institutions. The larger foundations are completely restricted within legal frameworks, much more so than in the United States, from what I know about how things operate in that country. So expect to catch up on structure, on history, and if it's a large one, it will be hierarchical. Programmatic staff will have to talk to their higher ups before making any decisions, so expect delays.

Younger organizations that are being founded are not really foundations proper, but are more like hybrids, they are more comparable to the US-based foundations. Also, Europe doesn't show up as a whole. There are vast differences between the capitalist West and the ex-communist East, where they have very few and mostly new foundations. In the West, you have foundations that don't always work internationally. France doesn't do much internationally, neither does Spain, Portugal or Greece, not in a significant way. They don't have the tradition of an international presence. In this way, Europe cannot be bunched together like the states; they would have to be discussed country by country.

Even in my home country of Germany, foundation law is not national, but specific by province. So what people can do in foundations is restricted by their provincial tax office. This is taken quite seriously because of the hierarchical system and the boards follow the legal frameworks religiously without challenging their relevance in changing times. It is not a very daring system.

Answer:

I'm not sure how I can answer that. I think the differences between bilaterals and private foundations are significant. I mean, it's their question, but I think that viewing European philanthropy money in Europe in one or two ways is dangerous or at least unwise. Just like with in the US, European foundations are all quite different. I think there are other questions that have to be asked. Are they family led foundations? Do they have an endowment or are they spending down? Who's behind the money or what's the mission?

I don't know if our foundation is different than some of the ones in the US. That said, I do think the philanthropy sector is younger than in the US. In the US, you can get a masters in philanthropy. There's a whole industry around American philanthropy that I'm not sure exists around European philanthropy as much. I think there are advantages and disadvantages to each approach. I don't know enough about how it works in the US to say, but I think there isn't one answer to that question.

The only thing to know is actually not about American or European, but just know about the foundation. I guess one thing that comes to my mind now that might help some American nonprofits is that European foundations wouldn't have the restrictions that maybe some American foundations would have around funding some direct lobbying work. They are not under the same constraints around funding advocacy that might restrict American counterparts. My understanding is that European foundations have this ability. That is about all I really know about differences, but I don't know about more red tape or less red tape than European governments or American foundations.

Question:

As a relatively small faith-based charity, we find that most donors come to us when they have a project to implement and want us to take part. However, it is more difficult to reach out to bigger foundations, including some of the same organizations that ask us to partner on their own incubated projects, and have them support our own programs or receive core funding. How do we position ourselves better to organizations that do not have a history of supporting faith-based charities?

Answer:

For nonprofits doing faith-based work, there's nothing wrong with being rooted in your faith. I believe that very much. You don't ever have to justify that or apologize for it, but that's not the work. As a faith person, you're doing the work of a faith person, but that work is still rooted in real world needs that exist outside religion.

You need to think of your faith as your motivation and your guiding light, but the work that you're doing is not about any particular faith; it's about justice. The motivation is your faith, but the work is how the community needs it to look in order for it to be a success. Position yourself based on the work and continue to do it based on your faith.

Answer:

I don't know what relatively small means to you and your organization, but our foundation is very concerned with impact and program outcomes. To a certain extent, we recognize the value of faith-based institutions for community change. However, cracking into the larger foundations is difficult when your operating budgets are small. I don't know the size of your organization, but the size of our smallest grant is $250,000 a year. That size award makes it almost impossible to fund organizations that have budgets less than one million dollars. That would be the very low end.

So the very nature of being a large donor or mover of significant money makes it a challenge to support smaller organizations who are looking for grants in the $25,000 to $30,000 range. I would say to really engage larger foundations, I would do that through peer networks, because I think that is the strategy most of the larger donors are using to identify appropriate change agents. If or when smaller faith-based organizations have partners that can combine their resources and do a joint project that would attract the bigger donors, that might be a really powerful way of being collaborative and yet still having the ability to absorb the gift that larger donors are used to giving.

Question:

Funders seem to be more involved in wanting to shape development and delivery of grantees. Have funders seen benefits to this approach and have the result of this approach been evaluated and the evaluation results shared with the charity sector?

Answer:

This feels very much like a Catch-22 for donors. We have been accused of not putting enough effort into how we grant in the past and now that we are more hands-on, we still receive criticism. The benefits to an approach like this is that there is more transparency between donor and grantee, and donors are willing to assume more risk when they can be involved more. Shaping doesn't mean taking over and donors don't have the time to do that even if they wanted. I think the evidence is shown in the success of fellowship and mentorship programs that offer young nonprofits more than just funding. They provide structure and guidance where an organization is lacking.

If you don't feel comfortable in the direction a donor is taking you, it is up to you to speak up and remind the donor why your own strategy on development and deliverables is the one to be followed.

Answer:

The message I give to funders is the same message I give to my advocacy organizations. It's very natural for people who are born leaders and born advocates to start an organization. There comes a transition point where you have to move and decide whether you want to lead that organization or you want to continue to work on the ground. The talent and work that it takes to run an organization in a very healthy and sustainable way is very different from the way you carry out an advocacy organizing campaign. Same thing for funders. If you want to do direct service work, then you need to go and do direct service work, and not tell your grantees how to do the work that they are doing on a daily basis.

Now, with that said, funders know their colleagues well. I think very much that there is value in funders partnering with grantees in a way that they kind of co-create a project together, but just remembering everyone's roles and responsibilities. It's to help leverage the talent of the grantee and the grantee is there to leverage the relationships in the sector. Just remember boundaries. That rarely happens on the donor side. Because we're the ones that have the money, the onus is on donors to monitor our boundaries and remain aware of the power dynamic. We have to own this piece and be responsible for not crossing the line more than the grantee doing the reverse.

A Thousand Currents does this well and talks very well about working closely with their grantees and co-created projects, so if you are looking for data on this, that would be a good resource. They bring their own money to it, but they also can bring other donors onboard. The grantee then brings the talent of how to make the implementation happen. One example I have from my own experiences was around the Ebola crisis.

With the challenge of Ebola, I was sitting in my office in the West and I had no idea how to begin to help. Not being a very huge foundation, we didn't even know how to leverage our funding or how much to put in to leverage with others. So I literally picked up the phone and called my grantee there on the ground and said, 'If you were going to shape the program, what would you do?'

She came up with the entire program on her own. Based on what she drafted, I was able to add pieces to it using my wider network in the region. It then became a project between us and another donor working in the region. It was a great example for me of how grantees and funders can shape development and delivery of programs.

Question:

I'm sure this will be asked many times, but why is there so little flexibility when it comes to core funding from individual donors? All other groups of donors like governments and corporates I can understand more, but not the individual ones. I know that for many donors, core funding only means salaries, but it really goes to creating a budget that allows us as an organization to respond quickly to a sudden change on the ground. We are not all looking to create a business model.

Some of us are trying to save lives and doing a damn good job of it with what feels like very little intelligent support. The rigidity on this has crippled our organization in the past. A few years ago, almost all of our core staff had second jobs to make ends meet. This included staff who were essential in creating some of the strategies that attracted our biggest donors and helped us win some major awards.

They were willing to take second jobs and spend less time with their families just to keep our organization afloat. As a founder of an organization that focuses on family planning and family care, that broke my heart that we could not be the model internally of what we were trying to promote. We lost many of them when bigger nonprofit opportunities came along. One of our former staff members who moved to an INGO told me that one of our donors who told us they didn't give core funding gave an unrestricted grant to that INGO. None of it makes sense to me.

We have to account for every penny we spend for tax purposes, so I just don't understand the reluctance or unwillingness around core support. If you're not willing to pay us to complete our goals at full strength, where we could do more at a faster and more efficient pace, then how can you also complain that we remain in the sector too long?

Answer:

I recognize the concern and I agree with the sentiment that it is difficult to attract more core funding. I've been a development person, so I've worked in positions where we were pursuing unrestricted funding. It was considered gold to get this, where you weren't stuck only doing restricted programs, so I recognize the value in it from experience.

Donors, especially in this time where the measurable impact is such a primary driver and foundations in general try to model the business world more, seem to have little appetite for core funding. In that arena, it's very difficult to identify how your resources move forward a certain project, deliver a certain outcome or outputs. I think there will be that tension moving forward, so long as that intense MBA-style assessment of projects is driving the industry.

There are certain organizations—and hats off to them—that only give core funding. I know that the Hewlett Foundation was one of those when I was on the development side. The grant that was awarded to the organization I worked with was purely unrestricted. It was to be used in order for that NGO to enact its vision. They were trusted to do that and used the money responsibly.

I think now there is a bigger appetite not just in looking at core funding, but increasing indirect funding, to control what proportion of money goes to indirect costs. The Ford Foundation led by Darren

Walker recently put out a pretty comprehensive plan about the foundation's new policies around the increase of indirect funding. I think that's moving towards this idea that the nonprofits and the social change makers that we're supporting are the ones with the expertise, intelligence and ability to make the decisions and to strengthen their organizations so that staff don't have to take second jobs. Nonprofits don't have to be thin on their administrative capacity and their IT capacity and all those other things that make businesses and organizations run.

Yes, there needs to be more advocacy on the part of nonprofits to talk with their donors and explain to them the constraints that restricted funding places on them. Try to engage with those donors who have recognized the limits of restricted funding. One, like I said earlier, is Hewlett Foundation and so is Mulago Foundation. So there are some leading foundations that have awakened to that need and hopefully things will move in that direction, if we can dial back a little bit on the whole business model of impact outcomes assessments.

Answer:

I admit I was somewhat annoyed at having to explain again why I don't give core support. Not every donor is in position to do so. Not every nonprofit can be trusted with it. I actually feel like not giving unrestricted funding would help nonprofit employees more because their salaries can be budgeted into program under labor, instead of creating scenarios where the founder is getting all of the money and staff are still underpaid. I have seen this. I have been to expensive resorts and I would run into high level nonprofit staff, ones that I donated to and ones that I know of. These are the same people who have told me that every penny goes to further the mission.

However, I agree that mission efficiency is just as important as financial efficiency, especially if one inhibits the other. I don't believe core staff should be forced to take on additional jobs in order to maintain a living wage. I've taken strong stance against donors being browbeaten into giving unrestricted funding, but your question has made me rethink my position. I think it starts with nonprofits coming to the table with this kind of honesty about specific needs for core staff. Nonprofits have a tendency to want to paint a perfect picture of their organizations, but an honest portrayal allows donors to understand the full complexities of the organization.

I plan to share this question with some of my smaller grantees to see if this is a situation they also face, but have not disclosed to me. Based on what they say, I would be more open to giving some form of core support.

Question:

Is philanthropy an art or science?

Answer:

Philanthropy is a science that is treated as an art. Philanthropy is self-regulated, making it more of an art typically driven by the passion of philanthropists and not by proven results. Since funders are only accountable to themselves and their boards, they are often motivated to develop their own systems of impact assessment that are not regulated across the field of philanthropy.

Answer:

Like art and science themselves, the answer is both. Great artists learn and methodically apply a range of tested techniques whether its brushstroke, perspective, color mixing, etc. Some of the greatest discoveries have occurred when scientists pursued something based on a hunch.

Rather than art or science, I would argue that philanthropy is human. Like our own psychology, it's a blend of rational and irrational behavior. Some of it is based on gut and some of it is based on evidence and will never be all one or the other. In general, I think the best approach starts with evidence, methodology and rigor, but leaves room for intuition, insight, and a good bet.

Philanthropy is human also means that, whether done by an individual or a multi-lateral institution, it is based on choices. Whatever the choice, be honest about what you are doing and why. The best artists and scientists are self-aware of their biases, motivations, assumptions, and intentions.

Answer:

Philanthropy is a delicate art. I've been on the other side of it, so I'm very sensitive to how donors drive issues. Now I raise the idea that donors can drive issues because I know that it is our comparative advantage, but again, this is very delicate. This is where the art comes in. How do you drive without imposing? How do you drive in a respectful way? How do you drive and build leadership without pushing too fast and know when to slow down or pull back? These are the things that go beyond the grant. This is the brokering role and the visionary role and so on. It's very tough. The skill level it takes to do that well is really hard.

Answer:

Philanthropy is not an art or science. I personally believe we have tried to create a structure out of something arbitrary. You pass a homeless person on the street holding out a cup and you put a few euros in the cup, but you probably passed twenty people asking for money and you might pass twenty more. Do you really need to set up an independent study to figure out why you chose that person or if there was a better way to do it? Yes, giving at a larger scale impacts the lives of many more in completely different ways, but it is still arbitrary and thank God for that. If we only gave on an artistic or scientific model, there are many areas of the sector that would never exist, like areas with huge risk or unproven innovation.

Philanthropy can be artistic or scientific, but it is not an art or a science. It is a gut feeling to do good when you are moved to do so.

Answer:

Philanthropy is not a science; it's an art. In that art, we make a lot of crumby pictures, but hopefully, once in a while, we can make a masterpiece.

8

'I Was A Bad Donor' – Candid Admissions of Donor Missteps

I was not the best donor...oh, let me count the ways:

Early on, it was simply inexperience. The first grant application form I created didn't have a dollar sign on it. Once I remembered to include the financial section, I 'helped' applicants fit their projects into our pre-ferred grant range. I had our web developer and receptionist reviewing grant applications on a particularly heavy cycle.

I can make many excuses for the mistakes I made, the shortcuts I took as an inexperienced donor; we were a small foundation just starting out, I was young (so young!), I didn't know about the resources that were available to help/guide/educate me toward better grant-making—and we couldn't have afforded them anyway, there was so much pressure to keep our own overhead down: the funders had their priorities and their pet projects. There was a legacy to follow, etc. But the truth at the core of those rookie mistakes is that some deep part of me believed that passionate good intentions were enough.

So I funded sexy projects in faraway places I knew nothing about (when I moved on to bigger and better grants, I got to visit sexy projects in far-away places I knew next to nothing about.) I pushed back on grantee 'overhead' expenses like staff time for program monitoring and evalua-tion, feeling all sorts of forward-thinking for helping these nonprofits behave more like businesses. And I served on a half-dozen nonprofit boards across a decade, with not one member of the communities they were intended to serve there as well. Not one.

I had so much to learn.

Often, though, my 'bad donor' decisions—and in honest hindsight I have to call them decisions, though at the time I often felt I didn't have a choice—were matters of expedience.

I remember a call from an Executive Director, in tears; they weren't go-ing to make their milestones, they were completely out of funding, and the program (a fairly public one we had fairly publicly supported) would die—tomorrow—without us. So I made a wire transfer. I hadn't learned that sometimes programs should die. And I'm still learning to walk with the weight of being the one who makes that call.

I remember feeling like a rock star sitting down for lunches during a 'capacity building' session with a group of grantees. I was speaking a second language without a translator, because I was that committed and we were way ahead on the agenda—everyone was just so in sync; no disagreement on anything, no resistance to the new skills/methods I was teaching, every one of them had committed to implementing the practices at their organizations!

It was six incredibly frustrating, expensive, and rather embarrassing months later that I was finally clued in to the linguistic subtlety (this region's version of the 'yes-no') that should have let me know my 'capac-ity building' session was doing anything but. I hadn't learned to listen first. I'm still learning how to make the conversation between donor and grantee really work.

The hardest lesson I ever learned in this work is that you can do more harm than good—and I have.

This candid admission from an anonymous donor was originally meant to serve as the preface to the chapter on peer advice at the do-nor level that follows this one. However, in several discussions—not just with this person, but other donors—it became apparent that call-ing out bad donor behavior without first providing tangible examples of what constitutes bad behavior and self-reflecting on our own mis-steps as donors, would diminish the intended impact.

As much as I like to think of myself as a nonprofit champion, there have been more times than I would like to admit that I, too, did more harm than good. The examples in this story are quite familiar to me. I have steered organizations down paths that looked promising from my narrow perspective without taking the time to fully see it from their view. I have also put up little to no resistance when I heard a bad idea because I didn't want to abuse the power dynamic, which—of course—didn't help anyone in the end. I've said and done and funded things I wish I could take back, but cannot.

I think one of the best things we can do in dismantling that power dynamic is not pretending it doesn't exist, but admitting when us donors have misused it, regardless of intent. We want to be seen as human and failure is just as an important aspect of humanity as anything else. The question is how we accept and respond to it. I know that part of my response has been to become (almost) as frank professionally as I am personally. If it serves you to hear the truth, I will give it to you.

If I cannot understand the point of a program or initiative within your organization, I won't just chalk it up to my ignorance; I will make you explain and go over it until I actually understand what you hope to accomplish. I am not afraid—ok, well much less afraid—to say 'I don't know,' because I've learned that sometimes it is less about my comprehension and more about improving the communication skills of a nonprofit or its representative. There are many more changes I can cite that I have made based on the abundance of questionable decisions I made in my donor role, but that doesn't absolve those mistakes. The recognition that I had engaged in bad practices means that I could do so again if I don't own it.

I talked often with nonprofits about the idea of failing forward, a concept I learned from the Open Road Foundation. It involves creating a space for nonprofits to learn and prosper from failure: take risks and benefit from the rewards, but learn from the obstacles that could not be overcome. I don't think we talk enough about how to create a protocol for donors to fail forward. We can create the space within our individual foundations and philanthropic giving to fail from our mistakes, but we don't have a common strategy to share lessons learned from that failure.

Donors can be too reactionary. When something fails, many of us are still too quick to look at it only as the nonprofit's failure. Then we change our funding strategies or grantees to avoid future failures, only to come across them again. At some point, we must be able to stop and see that the common denominator in organizational failure is us. From there, we can be more honest with ourselves about how we fund and the things we have done to contribute to undesired outcomes. Part of that starts with recognizing that we don't stop being capable of making mistakes just because we represent significant amounts of money.

With that in mind, I reached out to other donors specifically around this topic to see what they were willing to publicly own in their positions as donors. Yes, they would remain anonymous, but to admit this and then share it even with me was something I knew many would be hesitant to do. Indeed, some of the stories donors shared were along the lines of, 'I just care too much and am a bad donor for being too good a person.'

Fortunately and somewhat surprisingly, the majority of donors pushed themselves to delve deeper and delivered heartfelt examples. I offer a special thank you to those who offered stories that pushed the boundaries of anonymity, but were still willing to have them included. The majority of these were shared in-person and I was able to see the effect they had on the donors. A couple donors shed tears while others were clearly emotional. Of all the areas of this book where donors contributed, this was probably the toughest and by far most candid. This show that while it may be easier to be a donor, it is definitely not easy, and the weight of our decisions can be quite the heavy burden to carry.

●●●

There's a pendulum or rather a scale of the nongrantee-centric—like USAID—and the über grantee-centric, where everything is about your grantees. There is actually a balance in the middle and I think I tend to swing more towards the super grantee-centric. I think that the balanced middle still leans that way. I do believe that's the morally good way to be doing grant-making, but if it swings too far, especially as a westerner—or global northerner or whatever you wanna call me, a privileged white person—it becomes too paternalistic.

The view goes from more objective to something more akin to 'these poor organizations. They're in a village with no internet. How can I grow their capacity and make them look like an American NGO?'

I think there are times when it's easy to slip too far. My own nurturing instincts can get in the way of making an informed decision based on a criteria that is slightly divorced from the heartstrings. I have to constantly remind myself to be a promoter and a partner and an advocate for my partners without being a parent.

A more personal example of how I felt I let myself down as a donor occurred within my organization and not directly with a partner. We were having a conversation within our foundation about how to promote African-led foundations. We kept coming around to this idea that the missing link was that they didn't have a western champion to do their fundraising.

I let that slide and I think I should have stopped it, because the idea that we need to just make Africa-led organizations more western felt wrong. It feels like assimilation and is not what I believe in, so I wish I had reigned that in more and fought that notion more. I should have been an advocate more instead of being more like a parent. And not even a good parent. What parent would say 'Oh, my kid isn't getting this, so I'm gonna make them more like some other kid who is getting it?'

But that's what I felt I was doing instead of being the right kind of partner or advocate and saying OK, maybe they don't look like all the other organizations, but they are great in what they do. We have to make a better effort to highlight that greatness, and not in a way that compromises their greatness.

●

I think we as donors talk a lot about not wanting to create a power dynamic, but are unwilling to share or outsource power in relationships with nonprofits. Most of the times, we want to support and give to people who are dynamic, courageous and powerful, but when they exhibit power with us, we are uncomfortable and will reinforce the hierarchy when our position feels threatened. I saw this often from my days working on the implementation side and still see it done by other donors. As a donor, this is the one way I try not to be a bad donor, but I have had my bad moments in other ways.

A couple years ago, one partner in central Africa that had done amazing work and rose up quickly to be a credible threat to a corrupt government system came to us with a specific request that was possibly going to change the whole course of that system. The request required big bets on our part. We pride ourselves as donors on funding this kind of work. Where we would usually say yes, this time we said no. Mostly because it sounded too risky and dangerous, but who are we to know and say when people should take risks?

We were not afraid of the idea failing, but afraid of the repercussions of failure, which is not a good reason. We often tell our grantees, including this one, to take risks, to step up, to leave their comfort zone, and to address massive challenges. Then when this partner had done those things and was about to trigger a move to tumble the last fiber of the corrupt system, we said no. I felt we were hypocrites. I was a hypocrite.

To be honest, it was the only time I felt like a bad donor, because I didn't want to lose the work, but I didn't have the understanding that this was what the work had been building towards. Ultimately, the decision was in my hands and I was the one who said no. It was selfish and based not on the evidence or potential for success, but the potential for failure. I just kept thinking that this was 'too too too' of 'too too too' for us to go forward. This should have been a vote of confidence in the work we were happy to support when it was easier, but in the critical moment, with millions of people counting on the courage of this partner, I didn't show similar courage. That one moment when they needed a donor who was going to be flexible enough to understand the risks and weigh them appropriately against the rewards, we didn't do it.

That was a very difficult choice that I will have to live with for the rest of my life. It has challenged me to examine what I say I want to impact and what I do to create impact. I'm still reflecting on that, years later. It was a moment where we could have unlocked the future in a way we always talk about, but were proven to be only interested in talking about, not supporting fearlessly.

●

I remember one time sitting in a conference I co-sponsored and feeling really ashamed of myself. It was meant to showcase a new subject, but the convening used an academic approach that was not informed by the constituency. In fact, during the conference, the constituency was sitting in the last row like they weren't even there, and had not been involved at all in the planning process. My mistake was letting the funding take the place of my own participation in the process. Had I seen the approach they were going to take, I would never have given my consent. Whether it was from laziness or too much trust in the organization to implement without any oversight on my end, I'll never do that kind of thing again.

I strictly follow the principle, 'nothing about us without us,' so that was a clear mistake on my part. It wasn't much fun being there for me, so I can imagine how the constituents must have felt. The organizers should have also imagined how the constituents would have felt before the conference and it was my job to reinforce that. In the end, we were able to mitigate the harm that could have been worse. Still, the process was not a good one. Yes, sometimes there are different groups within a certain constituency and you have to choose who you want to listen to, but to ignore an entire constituency in the planning of discussing them is wrong. The entire conference was poorly organized and I should have been more involved in the process or never agreed to be a cosponsor.

●

It has been difficult for me to learn and accept that I do have this power, even if I don't want it. I have to be very careful about what I say to grantees and sometimes it doesn't work. There are moments when I'm thinking, 'Oh shit, I may have talked them into something they might not want to do or that they may not even be good at doing.'

●

As a donor, I inherited projects we were funding where the decision to fund was made before my time and I didn't feel I had the power—being so new to the foundation—to close those programs or challenge with any real force the relevance of their work to our mission. In particular, there was one project that brought support to individual children without addressing the real cause of the problem and without ensuring that there would be any sustainability in what was being funded.

It was making people feel good and the same funding could have brought more systemic change instead, which this project didn't. We were giving support to an organization that targeted the children of teenage mothers without ever trying to prevent future teen pregnancies. No one within our foundation ever pushed that organization to work with community leaders or government to address and reduce the high number of teen pregnancies. Nor did we realize the limited capacity of the nonprofit to carry out these more systemic changes. We eventually stopped funding them, but it took much longer and the chance to have a larger impact was missed.

●

Working for a philanthropic government department, any given day you can feel like a bad donor. Although we are providing key funding in large amounts in areas of serious need, the money comes with the biggest list of exceptions, clauses, waivers and rules and regulations on how you can and cannot spend the money or why you cannot spend the money in a way that you may have already determined best. I hate being the person who has to tell the organization it cannot put money towards something even when it's absolutely essential to what they're doing, just because of some stupid legislation that comes through out of the blue. I feel like a bad donor because sometimes I don't agree with the changes or the red tape, but I still have to implement the rules, even when the funding could do more harm than good.

Until we can redefine who makes the decisions on collective wealth on behalf of a nation, we're never gonna be able to get to that point where partnerships are really honest and really open, because there is still that dynamic of a systematic philanthropic hierarchy. We are stuck implementing rules and regulations that exist because that is where the money is coming from and they have decided to put in regulations that they don't have to explain. I don't necessarily believe that is the right way, but I do believe you have to work within the parameters that you're given. It still doesn't take away the personal frustration that I have with it.

●

I'm in a real position of power as a donor. I really do start thinking my point of view is the best. I can become overconfident because people don't challenge me as much. I have to be careful about what my assumptions are, because I'm not in a field where people are challenging me, because I have money.

Some people will challenge me within the foundation, but often my grantee partners won't challenge just because of fear, legitimate fear and unrealistic fear. I'm a bad donor when I am not every day reminding myself that I am in a position of power and not listening or questioning my assumptions. If I am not building a trust relationship with our partners in a way that makes it OK for me to hear things I don't really agree with, then I am not being a good donor.

•

When I was first brought on as a Program Officer in my foundation, I found myself not questioning our funding ideology enough, even though I was brought in, in part, to help redefine the programmatic role of our ideology. Instead, I was often doing more of the same. We, as an institution, and I think as a philanthropic sector continue to be guilty of this.

We do more of the same partly because we may not be knowledgeable enough to know that this has been done before, which points to a lack of philanthropic info-sharing and info-consumption. I think the question we are afraid to ask ourselves—and I was certainly afraid to ask earlier in my career—is, if it is not the project's obligation to document the project as such, shouldn't that be the donor's obligation to document what does and doesn't work?

Many of the projects do not have capacity or expertise to write papers that will be published about the work or offer analysis that a change has occurred as a result of funding at a level that justifies our initial and continued philanthropic support. If we don't do anything about it, then we are just replicating the same failures. I would like to think that I've have learned from my own evaluation and growth, but I clearly remember a time when I funded the mission of an organization and not the proof that the mission was working. I was guilty of keeping the problem status quo.

•

This may not be exactly what you were looking for, but for me I really feel like a bad donor when our grantees put on a performance for me, as if to say, 'Thank you so much for the funding you gave. We're just going to have a cascade of people come in and tell you how brilliant you are.'

It makes me cringe inside and I hate it because you can't stop it from happening, except giving as much notice in advance to say that I just want to come and not disturb. It makes me feel like a bad donor because it means that I haven't made them feel like a partner enough along the way where they wouldn't have to thank me in such a way. It reinforces that horrible stereotype of hierarchy that I personally abhor and try to navigate away from. It also makes me wonder if I'm the only one who feels that way and other donors love it.

There is no worse feeling for me in any donor setting. They sing songs and draw pictures and cater to the ego, and as lovely as the gestures are, I question the authenticity of it and then that makes me feel worse, because then I wonder if they really do want to make these gestures and I'm just being mean about it. I never know how to deal with the situation once it is happening, but because I go out of my way to not make it happen, I feel like I've not done my job in establishing the equal partnership piece enough.

●

We are really committed to getting this idea out there of risk management and that failure is okay. We promote radical transparency and all these other terms that identify donors taking on more risk. One of the ways that we do this is through press. We highlight our grantees and their stories. A few years ago, we were being interviewed by a reporter for a publication about our work and what we were doing at our foundation. He asked for a couple of good examples to highlight the work.

We had examples at the ready, because we expected that question. The grantees we chose were ones we felt the strongest about, who would have the most shocking stories to illustrate poor donor practices that required our intervention. What shouldn't have been surprising, but we hadn't fully thought through is that the reporter would say, 'Great, can I interview some of those nonprofits?'

We said yes, but let us check with them first to make sure they were comfortable speaking with a reporter and having their story publicized. We went to the nonprofits and told them about the reporter. We asked if they would be willing to speak to him on the record and they all said yes. One of those nonprofits had come to us because another funder had quite egregiously backed out of the funding commitment and jeopardized their entire program. We came in and saved it, which was the story we shared with the reporter.

The nonprofit worked locally in a very small community and the funder that had done them wrong in this egregious way was still a very prominent funder in the region, even though the funder wasn't funding them anymore. We knew all about that and were very careful in speaking to the reporter never to mention the name of the funder in question and to keep it anonymous, as did the grantee when they were speaking to the reporter during their interview.

Two days before the article was supposed to go to print, we got this very casual message from the reporter saying that he had planned to reach out to that foundation. Even though we hadn't mentioned it, being a reporter, he went back and looked at the nonprofit's 990 tax form and figured out who had funded them the previous year who had not funded them the following year. He emailed to say, 'Hey, I just wanna confirm that this was the donor you guys had been talking about, because I'm going to reach out to them for their comment on the story,' which, when you think about it from a reporter's perspective and in hindsight, of course that's what a good reporter would do: verify a story.

Of course the nonprofit freaked out. They begged us and the reporter not to go to the funder, because they did not want to jeopardize future relationships or funding from that network. They recognized, as did we, that they operated in too small a space to upset the few partners in it. What was meant to be a spotlight on both, the organization and the problem of leaving nonprofits in general in the lurch descended into one big mess. Being the ones who had set this in motion, we had now potentially jeopardized this nonprofit's standing in the entire community by being seen as a namer and shamer in one of the biggest publications in our sector.

So we spent the next couple of days on the phone with both the reporter and the nonprofit, trying to find a last minute solution. After a lot of back and forth, we finally got the reporter to leave out that example completely. He went with the two other examples where there were no problems discussing or verifying them. The crisis was averted, but it was a loss. It was a loss now for the nonprofit who didn't get the press, but the real disappointment is that this was precisely the story we wanted to tell. It was exactly part of this larger problem. Aside from the fact that we couldn't share it at the end of the day, it also put a strain on our relationship to the nonprofit, however briefly.

We failed in spending three days trying to convince the reporter to focus on the importance of putting that story out there without contacting that donor, but we also failed in safeguarding our nonprofits. We mishandled that completely, but we did learn a valuable lesson that promoting our partners and caring for them can be opposing objectives when they are not done correctly.

●

I think it's very dangerous from a donor perspective when you do things selfishly, because it makes you feel good instead of trying to create change in the world. I think there is a difference between creating change and making yourself feel like you're creating change. I've seen funding occur because the 'feel good' factor was scalable and not necessarily the mission. I've also seen funding not happen because the feel good aspect was too complicated to casually boast, which is very dangerous in philanthropy.

Personally, I supported an orphanage in South America where newborns and very young children remained until they were around four to five years of age, and then they went on to somewhere else. When I think of the impact I was looking to make with this project, it was much more for me than for the long-term situation for the children. I was caught up in the day to day, picture perfect moments that I could actually photograph and send to friends and family to show tangible proof I was making a difference.

Unfortunately, there was not enough effort put into reviewing the channels that the children were shuffled into after they left the orphanage. No oversight into the standards of education, health and wellbeing that I cared so dearly about when they were at the orphanage. I didn't challenge the orphanage to provide clarity on safeguards for children after they left the orphanage. That was an important recognition for me and made it possible for me later on to see the similar mistakes in how my colleagues approached grant-making.

There are so many donors now who focus on funding the tangible elements, like the equipment costs and such, because it looks like it is tied to a physical aspect of the mission that can be claimed as a success. That's the thing they can go to bed at night and feel good about supporting or mention at dinner parties, instead of something that might be less sexy or cannot put their name on physically. This usually comes in the form of the training or the unrestricted support a nonprofit needs, where donors can't always claim one tangible portion of it as a success solely attributed to their contribution, but is still necessary, especially to the longevity of the nonprofit.

•

There was one particular project we were supporting in a very difficult geography. The plan of the project goals presented an opportunity to make a significant difference. Because of the passion and the enormous opportunity, we were able to get some amazing people involved, huge names and A-list celebrity pull. Everyone wanted to buy into this project. However, the more the celebrity became associated with it, the more it felt ego driven, by all sides. Passion provided the entry point, but as it grew, more people wanted to be associated mostly, if not solely, with the celebrity names who had jumped onboard because of passion.

The project then became much bigger than it should have ever been and much bigger than the need demanded. This was the moment—or perhaps even before—when we as donors should have stepped in to protect the original tenants of the project. The project soon became so big that, at one point, it was destructive, not only to the beneficiaries, but to the organization itself. At no point in time did we or any of the supporters stop to ask how this was going to be supported in the long-term. We didn't question the lack of planning after the celebrity push.

The fault couldn't really fall too much on the nonprofit, especially given its experiential youth. The money, name, the star power, the energy and the passion are all very tempting and can blind anyone, especially an inexperienced nonprofit suddenly thrust into the spotlight. This was a huge mistake on the part of us donors, especially when there were very high level, very seasoned and very educated donors involved who allowed themselves to get star-struck and let this project descend into chaos, instead of questioning more and lending an expertise to the situation as financial resources.

Many years have now gone by and the project never happened because it was too large in scope. There were many points along the way where the nonprofit has tried to adjust its course to get back on track to be the right size, but the donor support has not been there, nor the celebrity support, mainly because everyone involved was still too attached to the original grandiose vision to let go and support a more realistic version. We played a small part in this, but all supporters share the blame for this never reaching its full potential.

•

We made an assumption that because we had invested in an organization prior, they understood how we had evolved in our thinking as a donor and our evolutionary process, which I think all of us as philanthropists go through. We went to engage with them with a grant that was probably about four times the size of our initial investment in them. They filled out paperwork and made budgets and processes without us explaining that we had changed our grant process to what we call a substantive engagement process, which meant we wanted to be a part of the budgeting process and a part of the ongoing activities.

So after they probably invested many, many hours of work time and energy together, they had presented something to us that ended up being outside of the scope of where we had now desired to go. They were taken aback at how much we had changed and became extremely frustrated with us. Then we backpedalled and instead of staying with our new core values of how we invested, we gave them a large grant for the old way of thinking.

Not even a year into the grant, the organization was so far off from where we, as philanthropists, were thinking, it was really hard for us to help them feel fulfilled. Even though they received the revenue they were seeking from us, we left an indelible impression on them of anxiety and inadequacy of not being able to achieve the impact they thought and had hoped we would together. In retrospect, we recognize that there is guilt in revenue sharing, but at the end of the day, the alignment of the values has to be there, even if you goof in your processes and in what you are trying to accomplish.

To this day, that organization doesn't want to take money from us. So we've lost them as a potential grantee and that's a shame, since we think that they do really great work. The amount of energy it took for them to engage with us had been too time and labor intensive for them to work with us moving forward. It's so sad and it kills me still that we could not resolve this. But it is hard to give away money well and you don't always get sympathy from those who need that money to do the great work in the world that many of us cannot.

We don't have enough theory around giving methods and metrics, even though we impose receiving metrics on nonprofits, mainly because we want those grant-receiving metrics to be our de facto giving metrics that tell us we're doing a good job in a replicable way. We continue to get lucky and unlucky, but still lack the information we need to know that we are successfully giving money away. Even giving away is not the right term. The language is also part of the problem, but that may also be part of bad donor practices.

•

When you work as the second hand of an individual donor, deciding who is responsible for being a bad donor feels like a chicken and egg situation. My donor promises a little bit more than he should and I'm the one who has to clean it up. But is he the bad donor for overpromising or am I the bad one for underpreparing him for those encounters before it happens? Whatever the answer, we come off looking like liars or the boys who cried 'grant' before making the appropriate assessments first.

•

Sometimes there are differences of opinion within a foundation on how to best help a grantee. Even if my way as a Program Manager turns out to be the way we should have done it, if the grantee suffers from our decision making, it is a shared failure on our part. We had a grantee we were trying to help, but were not really listening to her directly. During a scheduled meeting, I discovered she had a debilitating chronic illness that was going to impact her ability to run the organization for at least a year.

I normally request during the first meeting with a newly added grantee that at least one board member also attend, to see if they are focused on keeping the organization on track or are just 'yes' men and women for the founder. It was clear from the meeting that the board had no clue about the leader's illness or that she would need to take a course of treatment that would make it impossible for her to be a hands-on leader. Her board was not in a position to help and she was basically alone.

I shared the situation with my donors and they immediately went into savior mode. I told them that she had already handpicked an interim leader—a consultant she had known and trusted—who knew the work. They completely and totally meant well, but in trying to help her, they didn't listen to her recommendation or my suggestion that we honor her wishes. They were dead set on bringing in some hotshot interim person with loads of experience everywhere else but at her organization. I did not protest as strongly as I could have, as I saw the merit in what they were trying to do.

The person we decided to bring in ended up creating a huge mess. After six months, we had to let that person go and brought in the person the grantee leader had originally recommended. Of course, she was the savior and cleaned up a mess that we essentially helped create. I definitely don't own it alone, but from my role, I definitely should have pushed back a little bit more and paid more attention to my grantee. In the end, if we trust her ability to lead, we should trust her ability to delegate just as much.

•

This is incredibly embarrassing and it happened in my very first few months at my foundation, but I was on a conference call that I organized with a team from a nonprofit that I knew we would not fund. They were not in our mission focus nor in our regional focus. I decided on taking the call partly because I didn't know how to properly end the courtship they initiated. I had not yet learned that not every organization needs to hear, 'no, but...,' and sometimes it just has to be a no, especially when I was inundated. I also found the leader of the nonprofit to be very nice and personable, which was the other reason I let our communications continue to develop.

During the call, I was multitasking and barely paying attention to what the others said. At one point, I pressed the mute button in order to type emails without the sound interfering. A colleague came into my office to ask me how much longer my call would last and if she should wait for me for lunch. I told her that I would try to wrap up the call quickly since there was no way we would fund them anyway. I turned back to the phone to unmute myself and let the others on the call know I had to wrap up when I saw that the mute button light was not on.

Although I thought I had turned it on, I actually hadn't. They not only heard my typing away throughout the call, but my incredibly insensitive comment about them. What was worse was that the power dynamic was so strong that they didn't even dare call me out on my reprehensible behavior. I ended the call and sent a separate apology to my contact at the nonprofit.

As horrific as that experience was, it taught me many lessons about how to do my job. It injected professionalism into how I performed my job. It made me reconsider all future interactions with nonprofits who were not aligned with the foundation. It also made me change how I take conference calls, with more respect to the person or persons on the line, as well as my own time. And of course, I learned how to better use the mute button.

•

I am a bad donor when I am too involved in micromanaging partners and getting too involved in the technicalities of their work. We sit and we can see from the rooftops what's happening, which gives us a field perspective, so we see opportunities nonprofits may not. We're often in discussions with our partners about doing things that are not what they've thought of, but what we've thought of. There's a fine line between inspiring or supporting a group who shares an interest in innovation and going in that direction only to micromanage and get too involved, when we think we are leading from behind, but we are manipulating nonprofits to do things. They are caught in a space where they need to survive, so they go down that path, even if they know before us that it will potentially lead to more harm than good.

It is a fine line, though, because I think we can also inspire and bring people to new spaces that they thrive in and then they lead on. Because the line is so fine, the risk of reward is great, but so is the risk of failing our grantees.

●

In the early days when we started investing in social entrepreneurs, we had a very narrow definition of impact. Our mission is to improve the lives of children and we thought that meant tracking numbers of children served as opposed to quality. We sometimes selected entrepreneurs where the nature of their project was that they worked through caregivers and didn't have clear ways of measuring children or they worked on a systemic issue.

One group was working on publishing literature for children, but didn't actually interface with any children. They interacted with libraries and bookstores, but we needed a number of children to show to our board, because that was what they wanted to see. We unknowingly influenced this organization to change the trajectory of the mission with our demands for quantitative results. They went from having a literary prize for authors, illustrators and publishing, to creating book bags and trying to sell books to families. When that couldn't work, they gave the books away.

This caused the entrepreneurs to lose something unique about themselves and their big picture vision, and they didn't even realize it. They kind of took the feedback and the change was subtle, but after a while, we finally realized we were making them shift mission and that what they were doing originally was more valuable than the new course, whether or not it counted children in the way we had originally mandated for it to be done.

We still had constraints from the board in terms of what we supported, so after making them change the focus of their mission, we parted ways with them and exited that investment from the portfolio because we felt we were not good for them, not the other way around, but it's difficult to explain that to a partner. We sabotaged them and then left them.

It would have been worse had they stayed and just continued to bend to our suggestions. Some organizations become more focused on the donor or investor than on the mission that they morph into something too fluid and easy to change, instead of choosing their approach over the institutions in place to support that approach. However, in this case, we gave them bad advice and they believed us. We presented ourselves as the experts because we had the money and power balance was present, but based on lies, because we were not the experts we thought we were or that we told them we were.

●

I am still a bad donor. It is an ongoing struggle. There is a great organization that I've been in touch with for a long time. Great people and great programs. I really enjoy everyone who I know at the organization. Unfortunately, they are just too big. I have said in the past that our grants are just too small for them, but the response to that is always that no grant is too small and nonprofits always want unrestricted funds.

Instead of being firm by telling them there is no chance for a partnership, I allow them to keep trying for a partnership that will never happen. I give noncommittal answers that makes them feel like they have a chance and it's wrong. In the end, it doesn't help them at all. This is time that could be spent with another option for funds, better than us.

●

For one of our grantees in Asia, we were trying to put on their agenda a piece around alternative care. The partner was interested, but was really doing it more for the money that we guaranteed with implementation. Although the technical person was quite interested and committed, the organization itself was not.

It took up a lot of our time and it didn't lead to the results that we wanted in the end either. We ended up bringing in another partner from the outside. But when we looked at why it failed, we saw that we were too involved in things like reviewing Terms of References for consultants and helping to hire consultants, looking at the framework of the study and too immersed in their day-to-day. We should have recognized from the beginning that we were putting too much effort into trying to make this organization the organization we wanted it to be and not see it for what it was.

It wasn't good from our perspective. It didn't allow us to spend our time on other things and we were too embedded on the ground in an effort to be better donors.

•

Easily for me, I am my worst as a donor at conferences where I am expected to network with nonprofits. I don't know how to manage my time efficiently and I cannot say no even when I must. At the last conference I attended, I scheduled a meeting with an organization leader for the last day of the conference. I knew the night before that I was not in a good mental space to meet with him, but didn't want to let him down.

By the time we had our meeting, I was exhausted, mentally and physically. He came to the meeting so eager and full of all the energy I wish I had. I couldn't remember anything he was saying and was just trying hard just to stay awake. I failed. I nodded off during the meeting. It was only for a moment, but it was embarrassing and completely unfair to him. I should have been honest with him and told him that I was not in the right space for a meeting and rescheduled after the conference.

It was disrespectful to the person I met and he also didn't get the full capacity of what I could have given him had I been at full strength. Even if I had not fallen asleep, he would have only got me at less than 50%. I am not always happy with how conferences negotiate my time, but I have to learn to either be present when there or pass on attending in the future. That's on me.

•

I think of the money I wasted, well maybe wasted is too harsh—no, wasted is right—on only funding the traditional big nonprofits in my first years as a philanthropist. I went to the usual nonprofits and they just put a lot of sad looking things in front of me. The dialogue was always so basic when they described the problem, but then became either so technical or so vague when they described the solution. I didn't want to feel stupid, so I just nodded my head at everything I didn't understand. The reports were always glossy and pretty and so many amazing things had been accomplished, according to the reports, but when we went on site visits, I could see that there was a lot of exaggeration. I didn't question anything with my liaisons to these organizations. I blamed myself for not 'getting it.'

It was only after I spoke to other colleagues did I see that my naiveté was being exploited. I held fundraisers for some of these organizations and when my friends and other potential donors asked me about my support, I repeated the same vague language that didn't really mean anything, but sounded pretty or sad, depending on what the occasion called for. Other donors I met through networks opened my eyes to nonprofits that were smaller, but were able to explain what they did in ways I actually understood. This isn't to say some of the bigger nonprofits are not worth funding, but there was no diversity in my funding. I was dismissive of smaller nonprofits because they were about patient impact and I didn't understand that concept. I went for the impact for the impatient, which often turned out to be a mirage of short-term quick fixes designed to look like success.

It took me a while to learn that donor impact and nonprofit impact were not the same. Donor impact was more, 'Look what I'm doing in the Congo,' whereas nonprofit impact was more, 'Look what they are doing. I'm so proud of them and to be a part of the team that help gets it done.'

The ego of the donor impact point of view didn't feel so different at first. When you realize it isn't about you, you position yourself to support work that isn't sexy enough to brag about, but creates systemic change.

•

One of my grantees asked if I would host a fundraiser on its behalf. I loved the work they do and was thrilled to be able to do something for them in addition to my modest grant, considering their needs. I hosted a few fundraisers in the past, but I had worked closely with the nonprofit to make sure we put on the best possible event. This time, I let the nonprofit take the lead, although they had no real experience in putting together that kind of event before.

The people at the organization in charge of planning the fundraiser had decided to include local staff to discuss programs and provide a first-hand account of the situation on the ground. I agreed to pay for the staffer to be flown over and didn't ask any questions. I was busy with a bunch of other things and felt that if I just filled the room with potential donors, they would see the worth of the organization, especially with a local staffer who was also a former beneficiary. I didn't even think to prepare more than welcoming remarks and something brief about why I supported them.

I didn't ask for any updates other than light logistics. I didn't meet the staff person until minutes before the event. She had a very thick accent and I could barely understand anything she said. I had met other local staff before and had no problems communicating, so this was something I didn't even imagine could be a problem. None of the nonprofit staff in attendance were fluent in the local staffer's native language to translate, so she just spoke for what felt like an hour, while basically no one understood her. After ten minutes, side conversations developed and guests stopped paying attention. Then I began to notice other problems.

Instead of printing out the lovely one-pagers for guests to take, they left out copies of their latest annual report, which was maybe too technical for the guests to bother reading fully. The staff was not strategically placed to mingle with guests, but I didn't provide them with a list of people who I thought they should specifically speak to. It was meant to be a two hour event, but most of the guests had left just after the hour mark. It was a complete disaster and it was my fault. I had never ceded all the responsibility for planning to a nonprofit before and this was certainly not the first one to start with. I should have waited until I could have been more hands-on.

The nonprofit also saw that the event was a failure before any money tallies were done, but blamed themselves, which I hated myself for. This was squarely on me and I tried my best to assure them of it. The next event was much more carefully planned.

•

Although I had the best of intentions, I often go back and forth between thinking of this as a failed experiment and thinking of myself as a donor who poorly yielded power. I joined an affinity group for donors. One of the other members invited me to an initiative launch that united her grantees with potential donors around their mission. Her event was very well organized and I thought about doing something similar for my grantees.

After speaking with my staff, we saw the common thread of maternal health in a solid group of our grantees and reached out to them to see what they thought of a possible initiative between their organizations and other donors. They were thrilled overall, but one of our smaller grantees showed some reluctance. They didn't verbalize it, but it was clear they were not as enthusiastic as I was at the prospect of the initiative. Instead of asking them what they thought was wrong, I instead tried to reassure them that this was a good thing and could open their incredible work to new donors.

It didn't take long into the event to see why they were worried. The largest NGO there was a huge international NGO and their stellar communications staff who were tasked with representing their organization did so commandingly. They knew that this was an opportunity to partner, but they also saw the opportunity to pitch to new donors. They were respectful of the concept of the initiative, and positioned themselves to be the drivers of implementation. A couple of other smaller grantees in attendance did well to try and hold their own, but that big one garnered almost all of the attention.

The smallest grantee who originally showed reluctance might as well not have even been there. I had to make serious efforts to make sure they felt included and it still fell flat. They were afraid to assert their position, because the INGO was also one of their bigger donors. They told me only after the meeting that their biggest fear was that the INGO would propose that any funding meant for the smaller group be funneled through them. Funding disbursed from the INGO of the smaller group was often late. I wish I had spoken to them about these concerns instead of assuming we knew what was best.

The result was a stalled initiative as was presented, but the invited donors suggested a larger fundraiser for the large INGO, where any funds raised would go to the core of the initiative. When I revisited the successes of that initiative launch that inspired my own, I saw that all the nonprofit partners were a similar smaller size that complemented each other. Our initiative did yield some of the results we wanted, but it could have done more if I was willing to create a listening space for my smaller grantees.

•

There was a very good project that we funded in Africa, but then we stopped funding rather suddenly, only because we changed our strategy and that region of Africa was never really one of our major areas of focus. Even though we as a foundation still recognized that it was a good program, we let down that organization and the people who benefitted from their work and we couldn't even give a good reason that they could reflect upon. Instead it probably added more fear for them that such a thing could happen to them again without warning and through no fault of their own.

When we do have to stop funding due to a strategic realignment, we typically give a phase out grant. Even with that, when we do this and we know that there is not much money out there, especially if it is in a niche area or underfunded area, then we are being bad donors in my view. It's about ultimately letting down people when you don't have to, I find.

•

After being at my foundation for many years, I reflected on my time to identify the grantees in my portfolio and how they performed. There was always one that stood out as the lone failure. It should come as no surprise that it was also my first grantee. They were underperforming and did not have the capacity and sophistication that I expected of them. They really required me to do a lot of difficult negotiations and accountability follow-ups. I constantly had to do check-ins and send multiple emails for simple answers and the relationship became burdensome.

So I looked back to see why this grantee was so much less successful than the other ones that came after it. What I found was that I had very little prior experience with due diligence. I was also under pressure to move the first grant forward by the foundation. I was feeling that pressure to release funds without having developed the expertise on how to really assess the capacity of an organization, not just to do the actual intervention that they proposed to do, but to have the staff capacity and sophistication to interact well with a donor without causing extra work and anxiety.

The experience made me reexamine my version of due diligence. It was more than just calling the references listed on the application, doing one pass-through of the country office. I should have spent more time observing their processes and engaging with the staff I was partnered with to see if the organization had what I expected in terms of acumen, communication skills, follow-up and attention to detail, particularly in the financial areas.

●

During my first year of being a philanthropist, I went for a site visit in Africa. I could not have behaved more badly than I did. I was very impatient. Definitely full of white privilege. I was annoyed that there wasn't more gratitude for my being there. I walked in without understanding the history of the country. Not even the history, but of what was going on in the country's current climate at the time.

The entire trip I was horrible, but the worst part of it for me that forced me to self-reflect on what the hell I was doing was when I went to visit a women's savings and loan. I was told that I would be driving to see the saving and loan in a remote part of Burkina Faso and before I even got in the car, I just complained. I repeated that I didn't want anything to do with banking and asked why I had to go in the first place. I got in the car and the entire time, I kept looking at my watch, reminding everyone that I had a flight to catch and asking again about where they were taking me.

The car stopped and it was in the middle of nowhere. I asked the organizers what the heck was going on. They walked me out to a tree and there was a group of women who had a little box and that was the savings and loan. They started telling me about how they put the money into the little box and gave each other receipts. They had a very sophisticated method of insurance and method of repayment that increased returns through another savvy system that was embedded in their own tribal culture.

They knew I was in a hurry, so they did their best to present everything in a timely manner. In the end, they asked me if I wanted to fund them and I just bluntly said no. I didn't even know how to say no correctly. It was horrible. It was so shameful. If I could go back to those women now, I would be on the floor begging for forgiveness, but thanks to that experience, I've really turned around how I invest myself in philanthropy. I felt it immediately after I left the wrongness of my actions and that has informed my growth ever since.

9

Donor to Donor: Peer-to-Peer Dos and Don'ts

I think it is important to make clear one significant distinction in the donor and nonprofit relationship: donors do listen to their grantees when confronted, but donors do not always listen to nonprofits as a sector. It's evident in how I see the two sectors interact in my work, as well as in the process of putting this book together. Few people do well with criticism, so it is not difficult to imagine that donors would be less inclined to listen to and digest being told they are not as wonderful as they believe.

In earlier iterations of this book, I collected nonprofit experiences to match the ones given in chapter four. After about the third or fourth negative story, I realized that it would be nearly impossible to share them and not put the livelihoods of the organizations in jeopardy if donors recognized themselves and felt a need to retaliate in any way. That power dynamic reared its ugly head again and I did not want to be responsible for costing good organizations future funding. But I didn't want to walk away from something that would bring knowledge and insight to donors. This chapter is an attempt at providing that without the power dynamic getting in the way.

But just as I did not want any part of this book to be seen as a talk down to nonprofits, I don't think this chapter should be interpreted as a talk down to donors, especially since the advice is given from peer donors. In fact, when I first envisaged this chapter, I saw it as a way to help donors who were new to the field like I was: thrown into the fire with several mandates, but no rules on how to carry out or even interpret those mandates. I wish I had met some of the wonderful colleagues I know now much sooner. Some mistakes are growing lessons, which the previous chapter showed us. Some mistakes do not need to be made, and if this chapter helps others avoid those mistakes, then that is a win-win for the entire field.

Even with all the submissions from the hundreds of donors contributing, I found myself torn somewhat between wanting to include the most useful submissions of the peer advice and having an honest inclusion of what donors truly believe, whether or not I necessarily agree or even what is most widely agreed upon. It should be mentioned here again that I do not agree with all of the advice given, but I think it is important to humanize donors and show the differences in perspectives among them.

●●●

Do:

If you are under pressure from your superiors or board, be transparent about that with your grantees, so they don't view you as a hostile donor or frenemy.

●

We must hold ourselves accountable to our grantees. It goes both ways and I think if you are honest about wanting a relationship, and not just talking about it, donors must encourage grantees to hold them to equivalent standards.

●

When you tell your grantees to collaborate, be prepared to fund collaboration. It takes money to collaborate.

•

If you plan to address a specific issue with one grant cycle, then do your homework to make sure the issue can be successfully stamped out in just one cycle or focus your support on a small area within the problem to make sure your cycle counts the most. Funding one cycle on long-term needs, especially if you are a primary funder, can do more harm than good.

•

Stay on mission. Remember that people are watching every exception you make to your funding rules. They'll look to be another one of your exceptions if you come off as easily swayed.

•

Postpone a meeting. If you are in a position where you are a sole decision-maker about moving a proposal forward (private philanthropist, founder, ED or program director) and you are not in the right space to take a meeting, don't, unless it is difficult to reschedule. If you are not in a space to hear about an organization's work due to outside issues or complications, you are not bringing your 'A' game to a meeting that most likely the nonprofit representative has put a lot of pressure and meaning into.

•

When you make an introduction, be up front about whether you have a connection. Disclose if there are relatives or close friends on staff. If we fund that organization and we don't like the experience, we will look to the organization. If we feel we were led there because of undisclosed connections to you and not (as much) on merit, it could damage our relationship.

•

To the high net worth donor who has not retired from work, delegate more to a staff that has the capacity to focus on your philanthropic objective more effectively. And make it known that a meeting with you is not necessarily the Holy Grail that fundraisers believe it to be. Let it be disseminated through the staff that more traction can be made through meeting with them than meeting you.

●

Make sure your grant focus and grant size are formed to realistically complement each other. Small scale grants to areas where large scale grants are needed will make it difficult to evaluate the impact of your contributions. On the other hand, large grants can overwhelm grass-roots organizations.

●

Ask your grantees for an annual failure report. Have them list all the ways they came up short, hit obstacles that proved too strong to over-come throughout the year or made mistakes organizationally. This doesn't need to be a glossy report. Stress the confidentiality of the re-port and reassure them funding will not be affected by the result. I would add to not let such a report affect the amount you fund, but in-form how you continue to fund.

●

Funding the creation of new programs means that you must make a long-term investment into those programs. Do not make nonprofits chase funding to continue your pet projects after you leave in a year or two.

●

Push your grantees to collaborate together, but don't make it contin-gent upon funding.

•

If you are a donor who has started your own nonprofit, you have to be a major contributor to the budget. It instills faith that you believe in the mission as much as you want other contributors to believe. I won't make a donation larger than the founder.

•

Fund the mess.

•

Do fund risk, but please publicly define your version of risk. Although it could open you up for some scrutiny, it will provide context for other donors who are trying to be less risk averse. It can also improve your definition if room for improvement exists.

•

For donors who are new to philanthropy, bring in a consultant, but for info-sharing first. Weigh your quantitative expectations with personal leanings.

•

Funding capacity building also means funding the original area of implementation to completion. Capacity building means strengthening the core, not thinning it in the name of growth. Scaling up shouldn't mean scaling away.

•

Join at least one nonprofit board for a trial period to better understand the needs that get left out of the pitch. Consider offering a six month to one year board seat in lieu of funding to a nonprofit you're on the fence to fund. This could be beneficial to you both in the end.

•

When you fund a traditional nonprofit whose work already sounds familiar, you are basically funding failure, unless the evidence shows sustainable impact. Status quo grants are failure grants, plain and simple.

•

Conferences can be your friend or your foe, but that depends on you. If you are looking for potential grantee partners, act like it. If you are mostly looking for knowledge sharing, bring along a grantee most relevant to the theme of the conference and create a plan on how to collect the knowledge you want. Let people know up front you are there clearly in a learning capacity.

•

Be transparent about how you want to be contacted.

•

When you make a request for information, understand the scope of the organization you're asking. Will your request take away from the organization in a way that makes your possible donation not as desirable?

•

Communicate to your grantees if you are reliant upon your board for decision-making and they only meet 2-3 times a month or 2-3 months a year.

●

Understand that we have no insurance for impact.

●

Create a 'Why we support' of all of your grantees to be released at the end of your funding cycle. This is especially helpful for those organizations that could misinterpret your support for one organization as a potential alignment with theirs. For example, you could be a health funder, but one of your listed grantees is a secondary school in rural Kenya. However, the focus of your grant is to hire a full time onsite nurse for students. Education nonprofits who only see the grantee listed on your site will spend their already stretched time trying to make a connection.

●

Replace the annual reporting with a profile that is updated manually and not done repeatedly. Do it over email or online. There are tools for things like this.

●

Find a partner donor, especially if you can't give unrestricted grants, which is fine. Find one that is aligned with your mission to co-fund in a more agile way.

●

Ask your grantees about what could go wrong. Ask them during the proposal process and ask yourself what types of risk you are willing to take on as the investor. Rarely will your investment ever be used exactly as planned, so what is the range of impact that you are looking for? And what is the likelihood that the project will meet those goals? Exploring these scenarios up front will make for less unpleasant surprises and disappointment later on.

•

Sign up for newsletters from other foundations. This is especially helpful if you are a small family foundation or an individual. This will open you to other funding opportunities that have most likely been vetted and endorsed by your peers.

•

Fund at least one non-tangible program. A foundation that only supports humanitarian needs will never be a part of producing impact beyond a Band-Aid.

•

Check to see if your version of impact is one that mirrors what the beneficiaries want or need. That way, if you both have different versions of impact, make sure you get their buy in before you fund projects that have the potential to change their lives. It can't be 'for the better' if they don't know understand and believe that it's for the better.

•

Talk to your Board about what types of risks they are willing to 'insure.' Set aside a percentage of your budget, accordingly, to be available for emergency funding to grantees that might need it. Establish guidelines and share it with grantees up front about when and how to communicate with you if something goes wrong.

•

Make life easier for your grantees. There is no one way to do this. More universal reporting requirements, paying for M&E, regular diagnostic check-ins, advocacy for thriving grantees and better prep for the ones who need it. Your grantees have chosen to dedicate their lives to improving the lives of others. Your biggest gift to them is to treat them in a similar way.

•

Have a conversation with your board about how they define organizational failure. Then, as a Program staffer, you can provide feedback in moments where your grantees are headed in that direction. Your grantees might think the way they run their organizations and programs is satisfying to you, when they can be making errors that put the future of a grant extension in jeopardy.

•

Fund talent. What kind of nonprofit do you think is going to have the greater impact: one with a bunch of young adults straight out of the Peace Corps who want to make the world a better place for a below minimum wage salary or young adults out of college who have a plan to make the world a better place and want to be compensated if they are able to create the impact we all want to see? Every time you tell your grantees to keep overhead at 10%, remember that you are limiting talent to 10%.

•

Allocate one spot on your foundation board for a grantee for a year. Make it for a shorter time if you're too skittish about such a commitment and rotate your grantees into the position for whatever desired period you choose. This will help your grantees understand the innerworkings of decision-making for a foundation, but, ideally, can provide insight for other board members and staff with no nonprofit experience to have a more informed opinion from the ground about how they operate. A hard cap on membership alleviates any potential problems in case the experiment doesn't go so well, but also lets that board member know that he/she has to make the most of the time while on the board.

●

The grandchildren of your first grants are your greatest grants. To be a great donor takes time to learn how to do well. The experiences of the first few grants you give life to will help give birth to a new set of grants from a more informed place.

●●●

Don't:

Don't leave nonprofits twisting in the wind. Be clear from the start whether or not an organization is a good fit or not.

●

Ask questions, but don't second-guess your grantees.

●

Don't be an advocate for the type of grant-making that you or your foundation is not exemplifying just to be a crowd pleaser. It is easy to say all the right things, but the world gets to see what you fund and your grantees won't keep hypocrisy secret.

•

Don't believe that your job as a donor/Program Officer is only to decide on what to fund. You should be brainstorming and looking at solutions to problems more than just traditional models and methods.

•

Even if you are a niche donor, don't ever narrow your knowledge base to the successes or failures in your niche. Study how organizations outside your funding scope have been able to achieve concrete results. Bring in fresh ideas to better equip you in funding within your scope.

•

Don't ever think you are doing the world a favor. The minute you decide to be a donor, it becomes a responsibility.

•

Don't be afraid to innovate or fund innovation as a small or private foundation.

•

If you want an organization to be willing to change how it operates or works towards its mission, you have to be willing to change and accept suggestions for change as well. If you are a Program Officer and a potential grantee asks you to look at how you work, don't just say, 'This is not how we operate.' Take that suggestion to your boss or even your board and provide context for why the organization made the suggestion.

•

Don't micromanage.

•

Don't get lost in leveraging your smaller grants with larger ones. And don't confuse leveraging with bullying.

•

Don't be afraid of your board. Be willing to challenge them when there is an opportunity to broaden their view on passion projects or a chosen ideology.

•

Don't say you only support evidence-based work if you are not paying for the evidence piece. Earmark a part of each grant you award towards monitoring and evaluation if evidence-based work is honestly important to you.

•

Speak with other donors about strategies and practices, but don't copy and paste their methods as a template for your own foundation/ philanthropy. To promote a good relationship with your grantee, and if you think the methodology used by another foundation is a good one, try talking to some of its grantees about how they feel about working with that foundation.

•

Don't confuse wealth management with philanthropic management. While some financial institutions are setup to do worthwhile philanthropic services, many are not. Just because the service is offered, make sure that your vision is represented or else you should go to an institution that has strong experience as philanthropic advisors.

●

There is no such thing as a $5,000 restricted grant. I remember during my time at a nonprofit when we had a wealthy donor give $5,000 country-specific grant and demand that it be restricted and receive multiple reports on those funds. Back then, we had to tell the donor that there was no way the demands on his donation could be met, especially considering the sum. $5,000 is a gift, not a grant.

●

Don't provide a false sense of security to your grantees or those seeking funding by telling them that you are equal partners and they should feel free to have open conversations only to assert authority at every turn. The result is a donor/grantee dynamic where the organization is focused more on pleasing you than the original goals set forth.

●

Do not make too many meeting demands of a nonprofit leader. The founder of the nonprofit cannot be there all the time.

●

Don't let one bad experience with an organization shape your view of the entire field or the nonprofit space as a whole.

●

Don't have a strategic review every year. Commit, at least for five years. Otherwise, you are not being fair to the space or the constituents who rely on you.

•

Don't fall into the grassroots conundrum. Why would you fund small organizations who are not tested instead of scaling a model that has been proven to work? Don't create more congestion in the field by supporting only grassroots.

•

Don't become a fundraiser in the eyes of your fellow funders. When every conversation is about getting me to fund your favorite nonprofit, it begins to feel like an abuse of our relationship.

•

Don't take shortcuts. It takes time to build energy, momentum and vision, especially when you are funding the cutting edge projects. Give the grantee or project space to create the full process and not be rushed.

•

Don't follow a movement, don't be a movement funder. Fund the objectives of the movement or target the people who can effect change (government, politicians, leaders, etc).

•

Don't outsource your feel good story. Instead of relying on a nonprofit to provide the moment that you can take to your board, don't be afraid to go all the way to the ground and work directly with individuals within a community to see where you can invest smaller capital, but have huge impact in terms of buy in with the community on the change you and your nonprofit partners are trying to see.

•

Don't be deterred by a poor pitch. If you did your homework before taking the meeting and were intrigued by what you discovered, try to see beyond language barriers or nerves that come from an initial meeting.

•

Don't fund for results; fund for progress

•

Don't force potential or existing grantees to mirror your favorite grantee. Suggestions highlight best practices that might benefit the other grantees, but not every group can or should operate exactly the same.

•

Don't sit quietly through the awkward pitch. Stop the grantee and educate them on the inaccuracies there in the moment, especially if their mission is strong. That's more valuable than a grant sometimes.

•

As much as donors chastise nonprofits for overpromising, donors are just as guilty of it. Think before you promise introductions or anything outside of a grant.

•

Don't become cynical. Try to remain open.

•

Don't' join a board unless you have the time to commit to the role.

•

Trust is important between the potential partners, but don't assume everything you have been told is true and correct. Cross check all the information you have from the organization with other donors.

•

Don't put too much stock in public awards and public-recognition as proof of an organization's effectiveness. Reputation is important and can be a good indicator of an organization's credibility within their field, but big public awards don't always equate to impact. This was great advice I got from a potential grantee that was actually nominated for such an award themselves.

While honored and pleased to be recognized by such a prestigious forum, they acknowledged that the nominating individual (a 'celebrity' of the NGO world) had never visited their projects on the ground, had never spoken with staff below the CEO level, and had never partnered (beyond writing a check) on any projects with the NGO. So, while flattered, the NGO recognized that there was no way the nominator would actually know if the NGO was effective (and therefore deserving) of the award or not. To summarize: Looking good doesn't always translate into doing good.

•

I don't understand a donor who says, 'I don't fund advocacy.' All donors fund advocacy. Every grantee of a grant-maker has successfully advocated for the grant. It's all about the kind of advocacy a donor is willing to accept.

●

Don't let pre-conceived notions of outcomes for grants create stumbling blocks. Let the evidence speak for itself.

●

Being an ambassador for your grantees is great, but don't just be an ambassador who only advocates for his or her grantees, but is not interested in hearing from another donor ambassador. I've met donors who go on and on about their wonderful grantees, but when I want to give some praise to my own grantees, they tune out. It goes both ways or it goes nowhere.

●

Don't promise anything to support or indicate that you are interested to give grants until all the information and documentation are submitted and verified by your staff.

●

We have to remove the space for reinventing the wheel. Don't push grantees in that direction.

●

Get rid of the long no. Offering a significant amount of funds when there is a six month process to know whether or not those funds will be granted is really detrimental to nonprofit development resources.

•

Don't hide misdeeds or indiscretions you encounter during your funding relationships with NGOs. You don't have to shame them with a full page ad in a newspaper, but you do a disservice to other donors if you know there are serious reasons not to support an NGO and you just remain silent about it.

•

Don't make fundraisers compete.

•

This goes for donors as much as nonprofits, but don't make a direct introduction to a nonprofit without asking first. It's well-meaning, but it's in poor taste.

•

Don't force grantees to collaborate by tying your grants to collaboration. Create a space for synergies to grow and explain why you think there is room for partnership, but also create a space for pushback from the grantees to disagree.

10

The Conversations, Part 1:
Peer to Peer Conversations with Donor Colleagues

So what do donors talk about when they are together? Well, basically the same things most people talk about: family, personal life, and interesting things we've seen and done in and out of our professional lives. This holds true for when we come together for professional reasons. A typical 'formal' meeting for me with another donor usually lasts at least an hour and the first half of it is spent catching up on each other's lives in some detail.

When we get down to business, we usually exhibit the best practices we expect from nonprofits. We set the context for our separate or shared areas of focus. We discuss the issue and why it matters to us, something I think, above all else, nonprofits forget to do in both, their written and in-person presentations. We share entry points and strategies. We promote current grantees whose work we're proud to support. We suggest connections for each other, either from our portfolio if the interests are aligned or from our network. And yes, we also relay negative experiences with a nonprofit to each other, whether it is not liking the style of its leader or finding fault in the implementation. If there is something more nefarious to be told about the organization, it will be told.

We are colleagues. We are info-sharers. We are ambassadors. I've been known, whether I like it or not, as a connector. I often take a dim view of words like this because it doesn't denote that I connect good people doing great work to great resources; it just sounds like I can connect people to people, whether or not there is a good fit. It also implies connecting two people guarantees a match, which it doesn't. What I try to do is mostly mirror what I have learned from other good donors. What I have learned has mostly come from my peer level interactions.

No, not all donors speak to each other and that is more of a fact than a judgment. Donors vary, as some have full time commitments while others are smaller family foundations or individual donors who are not always aware of the networks that exist. There are also donors who prefer to take the approach of building a network of nonprofit peers to inform their giving structures and I think that's a brilliant way to improve giving.

This chapter is not necessarily an endorsement of peer level donor conversations. Instead, it is meant to shed some insight and context into how donors speak to each other, what we are willing to share, how we share it, and what we really think about our sector, from both the granter and grantee side. Up to this point, the feedback from donors has been direct, which was my intention. However, hearing donors speak about nonprofits contextually as opposed to just giving advice provides a framework that may be more valuable in understanding the mindsets and processes that form their ways of thinking and grant-making.

By now, we all know there are many kinds of donors, but when selecting the right kind of donor to highlight for a full conversation, there were some obvious choices. If I polled nonprofits and asked which donor they would most want to have speak candidly (I may or may not have), I think their responses would mirror the donors featured here in this chapter: donors from non-solicitous foundations, individual donors and donors from foundations with a narrow or very specific focus.

I feel confident in saying these group of donors are the ones who struggle the most to have their methodology understood and followed. Of the many conversations, I chose the ones I hoped best represented donors as individuals, but also as examples of their types of philanthropy. All three donors fund in three different regions in three mostly different focus areas with three fairly different approaches.

The first donor leads a private family foundation in Canada with a strict non-solicitation policy.

Donor 01

Me: You represent a foundation that has a no solicitation policy. Keeping that in mind, how would you frame a 'do' and 'don't' to address those who wish to engage you without the risk of alienating you as a donor?

Donor 01: I think, first of all, don't pretend that you know me. A lot of people who get in front of me and know that I am a donor will say, 'We have this perfect project that fits with your mission and fits with your goals.'

What do you know about us? Our foundation is private and discreet. Nobody really knows us. That's the first thing. The second is, don't believe everything you find out about us on the internet. Don't rely on the information on the internet. Rely on what our initial conversation can provide instead. From experience, the organizations that really get this are the ones that don't send their fundraising people to the first meeting; they send their senior leaders or senior managers instead. If you send your fundraising people to the first meeting, I know exactly why they are here. It is not to engage in a conversation, it's to get money, again without knowing much about us.

Me: I can already hear nonprofits asking en masse, 'Well how do we get that first meeting with you if we can't present our work to you?

Donor 01: Who says they can't present work to us? People think that because we don't accept solicitations that we are closed off to the entire world. We travel to conferences and to places where we can be introduced to the kind of organizations we want to support. Because we don't accept every proposal for money in the world doesn't mean we are insulated.

If you want to engage a foundation like mine where we fund privately and anonymously, understand that it can be a long process. Think of it as if we're dating. It may take a while before we sleep together, but every date and encounter is important and helps determine when that may happen. And we're a very conservative family, so it may not be until we are married and that obviously won't happen on the third or fourth date. I use this analogy to help those who choose to engage us to understand our process. The first few dates, you are still trying to figure out if there is a fit. We are trying to know each other. We are trying to understand each other. We're trying to find our areas of interest that we decide upon, not just what you tell me they are.

For the do, I would say have a genuine interest in learning who we are and what we do instead of waiting for the first moment to pitch. It may not happen in the first meeting and, believe it or not, that can be a very good thing.

Me: You started off, as many have done, with offering your 'don'ts,' then you snuck your 'do' in there at the end. Would you like to expand on the 'do' a bit?

Donor 01: Do engage us honestly. Don't try to bullshit us or don't try to hide an agenda in a meeting where you request to learn about us. I know those are more 'don'ts,' but they speak to what it means to engage honestly. Be assertive. I would say what triggers me to want to know more and be more engaged myself is if I feel you are self-confident as an organization and the staff I meet are an extension of that self-confidence.

Another 'do' would be to value your mission. Don't try to prostitute your mission, because you think you have an idea of what I want to hear. Be clear about who you are, what you do and what you're looking for. It isn't about money; it's about partnerships.

Me: As you're saying this, I'm thinking of my own experiences when nonprofits come to a meeting open, honest and committed to having a conversation, not just a pitch. I met with someone whose organization was not in our immediate scope and did so as a favor to one of my grantees. I scheduled 30 minutes with him, but three hours later, we were still speaking and I was actively looking for a way to work with him. He came ready to listen and ready to share himself, not just his mission or pitch.

He and I are still working together today and I foresee our relationship continuing for a while, but even if I wasn't able to create a partnership with him, I would have wanted to help him in some way, just from the impression he left. Our next meeting was spent brainstorming, which is probably my own contribution to the 'do' list. There have been many organizations I've met outside of scope that I have helped secure funding from another donor, while there are organizations who tell me that they are a good fit and are in our scope, but their narrow approach to the meeting and discussing their goals did nothing to excite me to partnership or provide enough for me to share with other prospects.

Donor 01: Exactly.

Me: But I recognize not everyone will be able to have four-hour meetings on the donor side and, often, nonprofit representatives who make long treks to meet with donors in places like New York or San Francisco or London don't have that luxury either. The trick in those settings is to make the impression, not the pitch. There is always email, Skype or donor visits to your projects. It doesn't all need to happen in one meeting.

Donor 01: This is where it pays to be concise in your messaging. You shouldn't need thirty minutes to explain your purpose and your plan. Budget time to let the unexpected happen in a first meeting. You know, what I'm also thinking about while we're talking is the issue of core costs.

Me: Ah, core costs. I didn't even plan to bring it up with you, to be honest. But feel free to tell me what you want to say.

Donor 01: I think this is going to emerge in the next couple of years as one of the main topics in philanthropy for donors. But I think there is a role to play for nonprofits to start sensitizing donors. If they can do it through a group of nonprofits, this may be more effective, because it is very difficult to do this alone, especially as a smaller organization. If they find a platform that can help get that message out collectively, almost as an advocate to donors for covering core costs.

There is a lot of hypocrisy and ignorance on the part of donors around core costs. It isn't true that an organization is efficient if it has only 3% admin costs. There is no business that can survive with using only 3% of its budget on admin costs and donors who come from the business side know this, but ignore it when entering philanthropy. But this is the fault of the nonprofits, too, that come boasting that they only use a low percentage of admin costs.

If I have a meeting with your organization and you tell me that you only have 3% or 5% admin costs, it makes me think you are lying to me or you are trying to hide admin costs into the project costs. Either way, something is wrong there to me. If you are proud of such a low percentage, I should be worried about how you treat your staff—if there is an implementing staff—how you plan for success and growth.

So, donors who refuse to cover core costs or create this culture of nonprofits proudly cutting admin costs have to look at the quality of work that they are directly responsible for, and if they are disappointed in it, they should ask themselves how they expected that work to be of a high quality without paying anyone a quality amount to do it.

Me: So what would be your suggestion to donors about how to shift their paradigms on core costs?

Donor 01: Honestly, I think it's on a case-by-case basis. You really have to look at the core of the organization, what they do, the number of staff members essentially needed to accomplish their goals and try to assess the organization as a whole to see if the percentage slated for core costs is reflected in a fair and realistic way. And like I said before, it has to start with nonprofits taking the leap to begin sensitizing donors. Too many donors have this magical way of thinking that they can only fund programs and the programs are going to run themselves. The example I use for donors I meet with this mindset is to ask them to look at the vital services that are provided in their communities.

The best ones have the people who are paid properly, because you are paying for their acumen. If you care about an organization's approach as a donor, you have to understand that you are not just paying for the program, but for the minds of the best people to implement the program. When you don't, they find people willing to take the low salary and no salary, which may hamper the project you originally loved and wanted to support.

Me: What is a memorable experience—good or bad—between you and a nonprofit that you feel comfortable sharing?

Donor 01: OK, so I have an example for both good and bad. For the bad, there was an organization that we started funding a year ago. As a whole foundation, we loved the organization. It was a local community based organization and one of our board members fell in love. Unfortunately, they were not aware enough to know that their internal strife with their board and their management was going to compromise that relationship. We would have been willing to not only renew our grant or even increase their funding, but because of their lack of leadership internally, we now question whether or not to continue funding them at all.

My personal experience with the organization is that we have—I have—had many discussions with the staff and given them many warnings over the course of the year that their internal problems were too public and was threatening the relationship. And I've been dismissed—politely—but dismissed. It always surprises me when the donor is willing to go out of his or her way to give a lifeline beyond funding to say, 'I know you are struggling and I want to help you before things get too bad' and be willing to support the organization on many levels, including shifting of strategy and the organization does nothing with that help. At the moment, it feels like a waste of time and money for us, but a waste of an opportunity for the organization, who will now be struggling internally and financially.

An example of a good experience would be our support of a local man who was an Ashoka fellow. He had amazing potential and we were the first to invest in him and now he is one of the most recognized success stories in the city and the country. What he did right was he came with his ideas, but he came ready to hear our suggestions. At one point, he was the founder and CEO and the Program Officer and the fundraiser and he was just diluting himself in all sorts of activities. I told him, 'No, you are the leader. You have to concentrate on growing the organization from that point of view and create a structure of delegation.'

Because he didn't hide this, we were able to see this as a problem and he was willing to take advice that was the opposite of what he was told to do in the past. He could have easily just said, 'No, this is my idea. This is my organization,' but he didn't. After many productive conversations about what he really needed besides funds to be successful, we decided to pay for a mentor for him and a coach. He was still rough in how he presented himself and we thought it would serve him for a much longer period than our funding would to put him through a coaching process. It was a suggestion that was not tied to the funding we had already promised. Even now, he recognizes that this was the tipping point for his organization from startup to being fully sustainable.

Me: You just gave an example of helping an organization from its infancy to maturity, but not old age. In situations where you are the first or sometimes only major donor to an organization, when do you know the time is right to move on, at least financially?

Donor 01: This is something that we must examine from the very beginning. We see capacity development as organizational development. We are clear with our grantee partners that we're not going to fund them for eternity. At some point, we'll have to pull out, so we ask, 'How are you going to ensure that in three to five years from now, when we pull out, there is not going to be any damage to your organization?'

Our foundation is looking at this from the very beginning. The grantee doesn't need to have those answers at the start of the grant, but must be thinking towards next steps early in the process. In fact, we work with our grantees to make sure they are integrating our exit strategy into the strategic plan at least six months before the grant is done, in order to see where we can assist in lieu of grant renewals. The goal is to educate the young nonprofit on how to move forward and become more sustainable beyond our help. Having said that, it doesn't always happen, but I think the intention is there and a lot of donors are not as sensitive or knowledgeable on how to properly view and invest in this kind of capacity development. Capacity development is the best way to maximize the impact of your investment into an organization.

Capacity development is not a stand-alone project. It is relevant when it is linked to programs and relevant when it is linked to the strategy of the organization. I'm not in favor of just funding staff without understanding the nature of the training. For me, I need to know that the training is not just targeted to training certain members of staff and once they leave, the knowledge base leaves with them. I need to know that the type of training and development is done in a way that can be replicated easily to new staff without need for additional funding every moment turnover of staff occurs. The knowledge has to stay in the organization, which is why I see it as organizational development, instead of capacity development.

Me: You're talking about capacity building in a way that dissects its stock definition and gives it contextual meaning. Terms like capacity building, scale and systems—even the word impact—are often used, but have no definitive meaning; they are more like placeholders for something that organizations hope to define at a later date. I have met with nonprofits that have serviced less than 50% of their original target area in a given timeline, but they are already discussing scale.

When I ask them what specifically they are talking about scaling up when they have yet to address why a large percentage of their original scope has not addressed as intended, they look like a deer in headlights. To be fair, I know that part of what they are thinking when I say this is, 'Isn't that what you want me to say? We're just doing what we've been told by other donors to say or do.'

In your view, is it on the donor to wade through the catchphrase jungle and not just accept a term like capacity building by asking the nonprofit, 'What capacity are you building and why?' or is it up to the nonprofits to go in with a clear definition behind any jargon that they choose to you?

Donor 01: I think it's a mix of both. If you have specific requirements as a donor and you're asking an organization to fulfill the requirements, you have to take the lead and make sure the organization has the capacity to fulfill those requirements, not just based on what they tell you, but also through your own research into the organization. You also have to be sure that you are not paying for capacity to be built that suits your own individual needs instead of the needs of the organization as a whole. It can't just be tailor-made for your own purposes.

For the nonprofits, they have to know their plan and be clear. Before a donor asks, they should be able to answer questions like, where are we going? How long will it take us to get there? What resources do we have to complete the plan and what resources do we need? If they answer these questions honestly, they will be able to accurately define capacity development for themselves and for donors.

Another word I would throw in with capacity building and scale is sustainability. There is push on the donor side to make nonprofits sustainable and then the nonprofits try to find a way to make this happen, even to their detriment. Sometimes, being sustainable for an organization is being stagnant and not able to adapt to changes that no one can predict. Not every organization is built to be sustainable, but their importance or impact is not less than one that is made for sustainability.

While I have the chance, I also wanted to talk about something else. One thing I see with nonprofits, but I think everyone is to blame for this is the lost voice of the people. A lot of organizations and donors think they know the needs of the people without really asking. They see the problem and come with a plan, but they don't have real input at every phase of the people. This is such a common mistake. Community participation is extremely rare.

Organizations come to us with some projects and proposals and I ask them, 'So how are you involving the community in creating and implementing this plan? Who has determined that this is actually a need for the people?' and they look at me with big round eyes and say, 'What do you mean?'

When they do say they have community participation, I ask them if they just tried it and asked the community if they liked it or did they discuss the plan before inception, and there is either stuttering or silence. How do you even know if it's a need if you haven't consulted with the community at the perceived problem level? I feel that so many organizations just pretend that they know what the people need. Coming from the nonprofit sector, where I was very close to the people and we would generate ideas together on programs and projects, I find this behavior of speaking for the people instead of with the people to be very strange.

Me: You're one of many donors I've spoken to who come from an extensive career in the nonprofit sector, but one of the few who works at a non-solicited family foundation. Thinking of your time representing nonprofits to where you are now, what moment upon becoming a donor did you say 'Aha! As a nonprofit, I didn't get it, but now, I get it?'

Donor 01: When I was on the other side, I was focusing on the objectives, rather than the big picture of what I was trying to achieve. I was trying to sell a list of activities, rather than a vision. Now that I'm on the other side, I think it's more important to share the end goal and say 'How are we going to get there together?' rather than coming to the table with a list of activities that are very narrow and donor-focused based on our research on the donor or foundation.

Me: And what is a mistake that you see nonprofits make that you used to make before, if you made any mistakes? You may have been perfect during your time with nonprofits. Is there a sense of empathy or frustration when you see it?

Donor 01: I wasn't perfect, not at all. But a mistake that I see many make that I used to make is not properly communicating the theory of change. It has to be more than why you're doing what you're doing, but why it matters. That includes research or something concrete that tells me that you know what you're doing and it isn't based on a wish list. When I had been in the nonprofit sector, I thought I was communicating my theory of change by listing accomplishments and projects we had done as an organization, and provided a list of stepping-stone goals for future work. I also spent a lot of time on the problem we were addressing and left little time to why our approach was worthy. From what I see now, this is still a problem for many nonprofits.

Me: We have focused a lot around practices that organizations should and should not do on an individual level, but is there one practice that you feel the entire field no longer needs?

Donor 01: There are certain types of data that we really don't need anymore. Seriously, most of the reports that I read, I'm not interested in them. They don't address what I really want to know as a donor. I don't care about how many people you have fed or how many malaria nets were delivered. That isn't what matters to me. I want to know what change did your actions and your efforts make in the lives of these people. So I think the nature in which the information that is reported—among 99% of the organizations—is irrelevant and doesn't need to be reported.

Me: We unexpectedly began speaking to the donor-to-donor dynamic earlier. I believe our relationship is a great example of sharing best practices between donors, even when there are few overlaps in our work. How we choose to approach what we do is more important to us than finding a way to work together. I know you gave your thoughts on what donors should do in terms of covering core costs, but I think that was more bilateral advice for both donors and nonprofits to re-think. Thinking exclusively of the donor, what would you say to do-nors, Program Officers, Boards or top level staff at foundations who might need a bit of guidance?

Donor 01: What they shouldn't do is pretend to have all the answers or 'the big idea,' choosing to work alone. They should map out what the other donors who are operating in the same area are doing and their success rate. They should not shy away from potential synergies, not just based on common interests, but also common cultures of giv-ing. From my experience, there is a tendency with many donors who come from the private and family foundation area to think they have the magic solution, but the problem is that they are often quite iso-lated and their solution may have already been thought of and imple-mented. They work in a bubble with their ideas and then when they are ready to launch, their work and their reputation for being a change-leading donor is discredited.

Based on that, I would say my 'do' would be, test the ground and be willing to ask donors in and out of your scope for ideas and support. Once you've tested the ground and incorporated other donor input, you will know more or less what has been done and if your ideas are indeed innovative.

I spoke about nonprofits being honest, but donors have to be honest. Do you want to be a donor who shares the work and the credit or do you want to be a hero donor? There is a competition between some foundations and donors. It isn't true that donors are all willing to come together and collaborate. Competition exists on all sides. So if you in-itiate an idea or project, be aware of the motives of potential donor partners, as well your own motives.

Another 'do' is to try to be emotionally intelligent. Try to see what's under the tip of the iceberg. What are the interests of all the parties of a collaboration, not just your own, but everyone from the beneficiaries to the nonprofits to the other funding partners.

Me: I mention general desperation early on in the book, mainly around the daunting prospects of fundraising for a nascent organization. With you, I would like to unpack a more specific side of desperation, one I've witnessed that you may have also seen. The nonprofit that made a huge splash and was able to get significant funding in its infancy is now not able to turn that early success into new funding. Meanwhile, current donors are leaving, the mission is not complete and may not be complete for many years to come. Survival looks bleak and, ultimately, desperation is high. What would you suggest to that organization? How could one avoid desperate behavior and actions while remaining in a desperate and possibly worsening situation?

Donor 01: Humility. Humility. Don't hide your problems. And I know that takes a huge dose of humility for some people and organizations to do that, but it's the only way. And be clear about the situation. I have to say, the reason why an organization in this situation is desperate is because it stopped listening somewhere along the way. Donors rarely stop funding without explaining why they are leaving or decreasing a grant. If you are meeting with potential donors the right way and not just sending funding requests to a rolodex of donors, then they will give you advice. If you choose not to listen early, you cannot blame anyone but yourself for the problems later.

As for what they should do once they are already desperate, they have to go with a level of trust, of course, but also with humility to the donors they already know. You have to engage by saying, 'We're absolutely conscious of our issues, our weaknesses, but we believe in our work, in what we do, and although we obviously have to change some things, the cause we are fighting for will suffer without our involvement. We are aware of the value that we bring, but we need help and in this moment going forward, we are willing to listen to how we can marry our vision with suggestions on how we can improve and reset our organization.'

I see so many organizations that are desperate and I actually volunteer as a consultant for an organization that is going exactly through this right now, in the homeless sector. They believe their priority is to get funding and that's where they want to focus all of their energy, but I keep telling them, 'Funding is not your problem. You don't have a vision. You have nothing to propose to a donor. Why is what you're doing necessary to the people, to the community? Work on that, then work on funding.'

Me: Shifting gears a bit, I will end with one last question. What is something that nonprofits should know about dealing with a family foundation that they may not know—not just a non-solicited foundation—but a family foundation?

Donor 01: Dealing with a family foundation involves a lot of arbitrary decisions and uncertainty about the focus. Although we have a structure and although there is some criteria, there will always be a part of our work that doesn't follow any specified rules or reason. This is just how it is. It is ruled by a family and many things pique their interests. It is much more personality-based than other philanthropy.

You can have the best project in the world with the best objectives run by the best people, but if the family doesn't connect, it will never get approved. This is why it's important to not come to a meeting equipped with what you find on the internet. That work may refer to a one-off initiative or grant that was done outside the stated mission or the scope of that foundation has changed since then.

●●●

The second donor leads a large European-based global foundation mandated to fund on a very specific funding mandate.

Donor 02

Me: Of the many areas you focus on as a foundation, you work heavily in South America. I think you understand better than most that this is one of the worst regions in terms of access to external donors. There is a perceived wealth, but not a history or culture of financial philanthropy. They don't have that direct line to donors that other countries have developed over the last few decades outside of their regions.

Donor 02: First of all, I think that the lack of many international donors in Latin America is not a complete disadvantage at all. I think there is an increasing amount of philanthropists from the region beginning to work there. But more importantly, there are a lot of resources that exist locally. The region is wealthy. Many of these countries contain a lot of wealth in government and in business.

Me: So how does an organization, especially a grassroots nonprofit working in Latin America find access to these resources? How do they make the first steps to a bigger donor outside the philanthropic community that we know exists, but is not significant enough to help maintain their organizational livelihoods?

Donor 02: They should certainly try to learn about the donor's goals first to see if those goals align, not just by who the donors have previously funded. Shared goals are how donors find new grantees and assuming a donor will fund you because you are similar to another already funded organization just says that you are similar to an organization that is already being funded.

Organizations must also articulate what they do in a way that doesn't ramble or rely on jargon in their elevator pitch. I also want to come at this in a way that also addresses what donors should be doing as well, in terms of how I frame the dos and don'ts.

Me: That's why it's a conversation. Feel free.

Donor 02: One of the things I would encounter with one of the Latin American organizations was the use of a lot of rhetoric, which is difficult to understand and feels alienating to people who don't have familiarity with the language of children's rights when, in reality, they could describe their work in many, many different ways without doing themselves a disservice. Even though I was familiar with that language, I understood the danger in speaking like this.

It is important for donors who encounter rhetoric to not just nod and walk away thinking that the organization's work seems too technical; as difficult and possibly embarrassing as it might be to do, they have to say, 'I don't understand' when they don't understand. There is always a simpler way to state what an organization does, or at least there should be. That simpler explanation will help see if they align perfectly with the donor's goals and values.

Conversely, top level foundations control a lot of how this rhetoric is created and used, mostly from a 20,000ft view. Donors should help simplify the language and lessen jargon, so nonprofits do not feel obligated to use it.

Keep in mind that it often takes a little while to find if there is an authentic overlap, because it is never perfect, but is often presented as such by the grantee who is in need of funds. It takes time to flesh out the realistic overlap from the optimistic overlap. There are also many occasions when both sides give and promise too much in terms of an overlap that turns out to be not so ideal. They decide to work together even though there isn't enough overlap and that ends up being worse for the grantee than the donor more often than not.

Me: Could you give me an example of that? Do you have an experience that you could share of such a structure fraying or even failing?

Donor 02: The first one that comes to mind, well, the jury is still out on whether it has been a failure, but there has definitely been some fraying. There's a group we support that works in Latin America on policy, but we found common ground on decreasing violence. Although we used different pathways, we thought the shared goal of reducing violence would be enough to make a relationship work. However, during the course of all our meetings and dialogue since entering into a relationship, they have only discussed policy and not violence.

At some stage, we began to wonder if we were on the same page of what we were funding. With hindsight, it appears to be a forced fit, which has led to many uncomfortable moments. We've had a little progress recently, but we may not know for some time if this relationship was beneficial and yielded shared results instead of just what they wanted to get funded.

Me: I wanted to focus a bit on your work in Latin America, but I think your perspective as being a donor with heavy experience in multiple regions around the world lends great perspective to some of the best practices and not so good ones that you have witnessed in your work. What are some of the experiences you've had that feel more universal, where grantees from just about any region could gain knowledge from that experience?

Donor 02: We had been working with a nonprofit in Asia and the national government on a program to have the government change its policy and scale up preschool education for tribal children that included being taught in their native language. We had been working on this for many years. We had demonstration projects, we had the longitudinal impact study and we were supporting curriculum development, as well as coordinating with other NGOs in the area. We had all the things you were supposed to have in the package. For one reason or another though, it wasn't really getting any traction, especially with the government.

So we hired a new Program Officer to help us reevaluate the portfolio. She told us flat out that those advocacy partners and those NGOs we supported were never going to do what we wanted. It was impossible, they just didn't have the political weight to do it. She said we needed

to find new partners, but there were no others working on these issues. Instead, what she did was go to a group of local tribal rights activists who had been working for fifteen or more years on land rights
and she spent time with them without even a mention of a grant. She
talked to them about how the agenda of multilingual preschool education related to their goals of identity, preservation of culture and
putting tribal kids on par with their nontribal peers.

She explained to them the brain science behind hearing your own language in the beginning of education and helped learn other languages
later, as well as a bunch of other facts until it clicked and the activists
got it. Then she made a small grant—I think it was equivalent to
around $50,000 USD or close to that—mostly for meetings and
transport, so they could organize their membership around this issue.
They started to have meetings and tell parents who were their members and other folks about this idea. They spoke with public officials
from the village level up to the state level.

In a matter of two to three months, over 100,000 people had gotten
involved, and involved from an educated view. The state government
then indicated that they were going to start a shift towards education
in multilingual based preschool education. That was more success
than we had when we funded NGOs for three years at a much higher
price tag with almost nothing to show for it.

Shortly after the success in this area, this tribal rights network connected to a national network. The membership in other states heard
about what was happening in the original state of interest. Two years
later, thirteen different states had signed on to this and began to officially advocate for it, with no extra money from us. Actually, we may
have put in additional $30,000 USD total. When the new national pol-
icy for Early Childhood Development was passed, it included a statement indicating that all tribal kids in the country, which would be
about 7.5 million kids aged four to six, should have access as a matter
of policy to preschool that's in their own language and that's in addition to more nationally spoken languages.

So I like this story for many reasons. For one, it really leveraged the
strength of the grantee. They already had in place enormous power in
their numbers and political savvy. Another is that the Program Officer
had to build a partnership before she made a grant. She had to use
other skills to forge common ground. Also because the grant became
secondary to the whole process. It was not an afterthought, but it was
just enough to enable them to do something that they really wanted

to do and saw the value in having once they had the conversations with our Program Officer.

Now we're in a position to work with the government to actually scale up the models that we helped create, which is a different kind of relationship. It also meant a different role for the Program Officer and a different relationship between the two parties that helped bring this to where it currently stands.

Me: This story sounds like yet another example of the outside-the-box thinking for which you've become known. But this Program Officer wasn't you, so this leads me to believe that when donors or trustees allow their staff to think and act without constraints, you create an impressive incubator of innovation. And this is happening, I might add, at a foundation that has a very specific mandate in terms of the kind of beneficiaries it serves. And yet, I would be hard pressed to think of a more forward thinking foundation.

Donor 02: Yeah, there is some reigning in, but we are allowed to present ideas and are given a lot of autonomy. I think we look at our lessons from when we've been successful and one of those lessons is that changing the grant-making strategy is not enough. You have to change a lot more about the institution, the kinds of people you hire and what's their job description. You have to become more operational in a way.

Do more advocacy in a way that doesn't mean setting yourself on fire or going to protests. Grant-making becomes a tool in a toolbox and that means you have set up staff in a way that makes them comfortable to use that tool and not just pass it off for someone else to complete the hard work.

Me: I mentioned your specific mandate and before we move on, I wanted to touch upon how that gets interpreted, respected and ignored. Mostly, ignored. What do you think nonprofits should know about trying to find synergies even when their core mission exists outside of your mandate?

Donor 02: First, I think the onus goes to the donor to not have a lot of examples that nonprofits can point to where the donor stretched the parameters of the mandate. Restricted mandates exist for many reasons and even if they feel arbitrary, the staff is still obligated to enforce it. You can't fault a nonprofit if they can show how you left your mission and were successful in doing so and want the same opportunity for a successful partnership.

As for the nonprofits, when there are no examples of the foundation diverting from its strict mandate, it is unlikely that you will be the first. Either come to the donor with a clear strategy that still sits close enough to their mandate where taking the chance looks more rewarding. Otherwise, don't waste too much time looking for funding there.

Me: I know that you work in Africa, as well as Latin America. From my limited experience, I already see quite a significant difference in funding and working in the two regions. Given your much lengthier experience in those regions, you have seen a lot more of the best—and worst—practices on both sides. Are there practices that you think African-based nonprofits can learn from Latin American-based nonprofits and vice versa?

Donor 02: It's difficult to answer that question, because I think there are things that Latin Americans do very well that are harder to do in Africa, but I don't think it has anything to do with Africans or the NGOs. I think it has something to do with the dynamics of aid. In an effort to answer the question, I think that one of the nice things for our foundation to work in Latin America is that we have less power. People are less likely to tell us what we want to hear when negotiating a grant, possibly out of a sense that the work they want to do will get done with or without us out of sheer will.

In my personal experience of working in Africa compared to Latin America—and, of course, this is a generalization and is not the case with everyone—is that it takes grantees in Africa longer to get to a point where they are willing to tell me or our foundation staff that what we are trying to do or accomplish is a stupid idea or they disagree or don't want to do something that has been suggested. I think it's extremely important to build a relationship where the implementing organization can be critical of the donors and have a dialogue that's constructive. I found that this happened more in Latin America, but, again, it may be more about the dynamics in aid, where there is a lot more dependence in Africa than other places globally, including Latin America.

Me: You mention the aid dynamic being different in Africa and Latin America and the dependency aspect. Could you go into that a bit more? Why is there less dependency in areas such as Latin America? What could donors do to move Africa to a model that mirrors the less dependent structure or is there a cultural element that makes this less possible?

Donor 02: These countries have stronger economies. The domestic government budgets dwarf any foreign aid so foreign aid matters less. Also, there are fewer foreign donors precisely because the stats are better. On average they also have better functioning governments and stronger democracies. I am not sure a donor can change these things other than to consider whether their investments and their tactics help strengthen the economy, equality and democracy.

Other than that, I think it is more about the kind of people they hire that represent the donor in the countries. That, or those people will determine the power dynamics of the relationships they get involved with. And of course, what kind of messages the donor leadership sends to staff is crucial.

Last point on this: I think that the entry of China as a major donor in Africa, who does not ask for much accountability, will actually change the power dynamics immensely, making western donors less powerful in that region. So will the rise of African business on the global stage.

Me: As I've already said to you many times before and even earlier in this conversation, your foundation is quite a forward thinking and innovative organization, but you, as an individual are one of the most innovative and outside-the-box minds and donors that I have the pleasure to know. You don't just fund programs and make suggestions; you've created your own programs based on what you hear from beneficiaries and people you meet on the ground. You also convene your beneficiaries in an open and intelligent way. How do you sell that kind of innovation to other donors or make them buy into your unorthodox methods when you can't fund something alone? And how do you sell that to your board, since most donors or Program staff have to answer to a board?

Donor 02: We only go to the board if the project is above a certain amount, so we don't always have to go to the board with our work. A couple things to say about that. Among a lot of donors you'll hear the term 'just a donor' or 'We shouldn't have an opinion. We shouldn't have an agenda.'

I think this is total bullshit. I think everyone has an agenda. As one person said to me just the other day, 'Planting a tree is political.' We have to be honest with ourselves because having opinions and agendas is a good thing, especially when explicit, but you also have to be cognizant of the fact that you are often in a position of power, because you are giving out money. You are at the table not always because you have the best ideas, but because you have the money. Finding the right balance between speaking and listening is not that easy, but we, as donors, frequently err on one side or the other instead of striking the right balance. That doesn't answer your question completely, but I need to identify this first. Donors have to be more reflective of this balance. No, we are not just donors, but the money we represent doesn't make us all-knowing.

In terms of starting up projects or looking for fellow donor partners, it can be tricky. What do you do when you believe something needs to happen and there is no one to fund or co-fund it? My first point of entry would be explaining why this initiative would achieve their goals.

Me: Just a slight digression to speak more to that point, I think the reason donors can go to each other with more ease than nonprofits is not because of the money hierarchy, but because we understand each other's institutional goals and objectives together. When I go to a fellow donor, like yourself—and we have partnered on projects in the past—it isn't fundraising for an organization, even if we have identified one or more implementers who will receive a grant. The purpose of the donor partnership is to address one of the explicit core tenants of our existence as foundations.

This is quite nuanced, as nonprofits will see this and say that their organizations may be in line with a foundation's goals, but are not privy to the same accessibility. The part that gets lost to those on the outside looking in when they see donors partner is that the homework is still done. If I go to you to co-support a nonprofit's work, you are expecting that I have put that organization through similar due diligence that would exist had they applied for a grant directly to you, as I would expect from you in reverse. Donor partnerships should not be seen as a disadvantage to nonprofits. Unless donors are just funding familiar INGOs that have more name recognition and perceived influence. End of digression.

Donor 02: Well that's the beginning of any partnership or negotiation I have in my life. Negotiating with a friend or with my wife or eventually with my children as they grow is starting with what they are trying to achieve and then helping them see what I want to bring to the table—if authentic—can contribute to that, as opposed to selling whatever I'm selling.

Me: When you find innovation and create or discover projects that have been built from talking directly to people on the ground as you do, how do you find implementers you believe will not feel slighted when you request direct access to the beneficiaries? Better put, how do you identify the best implementers from your interactions with beneficiaries, especially when your interactions may reveal that the current implementer may not be best at addressing their needs? You already gave us a great example of that, but is it always that simple?

Donor 02: There are a variety of ways to do that. One way is via competitive processes, where a group tells you someone should be working on something different or they are not getting a more pressing need met from the implementing organization. So you set up a competition for proposals to find out who can best address those needs. This also alleviates the possible tension with the nonprofit since you have not stopped funding, but opened up an avenue to address more of the needs of the beneficiaries, while recognizing that the organization is still addressing important needs.

Another option, which our Program Officers often use, is to weave the beneficiaries together with a group of implementers so that they can have an open conversation. One of our Program Officers did something quite unique. A group of kids in one of our Latin America countries did their own baseline research and then held a workshop where they presented their results to a number of nonprofit organizations and other people in government and media. Some of those nonprofits got excited about working with the kids based on the research and once we saw how they planned to move forward with the kids, we funded those organizations. So setting up an interaction between the beneficiaries and the potential service providers to them and seeing where there is a match is another way to support beneficiaries more.

And in some cases, you have to look outside of the normal nonprofit construct to find someone who is capable and willing to support your vision. All that being said, when you start to do any of the things that I've described, your work becomes heavier than giving grants. You actually have to do advocacy, build a partnership, etc. That's why it all comes back to the idea of not being 'just a funder.' If you run your foundation with this mentality of just being a funder, your Program Officers will not be able to do this kind of work and it won't be supported, at the possible loss of many great ideas.

Me: To close this up, what are some lasts words you would like to impart to other donors around their own philanthropic practices?

Donor 02: I would say don't present yourself as neutral, because I don't think anyone is and everyone knows that. Do spend more time making sure your narrative and goals are clear, as well as your agenda for your role in philanthropy. Also, fund advocacy. This is under the assumption that the foundations are not huge. The way that we have an impact on the world is by using our comparative advantage. Our comparative advantage is that we can take risks, we can be flexible, we can support unpopular ideas, we can move more quickly and we can be patient in terms of waiting for results. Everything we do that can be supported by another foundation, including bigger foundations, makes us advocates for what we support, so we have to embrace it.

Me: Many donors have surprised me a bit in this process by encouraging nonprofits to be more assertive and persistent. My only concern is that this message might produce a bit of fool's gold for those who will take this to mean a 'no' could be a maybe, when it most definitely is a 'no.' How would you suggest balancing assertiveness with acceptance that a partnership is not possible?

Donor 02: Not sure how to answer that. I would say try to open an honest dialogue as soon as possible because that is hard to reset. Really try to understand whether there is a match in agendas. If there is not, then no amount of pushing will help and I think persistence and assertiveness becomes pushy and annoying when one side has been clear that there is not a match and the other side is unable to hear it. I think a no is usually a no. I would suggest always leaving doors open. I usually say I would love to keep in touch in case something does come up that is a better fit. Most polite people say yes to that.

●●●

The third donor is an individual donor based in the United States. The donor has a mainly Africa focus, but also looks domestically for smaller projects.

Donor 03

Me: I have spoken to many nonprofits that started with a seed grant anywhere from $10,000 to $25,000. Most were successful in growing their organizations exponentially from that, while others have not been able to attract similar investments from other donors. I think I've identified the difference, in that the successful nonprofits knew how to leverage that first big grant, while the others, sometimes selflessly, put that money to immediate work. They thought if they just did the work, donors would come based on results. I know of a few nonprofits who used part of their seed grant to hire a professional fundraiser and that is a concept I think most grassroots organizations wouldn't even fathom to try. As a donor who does give seed grants, what are your thoughts on how to spend that first big grant, knowing there are issues on the ground, but wanting to grow at the same time?

Donor 03: I can't really tell you a definitive answer to that, because for me, it's about going and vetting and seeing the work. So I don't feel that I'm the person who's in the position to direct or determine where that seed grant goes, but I am the one who can say that this fits my theory of change and our agenda as a foundation and what we are looking for. Therefore, when we give any grants, they're given with no instructions. They're given because there's trust, because the work that's already been seen is trusted, and that they know what they are doing.

It's not about me. It's about the work that I'm seeing in front of me, because if it was about me, then I'd be doing it. So, I can't say to someone, 'you need to be doing this in order for this seed grant to help you grow.'

If I want to get engaged with and help an organization and the first thing they say to me is that they want to hire a development person, then I would give my opinion. From my experience with working with these type of young nonprofits that decide to do that, in my head, I would have to say that I don't think that's the greatest idea or I'm not sure that's what you should be doing. Honestly, how do I know that's not the right or wrong thing to do? I think that context has to be taken into consideration and that's something that many of us funders do not do.

What I usually will do is, I'll just start asking questions. Just asking questions and asking questions. And then, as we start talking, I can start hearing what this organization's goal is and what their drive is. What it is they want to do, either for a particular demographic or community. We'll come to a point and I'll say, 'What do you think about this? How does this resonate with you?'

So it's more that we've decided together how that money might be spent. Or I will ask them how they want that money best represented and we listen together. It's about developing a relationship where we can have that conversation in a way that it's not a struggle or a power dynamic, but it's more that we're doing this together if it's something where I think it's not the best place to put the money, especially if it's a seed grant like $10,000 or something like that.

It really is a wonderful opening to build a new relationship and I feel the burden is on me. I feel that very strongly, that it is about the funders doing this work. If I want to give organizations money, of course I want to make sure they are using it properly, but that burden is on me to assess and evaluate what I see as something I want to be funding.

Me: I think it's tough, though. You're in a position where you choose to be very involved. You do site visits, you have ground level relationships and even have a fellowship program that requires more involvement on your part. Not every donor has that opportunity. When you say the onus is on the donor, how does a donor who is also running a financial institution or is also on the board of many other organizations find that time? Or how do they compensate for the lack of time, but still give grants in a good way?

Donor 03: Hmmm. My feeling is: listen, it's up to you how much you want to do or don't do in your life. If you want to go out there and make grants and you personally don't have that time, then you either need to reevaluate the amount of grants that you're making or you need to hire someone who can do that for you. It's not, 'let me tell you how to make good grants in three easy steps,' you have to want to do this. You have to have that desire to want to build your philanthropy in a way that is not transactional, but is transformative. For me, that has never been anything different.

If I was a checkbook philanthropist, I would probably hire someone to make sure I was making grants that were doing great things and I could pat myself on the back and say that I'm satisfied our money is going somewhere good. I really can't say that this is the template for how you do it. You have to find the time. You have to make the time. You have to have it happen. If you can't, hire somebody, but make sure that your philanthropy is about transforming not only the organizations, but you, yourself and your foundation.

Transactional can be used in certain sectors, like impact investing or investing in your endowment and so on, but if I really wanna talk about what I'm doing as a philanthropist around my money and how I represent myself, that—to me—is something that takes time and reflection and it has to be done. I really can't say to you that I have that empathetic bone in me that says, 'Oh, yeah I understand, you're on sixteen different boards and you've got this going on and that.'

Well, figure it out. Hire someone who can do it for you. Then you can be happy and satisfied with the work by reading reports. And hiring someone is not a bad thing if done correctly. If I had $100 million to do what I'm doing, I know exactly who I would hire so I could have the same experience I have now being more involved.

Me: It's funny you say you don't have the empathetic bone. You were one of the original contributors to the PDF of dos and don'ts that led to this book. While most of the donors who contributed saw that as an opportunity to vent, I felt that you took it as an opportunity to nurture and empathize. I bring this up because as much as I think the sector needs to be prepared for its new reality of a closing civil society, shrinking government grants and more competition for fewer funds, the space also needs that nurturing and with more empathy. How do we as donors provide that empathy when we are also providing fewer financial resources?

Donor 03: I'm not sure I do believe there is a shrinking of resources. As a matter of fact, out here in California, we're bleeding money out of these donor advised funds. I think where the money is going and what it's being used for is a different story.

Me: You bring up a really good point. Sometimes it's not about the lack of resources, but knowing where the resources are. I'm thinking more about government aid, which is being slashed in the USA—

Donor 03: Oh right.

Me: And you have government donors in Europe who have diverted aid from Africa in order to focus on the growing refugee crisis domestically. We're now seeing traditional funding streams that have always been consistently available disappearing quite abruptly. You then have organizations competing for what's left without having the full knowledge base of where to look beyond the obvious channels. Just as a point of clarification.

Donor 03: Oh, those big bilateral donors (chuckles), honestly and truthfully, I look at the partners that I have. Some are very savvy and some aren't. I shouldn't say savvy, but rather are not prepared for the changing landscapes. When I run into an organization or a particular nonprofit that is ready to take on that type of funding, I do everything in my power to have them really vet it and to think long and hard about what that means for their future. I tell all the folks I work with, think about who you're getting in bed with.

Even though you may be literally under your desk crying in a curled up ball position because you don't know where the next amount of money is going to come from, you still have to be aware. I hear it from nonprofits all the time, 'I just have to take it where I can get it,' and it ends up being a big mistake, because you really want to make sure that your funders are in alignment with your mission and vision, instead of trying to adapt your mission to theirs. If, for example, you're starting a feeding program for children and USAID doesn't give to that, then you're going to have to think long and hard about how your program is going to survive and thrive if you try to manipulate it to fit what they want to fund.

So to answer your question about shrinking funds from those bilaterals, I say don't take it. It's a really ugly relationship and you really have to go out there and build relationships with individual donors and foundations that can and want to grow and adapt with you. It's something that I'm engaged in now, which is to work with individual donors. The largest amount of assets being held are donor advised funds and individual donors, and I'm trying to get them to understand what the relationship is between the donors and the nonprofits. What is it that they are looking for and what does their money mean and what is it they are trying to represent? What are they bringing to the table so that there is more empathy around the work that's being done? I want to move us from ego to empathy.

Those funds, I believe, are not shrinking. If anything, I think our problem is that, as funders, we have given this false impression to nonprofits that there is a finite amount of money out there, when in truth, the funders have all the power to be able to assert that myth. It is hard work, but what I encourage very much is for funders to be transparent. Go out and find out who is out there. Listen to people. Don't feel that holding all that power is what's going to bring you, joy because it won't.

I recently met with a gentleman who made a bunch of money in the oil industry and when we were discussing his philanthropic plan, in the beginning, all he said was, 'Metrics. Metrics. All I want are metrics,' but at the end of the evening, he said, 'I have never experienced joy in my giving.'

What I'm trying to get to in all of this is to encourage other donors to open their hearts with the same capacity they open their checkbooks.

Move from the transactional to the transformative so we can bring back the joy in giving. This way, nonprofits won't have to feel the squeeze if we can work on funders from that perspective. As much as I'm a cynic, this is a bit of my inner 70's hippie coming out. However, I still think it's a tough world to go out there and think you're going to get $100,000 or a million dollars from these bilateral donors and that you're not going to be getting in bed with the devil.

Me: We're talking about the donor experience and the many ways donors who can't get involved the way you do, but I'm just thinking about the nonprofits who bear the repercussions of donor inconsistency. The nonprofit experience I hear about often is when they reach out to a big donor and that donor tells them to do everything the opposite way they thought they should do, so they change to appease that donor. Then that donor goes away and they become an organization with no identity or multiple identities. How do we repair that identity crisis as donors or do we even repair?

I'm thinking specifically of some great organizations that have been changed due to following donor dollars. What I see now is some hybrid of what they used to be mixed with what they've become now. In discussions with them, I tell them to go back to who they were, but the feeling I get from them is, 'You're telling me to go back to our original strategy and you're offering me a $20,000 grant, while this other foundation told us to change or 'innovate' and gave us $250,000 to do so,' but they've also left.

I feel like nonprofits get so much contradictory information that it's hard to follow and hard to blame them for making some of the decisions they make. Even in putting this book together, the levels of contradictory info I received was staggering. I understand why nonprofits gamble; a gambler doesn't focus on what can be lost, but what can be gained. Besides not taking bilateral money, what do you say to those nonprofits?

Donor 03: Again, I very strongly feel that the burden is on the funders, so that is where it has to begin. One of the reasons that I've turned this corner is because relationship building with my grantees and fellows had become so informative of all the work that we do and that I have done. It has now made me want to help eradicate as much of this self-centered and Special Forces type of behavior of funders. The reason why those organizations you described get put into those positions is because they feel like they need to listen to the donors and do what the donor says in order to get that big grant. And I've built good enough relationships with my grantee partners where they are telling me all about this bad behavior, very openly and very honestly.

It's frustrating for them and infuriating for me. I've just become more and more disgusted with it the more I hear it. So I've committed to talking about it more, but I also started to think, what can I do? I don't just want to spotlight bad behavior; I want to teach good behavior. Along with my own grant-making, I began working with other donors and built a curriculum to help funders realize—philanthropist to philanthropist—the types of risks, the vision and the passion that these people are putting into their nonprofit work that's being done, and donors must learn to trust it. I really think the solution is to get donors to do more trust-based grant-making.

For my part, I ask my grantees not to give me any report specifically for me or my foundation and to just give me something that has already been created for another funder. If you're staying engaged with the organization, you will see what an inconvenience it is for them to do the extra work that we make them do. Besides, you won't need a specific report because you are seeing the results up close and personally. And the grantees, they don't just want your money. They want to have a better understanding of what's out there.

I've made grants of $10,000 and even $5,000 and turned them into $50,000 for my grantees because I've gotten them connected into networks that have awards or have connected to donors who know that if they come from me, they have already been vetted and they don't go through that process again. Relationship building has given me this understanding that I need to go back and work with funders. As well as being someone who makes grants from personal money, I am now working with other funders and the money I get from that work, I put back into philanthropy, because I don't need it to live on. I live a really wonderful life. I guess what I'm trying to get to is that if we can start with the funders, then hopefully we won't have those situations happen anymore.

But once they do, EJ, going back to what you said, I totally agree with you that if you can rebuild that relationship with a nonprofit who has had those bad experiences with donors, it is worth giving them that smaller grant to say, 'Go back to your original mission.'

That is the way to do the repair work, but be willing to guide them to more likeminded donors who won't pull them off their path. They can go back and find their heart, find the thing that drove them to do the work in the first place. We can all start all over again.

I can guarantee that if there's a nonprofit leader who really listens and goes back to do a realignment with their original values around the work that they're doing, they'll benefit from the failure of taking the large scale grant that totally shifted their mission. I totally agree with you that we do have to repair. We have to go to them and say that we've seen what happened and believe in their original vision, because if we don't come in and be the correctors, it just perpetuates this power dynamic between the funders and the nonprofits. I personally center myself in relationship building because when there is trust on all sides, we can have that conversation about what money is good money and what money is not good.

Me: We're touching upon some of the donor errors that lead to nonprofit chaos and frustration. You mentioned the donor who was only looking for metrics, but later admitted to not being happy in his philanthropy, but what are some of the more common mistakes you've seen donors make face to face? (Donor laughs) Not some of the horror stories that you've heard, because I've heard those, too. Often. I'm thinking more about something you've seen a donor do or attempt to do and you were able to step in and give real-time guidance, especially in your moments of collaboration or advising other donor funds.

Donor 03: Right now, the mistake I see the most is sacrificing—no, not even sacrificing—ignoring and disregarding qualitative outcomes for quantitative outcomes. What my experience is showing me is that this is actually becoming harmful. Metrics are not wrong, they are not bad. Of course we need data. But data will give you true or false. Data cannot or has a very difficult time telling us what is fair, what is just and what is right. So if we let data drive all of our philanthropic decisions, it can come at the cost of not only missed opportunities, but missed solutions.

I'll give you an example. The agenda around prison reform is being set by men. The narrative is set by men. As a result, money has been funneled into the metrics and the data around prison reform from the perspective of men at the price of women. Now women—and I mean women of color—are being incarcerated at a rate higher than men and are actually having a more difficult time integrating back into society once they have left the prison system. That's just one example of many that I see where talk around metrics leaves people behind, whether or not it's well-intentioned. Right now, metrics and data is the biggest shiny new object out there.

Me: And why do you think that's happening? How do you think we came to a point where quantitative over qualitative went from the shiny new toy to the new norm?

Donor 03: Yeah, and it's not even a combination of the two. It's not like all data has to be metrics. It's doesn't all have to be numerated. What I think happened is that a number of very, very large foundations—a couple of which are located in Silicon Valley, as well as one very large one on the east coast—just woke up one day and said, 'You know what? We want metrics,' and every other funder behind them said, 'Wow. They're doing it so we have to do it.'

Going back and watching this happen, talking to my grantee partners and looking at the dates and the years that this started to happen to them, it is clear that it was driven by some very large funders. That's my theory and I think it's right. Again, that isn't to say that data isn't important, but not only has it pivoted focus, it has made philanthropy become far more transactional and I've seen it have harmful effects to entire populations. There's been a lack of wanting to hear narrative or to incorporate narrative into the metrics that they're collecting.

I will also say out here as well, the young folks—the millennials—who are getting into philanthropy for the first time, this is their focus. They just want to say, 'I'm making a difference' and the money they're putting into philanthropy is tied completely to outcomes and metrics-only giving.

Me: Do you think we'll come to a point where we might see donors funding nonprofit advocacy toward philanthropic reform?

Donor 03: If that happens, I will be dancing a jig. I would love that more than anything. I would jump on that train. I don't see it happening, because who holds all the power? Philanthropists.

Me: Yeah, but you're a philanthropist and you don't think that way. This isn't a solicitation for you to pioneer this, but just to say that there could be donors with access to more wealth who might share your view. Nonprofits speaking up on this for themselves is not really going to make a dent with the people who really need to hear it. If I were to put the power dynamic into a rather crude analogy, the philanthropist wouldn't be a democratically elected leader, but more of a dictator or monarch. When would you ever have dictators implementing changes based on the will of the people who want to change how they dictate or even if they can dictate? So is it something that has to be funded or led by other donors or financed in some other way?

Can we find a way that allows nonprofits to be able to join or lead the conversation about how donors give and when something isn't right, have the ability to say, 'no, this is not the way,' when they see bad practices, but also know that they have the backing of other donors? I don't like to use the word impossible, but I think it would take someone really courageous and with money to do that.

Donor 03: I think those folks are out there. You're asking me a question that's based on such a brilliant thought that you have there. Before I make a response, I need to think about it. Like you said, I don't want to use the word impossible, but I see it as really difficult. However, I will say on a hopeful note, when I start working with donors, when I sit with them and start reflections about what is their relationship to their money, there are shifts in ideology. It's important to note that giving away your personal wealth is entirely different than giving away an endowment at a foundation. It just is.

These things matter when trying to figure out the relationship we have to the money we are giving away. There was a huge grant given to an already wealthy institution recently and what I heard from someone very close to the funder was that it was basically a pissing contest. That's what it comes down to in some of these cases. I look at someone like that and I think, 'Great, at least I know now where you are coming from, but let's do that and still give you that reward while doing it in a way that's far more transparent and transformational.'

Wouldn't you like to know that your funds have affected an entire community and they'll give you all the plaques that you want? Or that you used your finances as a means to make an impact on something concrete like violence against women? There are so many ways to find the mechanisms to fit each particular philanthropist. I know that my language before was crass, but, it's honestly the truth.

Me: No, don't worry. That's what I want is honesty. That's the whole point of this, to be as forthright as possible. I couldn't ask you to censor yourself when the whole call to action under anonymity was to be uncensored and unfiltered.

Donor 03: Well it's hard for me to censor myself in any circumstance anyway. Going back to what I was saying before, it is better to at least know the philanthropic environment than to ignore it. And let's face it, it's white. It's male. It's Special Forces, top down. I've been invited to this big conference for many years and finally went for the first time this year. There were people there who knew me, big name folks who I'm sure we both know from really big foundations who just blew me off and acted like they didn't even know who I was. They literally couldn't be bothered to talk to someone in that setting who was not in their league. And it's not personal wealth; it's foundational wealth. I just said to myself, OK, I know where I stand. Whatever.

Me: You've touched upon a good point there. I probably know some of the people you mean. Sometimes I think it is worse when we're representing money as opposed to having our own money. I'm saying that as a person who is representing wealth and I don't necessarily have my own. When you're representing wealth, you're getting caught up in a world that you're not used to, at least not in the beginning. And it's very easy to get caught up in the trappings a bit.

You're getting invited to go to extravagant events in exotic locations. You get to meet big names and celebrities, as well as travel to places you may have never seen on your own in a way that you would have never been able to afford to do before entering that world. Sometimes, you lose sight that you're doing this for philanthropic reasons and are just happy to reap the benefits.

Donor 02: Yes, that's exactly it.

Me: I've seen it. I wouldn't say that I've experienced it myself. I have a wonderful boss who has always kept me in line with what we're doing. I wouldn't say I've shied away from those events, but I've tried to keep a level head about it. When you're talking about who represents foundational wealth, it's tough because they have to create their own relationship to a wealth they have a limited control over and, at times, with little guidance. I know many people who have left philanthropy because they were more frustrated with the process than they ever imagined. Then you have some like the ones you mentioned, where it becomes an opportunity to perpetuate a new class system among the elite. They are in it for the lifestyle that it brings and not—only—to change what needs to be changed. I don't know what we do about that. A lot of foundations now hire from the nonprofit sector. That's not where I got my start, but it could be one of the answers.

Donor 03: It just sort of uncovers itself like an onion and people are exposed to their own layers as they try to figure out the driver of this particular money. Rightly so, there are tons of controversy around donor advised funds and donor advised funds are where tremendous amounts of wealth are being held, more so than in private foundations. It's just enormous. So I have decided I would really like to influence that money. Now, I can't change the fact that the United States has a tax system that allows people to put their money into a donor advised fund to tremendous benefit. What that does is take that money out of the common good and allow the elite and the wealthy to choose what they think is the common good, because it is not going into the pot of what is being used for the rest of society, where more people have a say. And they get these gigantic tax breaks, so it's like a double dip out of the tax system that would be used socially. I can't impact that. I can't effect change there.

What I can do is say, let's at least generate interest in better deploying those funds. When you can have those conversations that really ask you to reflect on your relationship to your money, how you want to be seen and how you want your philanthropy to look, then you can begin to see a change in how things are currently done. I believe that in the end, people really want their hearts to be in this. They want to be doing things that are heartfelt.

I also think that is the piece that is hard. It's sort of like going to rehab. You see people who go through rehab over and over again. They'll come out of rehab weeks later and say, 'I'm cured,' but it takes a long time. You have to keep doing that deep reflective work. Once you do it, it just becomes that much easier, because you know instinctively what it is you want, what it is you're looking for.

That is where I think or hope I can make an influence, because me just making grants all the time to nonprofits isn't really getting back to the relationship. It's only one side of the relationship and I want other people to feel how unbelievably joyful and cool and wonderful it is to learn from grantee partners. They are front and center in my work because they have taught me and informed my work and shaped who I am as a philanthropist. If I could go back to all of them and give them a round of applause, I would. It's just something that I think once you've tasted, it becomes engrained in your philanthropic DNA. You want to continue on that path.

So I try really hard when I work with folks that say things to me like, 'I would like to endow the athletic department of some university for the rest of the life of this foundation,' and although that might not be my choice, I can say, OK how about we start talking about why that is so important to you. Is it because you like sports? Is it because of recognition? Once you have the reflection, you can have them reimagine how they accomplish what they want in a way that maximizes the potential of their giving. In that situation, once we dug deep, that person said, 'Oh, you know what I'd also like to do? I would also like to fund a scholarship for underprivileged girls of color around sports.'

That came from reflective discussions and discovering that the donor's daughter did sports and she is a very quiet person in the family, while everyone else is a bigger personality. She went to that university, so the donor thought that endowing the athletic department would be a great gesture. Once you start asking questions around what they want from their philanthropy beyond what they originally say, you find a way to capture what the funder wants while increasing the impact of good.

They even agreed to keep it anonymous and it was them who came to me and said, 'You know what? We don't need to have our names splashed over it. We'd like this to be something that girls can have that transforms their lives by having this opportunity and we don't need all the accolades for it.'

Does that make sense in terms of entry points into changing philanthropy?

Me: Absolutely.

Donor 03: What I want to do is stop being angry about the bad behavior, because it does make me so angry and bitter. What good is that? That only hurts me and improves nothing. I want to get out there and say to funders, 'I want you to find that great life-giving feeling from interacting with others and helping those who can transform lives just by giving them some money, but more importantly, some understanding.'

Me: We speak the same language with that. I mean, the one thing I've tried to do since I've gotten my feet fully entrenched in philanthropy is change it. I wouldn't have known how to do it the old way because I came into it from a different lens and worked with a progressive donor who understood that good philanthropy didn't need to be a separation from the heart and the head. I think there are some people who are so resistant to change on both sides and not for bad reasons. They have their own experiences or they feel like, 'We're happy with how we do things and the results we see,' and their thought is, 'Why are you trying to change that?'

I'm not trying to change anything in terms of needlessly making life harder. It's more about figuring out how we increase what we're doing in a way that doesn't look like 'metrics' or another slogan, but actually changes how people do what they do. You gave the perfect example there. It wasn't about changing that grant or taking that grant and moving it to some other part of the world; it was about engaging on a deeper level, asking and answering the question, 'How do we make this grant mean more to more people and still have it mean more to you?'

It was the same grant, just looking at it through a different lens. That's the idea you hope to do with this which is to get people to reimagine—no, not reimagine or not only reimagine—but refocus what they want to do with their philanthropy. I say philanthropy, but we speak of non-profits and philanthropy in such absolute terms. For beneficiaries, nonprofits are philanthropists. It's all about the view. When beneficiaries are looking at the people who are helping them, they are not looking at you or me or Ford Foundation or USAID; they are looking to those people coming into their communities and implementing the necessary changes. Whether it's someone who is from the community who has been funded to improve their community based on their experience and ideas or if it's someone else who has decided to make a new home in that community in order to bring about positive change.

It's all about perspective and I just want to make sure we are looking at all of those perspectives or at least as many as possible.

Donor 03: I absolutely agree. I just wish philanthropy had more of a trust and more of a taste for risk. It really hits me hard. That conference that I told you I went to for the first time this year, it wasn't any more or any less than I expected. The button for me got pushed when I was watching the awards ceremony. It was so disingenuous to sit there in the audience and watch these high functioning grounded non-profits with a lot of traction and teeth in the communities where they work getting about a million dollars, when that foundation is capable of so much more. Give them five or ten million dollars and show what they could do from there.

Or they should start exploring the Global South in a much better way, where one million dollars would just kick them right over the edge and put them into a position where they are not focused on fundraising, but instead on implementation and eradication. The conversations swirl around scale and impact, but this is where we can put those in the best positions to happen, instead of this very disingenuous gesture that feels more like a donor or foundation leveraging already established nonprofits in a way to pat itself on the back. I actually found it insulting, what they were giving. It's like giving Google a million dollars and saying show me what you can do with it.

You have to be true to yourself. You have to do this reflective work. You have to understand where you stand in your position as a philanthropist. That can be tough work. I actually have found it to be so rewarding and have expanded my thinking around it. I'm so engaged in finding these really fascinating outside-the-box nonprofits that are doing work that I would have never even thought of those people before that are working on true systems change or working on real root causes of a particular issue. Even if it's an organization that has a budget of only $35,000, they are out there. They don't always have to be these six, seven or eight million dollar organizations, although there are some that big who are doing the same kind of great work as well. To work with these types of organizations is such a huge high for me.

Me: You're such a champion for nonprofits and we've spoken so highly of nonprofits and your grantees throughout this entire conversation. I wonder if there is something you might want to say on the opposite end. What's a common mistake that nonprofits make when they meet with or engage you?

Donor 03: Oh goodness gracious, there are a million of those. Arrogance. A lot of arrogance. Lack of self-reflection. Not understanding the perpetuation of the western savior. Why is it that you are in India as an American or westerner after going there on a summer vacation or for some service work? Why, other than you are from the West, do you think you can do what needs to be done better than someone else? There is a lack of connecting the dots before they approach me or donors in general. Think long and hard before you approach about who is already there doing the work who I might already know. When you tell me your organization is the only one there doing what you do and I know that is not true, I can't take you seriously.

That also upsets me. There are people in country who are movement builders, who are indigenous people. You're never going to mimic that perspective because you are not an indigenous person, so be clear about who you are and what you want to accomplish. Selling me a big idea as an outsider without any proof that you have really connected to the area where you want to work won't work.

I know I go back to this, but I put this back on the funders. They are the ones who have driven this agenda. They have pushed nonprofits to come to us as say, 'Look at the metrics I have,' or trying to bend their work to fit anything. I remember one time someone came up to me at a conference who was doing some work with batteries and said, 'You know, girls need batteries to have lights for when they go to school, right?'

I just looked at him and I just started to laugh. He went, 'Come on, you gotta give a guy credit for trying,' like he was hoping I would give him a shot. It felt like I was being hit on. I'm thinking the whole time, Oh my God, no. Stop.

I know it isn't your question, but I just thought of something great that I've seen a nonprofit do and I just found this out. An Executive Director of a nonprofit who, after he receives a signed agreement or MOU from a funder, will send the donor his own agreement for the funder to sign.

Me: That's brilliant.

Donor 03: It *is* brilliant. When I heard that, I screamed, 'Yes!' I really like this. It wasn't anything showy. It basically said stuff like, 'We would like to have two weeks' notice on this' and 'You promise within the span of the grant, the terms will not shift.'

Me: I love it. It's a way of saying I'm going to keep my power. I'm not taking any extra power, but I'm not ceding any power either. I'm maintaining the power I have. I think that's the thing other nonprofits— certainly not this one—have a problem doing. There might be some donor who receives that and thinks, 'Who does he think he is?'

He thinks he's the person that you decided to work with. He doesn't get diminished because you've given him a grant now. And you didn't just 'give' him a grant; you saw the work and you are investing in the merit of the mission and program that he helped create or implement. You're not bestowing something magical upon him; you've basically come to an agreement with him that this work needs to be done. His part in getting it done is putting it into action and your part is putting up the capital to increase the potency or scale of that action. That's why it's called a partnership and he is making sure you are both equally bound to the partnership.

Donor 03: Yeah, he's not giving them anything they didn't already know. He's just saying if something changes on your end, that you also have responsibilities and this holds you to them. If things do change, they need to be done in this timeline.

Me: I say well done.

Donor 03: But I know you asked me about mistakes, not things I love, because I can talk about that forever. One of the other big mistakes I see nonprofits make is not understanding the context of where they are working. Are you trying to bring water pumps to farmers in a remote area of the Congo or are you trying to make an impact on a root cause where the pumps represent access to a whole new life?

Me: I think it's interesting that even when I ask you to say something negative about the nonprofits, you still find a way to tie it back to the fault of donors.

Donor 03: I know. I can't do it.

Me: You remain a champion for nonprofits.

Donor 03: But you know what? I haven't seen anything different. I mean, yes, there are funders out there who are actually blazing the trail. A Thousand Currents, probably everything I've learned, I've learned from them. It's phenomenal what they're doing. So there are some great, great foundations out there. Another thing I think funders can do that I forgot to say earlier is convening. When I talk to nonprofits, the one thing they want almost as much as money, but not quite, is having convenings and learning exchanges. They want to be brought together so they can talk about what donors are looking for and be on the same page.

This is how bad it has become. I had a group of grantees who I put in touch with a very large foundation. The foundation contacted me and said, 'We really like who you're funding. We really have so much money, we don't even know what to do with it all. Do you have that same problem?'

I was like, no. They told me to send all my nonprofits to them because they had all this money and really had to start getting it going and they trusted who I would bring to them. So I did. A little while later, when I was with a number of my grantees, I came across one of them working with a small group discussing how to fill out the application for the grant to this foundation. I overheard her say, 'This is exactly what you write. This is what they want to see and this is how you bullshit your way through the application.'

Me: Wow.

Donor 03: So these nonprofits have learned how to bullshit their way through a process that is meant to vet who is credible and deserving of support, but who is being lied to? And who is driving this bad behavior?

Me: And what do they learn when they go to the next donor?

Donor 03: Yeah, so I tell many funders if you're getting reports with zero balances, you're being lied to like nobody's business. If you don't have a relationship with them and you don't stay in touch with them, then you're living in a dream, because they're not telling you the truth, because you haven't given them that opportunity.

You know, I don't want to be the donor anymore that hears over and over again, 'you're so different. You're different. You're different.'

Yeah, there may be some truth to that, but that isn't always a good thing. When I hear from nonprofits the horror stories they experience from people in positions to make their lives and the lives of their beneficiaries easier who, instead make their lives harder, it breaks my heart. It is worse when they don't even know why they are making life harder for these people.

Trust, for God's sake. Trust the expertise of the work people are doing. It's philanthropic dollars. This isn't going to make you go poor. Let people try things. And if they fail, they fail. It's not the end of the world. To see people micromanaging a field they don't even understand, it really does break my heart, but it also fires me up.

11

The Conversations pt. 2: In-Depth Interviews Between Donors and Nonprofits

You can't write a book called *The Conversation* that is meant to represent conversations between donors and nonprofits without having actual conversations between donors and nonprofits, can you? Well, I wasn't so sure about that in the beginning. The running theme for me throughout my process of writing this has been facing my own perceptions and misconceptions of the field. Although I obviously saw the worth in having virtual conversations between donors and nonprofits, I saw all the trappings of trying to facilitate proper conversations.

I have attended and overseen many a convening between donors and nonprofits, and while many were wonderful examples of organic dialogue and solutions-based discussions, the majority have followed one of three familiar patterns:

- Donors do all the talking and nonprofits are just too afraid to engage in a way that is necessary, but (in their minds) could lead to an end of a relationship before it begins.
- Nonprofits do all the complaining, while donors feel threatened and shy away from engagement of any kind. Those donors are later lost to the conversation for fear of being scolded for their sins or the sins of the entire sector. One donor unfor-

gettably told me that she would no longer attend one particular annual conference because, to her, it was a week-long gang-bang on donors. She also said that the entire time she was there, it felt like open season on donors.

- Donors and nonprofits start with talking to each other, but end up talking at or yelling at each other. Unless you are a fan of this style of Jerry Springer format, shouting matches are uncomfortable to watch. It is still insane to me that people who are in the business of making the world better could be reduced to such behavior, but I've seen plenty of heated exchanges erupt and escalate like wildfire.

So forgive my reservations about putting donors and nonprofits together and expecting a Kumbaya-fest where all the solutions we need floated from everyone's mouths on candy-flavored rainbows. Yes, I'm the one who chose the participants, but that guaranteed nothing. Nor did I want to present something artificial in order to have donors and nonprofits appear more collaborative and like-minded here than the majority of the field has experienced. What I wanted to do was invite nonprofits to the table who best represented the questions most asked from the Q&A chapter and put them in front of people best equipped to provide honest responses.

I reached out to a select number of nonprofits and donors to see if they would be willing to try this crazy experiment. Some conversations flowed better than others. They were, after all, trying to have a pre-constructed organic conversation about fundraising without knowing anything about each other. That was part of the criteria. I wanted to match people who were not necessarily philanthropic matches, but would still be able to engage on the state of overall philanthropy in a thought-provoking manner. I told both members of each conversation that they would get no information about the other, so as to have no time to prepare. Before and during the conversation, neither would be allowed to reveal their affiliations, but could speak about their specific work and the issues they faced in doing that work in the most effective way.

This chapter—as has been much of this book—is an experiment on whether or not donors and their nonprofit counterparts could engage in a proper conversation without fear or hierarchy. I cannot be the judge of the results. In fact, it is incumbent upon me to repeat, probably more so than in any other chapter that the views and opinions expressed in this chapter are not my own and I do not express an agreement or disagreement with any of them, at least not publicly.

•••

Conversation 01:

As an international Human Rights donor, probably the number one criticism I receive is that we and many other US-based foundations overlook domestic Human Rights nonprofits. There are many possible reasons for this, including the feeling that Human Rights is more of an international issue and that domestic nonprofits have an easier time finding domestic donors. I can say that while I personally support many US-based nonprofits working domestically on Human Rights, our foundation has a mandate that keeps our focus primarily in one region. We also don't have the kind of funding to be ubiquitous. I can't speak for every other foundation, so I invited another US-based international donor to come and speak with a domestic nonprofit and see what might come up in conversation.

Nonprofit: We work in human trafficking and there has only been federal legislation in the United States on it since the year 2000, so it is still a very young field that has not been able to demonstrate a tremendous amount of impact the way other fields have, such as global health, global education and those sorts of things. A lot of the things we struggle with and work hard to do, especially as development and communications staff, is convey our impact. This is very tough, because there is very little data on human trafficking in the USA. We are an organization that is trying to change that. We are trying to use the data to educate the public, so that they know that trafficking is happening in their neighborhoods and is not just an international issue.

Even the foundation requests for proposals (RFPs) we receive and many major donors want to talk about impact and metrics and how we know what we're doing is working. A lot of the truth around that is we can talk about outcomes, but we can't talk about impact as easily. I guess I would say that I wish major donors understood this context and how it's a complex issue. If they want us to report on impact, they would have to get educated on it. I certainly had to get educated on the issue to understand how difficult it is to talk about impact. But I think it would help donors to come into it with a more open mind about the challenges around that.

Donor: I'm trying to think about how best to respond because there are so many things firing in my head. I've been in the social justice space for decades, the last several of which have been as a donor. The majority of the rest of the time was spent on the NGO side. In that time,

I mainly did advocacy, which is extremely hard to measure. So I'm quite sympathetic philosophically to the challenges that you talk about in terms of a new field that is hard to measure and in terms of the data and weighing it against outcomes vs. impact.

Something I also found true of the trafficking issue, because I did work on that issue, actually before the legislation—

Nonprofit: Oh, great.

Donor: —that is was kind of an amalgamation of other issues.

Nonprofit: Yep, you're exactly right.

Donor: In some ways, it's like a composite indicator, but then you have to see, is it about migration? Is it about violence? Is it about school exclusion? Is it about nonpayment of wages? There were all these other issues that were wrapped up in it that were often related. That made it very hard to get the aggregate indicators because it was so much easier to get the related data portions instead. That makes defining it as an issue and not an outcome of other issues all the more difficult, so I'm definitely sympathetic.

What I feel is interesting is that even a place where I work, which is a small to medium size actor that does both domestic and international work—although I am only on the international side—is changing its direction on how it is funding. In the old days, my organization used to support good organizations doing good things. It was a little bit simpler. Now, we are increasingly asked to show how to strategy, how to theory of change, have sub-strategies, have each grantee map to a sub-strategy, be measured ourselves within our philanthropy on how we as grant-makers are doing in that sub-strategy. So it's not just that the grantees are being asked to be measured. We're getting measured on whether our grants accomplish the sub-strategy. This makes us way, way, way, way, way more narrow than it has to be and then we're kindly asking people to comply with our theory of change.

It's a weird thing because, on the one hand, it may make philanthropy more accountable, but on the other hand, I am sympathetic to the headaches it causes. Donors might be doing better social justice work giving general operating support to really talented leaders who are doing good work. I feel like the Gates [Foundation] phenomenon has sort of swung the whole field towards metrics and I'm wondering if, at some point it will do measurement in a different way.

Well, as I think about it, we also work with a lot of groups that haven't measured at all. At all.

Nonprofit: But was that part of an agreed upon, 'we're gonna take this part of our assets for risky investments' approach?

Donor: No, but we do have that. This is more like we have intermediaries and they are going to support Community Based Organizations in such country and they really don't measure. So we as donors do recognize that sometimes that not every situation calls for measuring and our Board also sees that.

Me: I find it interesting that you mentioned your support of organizations that don't measure impact or you don't require it of them. I tend to find that these types of organizations, whether community based or more prominent within a region are based internationally. There's a feeling that when the organizations are domestic—no matter the size—they should inherently possess the tools to measure and evaluate their impact and outcomes. I could be wrong, but I represent an international foundation and the mandates we place or rather don't place upon our grantees based completely in country vs. those grantees based in the states are significantly different.

We as donors seem to be more sympathetic to the impediments to measuring and evaluating on the international grassroots level than we are to domestic organizations with similar impediments, such as the issue is too new and the data is lacking or nonexistent. I would love to have your thoughts on that, whether you agree or disagree.

Nonprofit: No, I think the obsession with M&E is just something we have to grasp. Internally, we talk about and talk about it, but we still have trouble articulating it. We're getting better at it, but—

Donor: Do you do direct services or advocacy?

Nonprofit: We do direct services, but we also do systems change work. We're just at the infancy of sharing that data, pushing it out and doing some of the disruption activities ourselves. I think that's an exciting opportunity for donors to be a part of. We have two major donors who came in and were willing to invest in what was essentially entrepreneurial experimental work, but donors like this are really rare.

Donor: And is the hard part measuring not the direct services, but the systems work or both?

Nonprofit: Both. I mean, direct services is about how you measure success. Is the person we help fully employed and housed? That's a huge thing for a trafficking survivor, but are they psychologically and mentally in a good place? Maybe not, so how do you find that out? I think the world would say the measure of success is that the instances of trafficking go down, but it's going to take 50 to 100 years to internationally wrap our minds around measuring that and getting prevalence data and then being able to track progress.

But there is another challenge we deal with. In this field, as you probably know, there's a very heavy focus in the US on sex trafficking. There are a lot of organizations in the field who are also exclusively focused on children, so there is a perception issue. We encounter this especially with donors who really only want to work on child sex trafficking. And that's not necessarily the right picture of what's happening in the US. So there's an education piece we have to do before we can get their investment. That might be true in many fields actually, but we have to go through that a lot of the times and it's been difficult to overcome.

Donor: I think especially in your field, I would say, more than others. Right now, we're fighting that with the UK government, who wants to work on online sexual exploitation only. I'm like, 'Okay, but the Sustainable Development Goals (SDG) is about all forms of sexual violence against girls and boys,' and actually, that is not the most prevalent or possibly the most destructive kind, but that's very problematic because they are contributing to a fund and they are trying to influence all the money from other contributors so that it goes to that niche issue, too.

Like I said, my organization funds domestically and internationally. I can really only speak to the international side. Interestingly though, because of our board, the national side has a much more narrow mandate than we do on the international side. Again, to your point of donors framing the issue, because the board is US based and know a lot more about the US system, the team working domestically has a lot more constraints and oversight on them.

Nonprofit: Can you tell me about them?

Donor: I can't reveal anything about our board members—

Nonprofit: No, I meant the constraints.

Donor: Well the constraints are that there is a bit more of a conservative approach to things, I would say. In our organization, if you're trying to help children, you work on the tax code, as an example. There is evidence based that shows that the single best way to get more resources in the hands in families is this way, because they don't have to pay taxes. But that's very narrow.

Nonprofit: And very upstream.

Donor: And on the international side, because they are not as familiar with the dynamics, we are given more freedom to interpret the mandate as we see fit.

Nonprofit: So the tools feel more predetermined in the US?

Donor: Yeah, because our board lives [in the US], they are more familiar with the context and the domestic work would be subjected to more rigorous monitoring and evaluation and measurement. There may even be a more ideological perspective on things than with the international work, so in that sense it can seem more predetermined. They have to jump through some hoops that the international team doesn't, although we're a little afraid that some of that might spill over onto us.

Nonprofit: Have you ever been in a situation—or maybe your colleagues on the domestic side—where they sort of have a gut feeling an organization is doing some great work, but there may be some possibly arbitrary obstacles or not arbitrary obstacles in investing in them? Have you even been in the position of, 'I really wanna fund you, but I can't because of x, y, or z?'

Donor: Hmmm...

Nonprofit: Or maybe, again, the domestic counterparts have more scrutiny in their programs and their investments. Well, do you ever go back to a donor and say, 'I think you got this wrong?'

Donor: Oh you mean telling other donors that?

Nonprofit: Yeah.

Donor: There are a couple of different threads of that. I would say that my initial instinct was more the opposite. I've been in positions where, like at my last job, somebody had a pet project that they wanted to fund. I didn't necessarily think they were that effective, but I was leaned on to give them money. We as the technical experts in the area didn't think that it was the best program design, but somebody's friend of friend or college alumni yada yada comes along and all that due diligence we talk about goes out the window. So I've seen that more than the other way around.

Me: To flesh that out a bit, can I ask you how you try to get around or mitigate that or do you feel you did not have any choice in that position, especially as a Program Officer or Program Manager or staffer to the actual donor?

Donor: I'm fundamentally an advocacy person, so I would view my role as to try and educate the person who was trying to pressure me. In the same way—I think we'll get to that part of your question—if I had something I really wanted to fund, I would try to fight really hard to fund them or try and line up other donors to fund them if I couldn't fund them. It isn't just about money; I see myself as trying to offer thought leadership in the space. That's part of the job.

Me: One thing I can say is that this donor has actually done the same with me, bringing people to me and saying, 'We can't fund them, but maybe you could,' or 'We have funded them up to this point, but we cannot renew, but I want to make sure their mission continues to receive support from good donors. See if you can take the reigns over or just have a look at them.'

I think I was called a good donor just to butter me up, but it works. So donors do speak like this and I think it's great to have an example of that to cite for a nonprofit. We always say donors speak to each other, but what I hear from nonprofits is, 'Are you speaking in hieroglyphics, because we don't understand?'

Nonprofit: Would you say that you sort of, and I mean this in the most positive way, horse trade in some regards? If you can't do it, maybe the other can, but maybe the other has something that can't be done so the other reaches out to you or something like that.

Me: I think it happens like that, but organically. All I can do is speak for myself, but if something comes to my mind that their organization could fund specifically through this donor, then I don't have a problem reaching out, but if I have something that I think their foundation could fund, but it is not in the purview of my direct contact, I won't choose that as an avenue for engagement, because it isn't a beneficial use of either of our time. I think, as donors, we respect these nuances in the relationship, where a nonprofit might view the same scenario as not a big deal to reach out to someone else within the same organization for engagement. Of course, that is a generalization, but does happen. I've had nonprofits ask me to make connections to foundations even after I've indicated that my contact covered a different sector.

But if something is a good fit and can go through my specific contact, then I don't have a problem reaching out, just as I don't mind when the request is made of me from other donors.

Donor: Yeah, there is some level by which once you know the other foundations well enough, you are not trying to find a fit because you already know for the most part. I did this just yesterday where I saw some great programs in Africa that were frankly too small for us and too direct services for us, but I sent it to two other donors telling them I thought it would be perfect for them.

The horse trading piece, I can say that we co-fund a lot of things with another major foundation. I have a lot more leeway than they do to pay high salaries and high travel costs. They have some internal accounting rules that make it so they can't. So oftentimes, we're funding an organization for a million dollars and sharing the support 50/50. Core operating support for a research center or something similar. We'll pick up the salary, because we can get the western level salary for the person we want that will be best for the job and not be constrained by only who we can afford. They, in turn, will fund more of the program, but we'll make sure that our interests are also well represented on the program side as well.

The other way I see donors horse trade is not as much about individual organizations, but to be in a pooled fund. I ran a pooled fund one time with five big donors. One donor put in $25,000, while every other foundation put in about a million dollars, but there were five donors sitting around the table deciding how the structure of the program was going to be. And that one little...$25k donor.

This little donor paid $25,000 to join a multimillion dollar pooled funding, but because she was also involved in the government, could redirect all of the money to how she thought it should be spent. So that's one way I feel donors horse trade in these kind of pooled funds, to be able to pull more money to their issue, even though they are contributing a relatively small amount.

Sometimes, I do have a lot of friends from my old jobs that I can't fund in my new job because I have a certain mandate. But I try to get someone from my foundation to fund them all the time, which is relatively harder to influence (laughs), but I will try and connect them to A, B and C person and say this is a great organization to support.

Me: I'm glad you mentioned that for the purposes of this conversation and the greater one. It goes back to my earlier point. Even though I represent an organization of one, I'm well aware of the workings of organizations with multiple staff. I know that it's not as easy as turning to the colleague on your left and saying, 'Hello, I work on this, but you work on that. I have a grantee for that. Can you fund that?'

I think there is this idea that programmatic staff sit in a circle all day and sing nursery rhymes together, sharing information from very different fields rather easily over a plate of quinoa like it's that simple.

Donor: No, it's about timing. It's about fit. It's about what's complimentary. It's about all the objective reasons, but it's also about all the non-objective reasons, like ego and control and discovery. Many times, they have to think that it's their own idea.

Nonprofit: Are there things that you think organizations consistently do poorly, from the self-promotion perspective? I won't say just the fundraising perspective, which is my perspective, but overall, that I can bring back to my organization.

Donor: Thinking of some of the problems I see in my work internationally that could apply nationally, some of the organizations we support in Africa are not nearly as good with the storytelling aspect as they could be. You go to the field and they're doing amazing work. And the reports that you read over here are sometimes not written in clear English, but they also don't capture the design, the people, the stories, basically the essence. So I feel like the whole field could come up another level on that, not just there.

Nonprofit: And do you have something that you have from your experience domestically that you think we can improve upon?

Donor: (Long pause) Well, I guess. I did find that at my last job, we were trying to get a bunch of groups to work together domestically, but there was so much competition at the top that it made it very hard to present a unified front to the US government, who we were trying to convince. That kind of in-fighting in the field, sometimes undercuts their capacity for effectiveness. Sometimes it was over a legitimate substantive issue, but a lot of times, it felt like it was about ego and recognition. I mean, that's sort of easy to say, because donors have the same problem, as I was just saying in my horse trading example. It's on both sides.

Nonprofit: Yeah and every Executive Director has their separate set of priorities.

Donor: They have to succeed to their board, too. It's not just about what your contribution is to the field. Right?

Nonprofit: Right. It's about keeping people employed.

Donor: It's the financing thing. It's very competitive.

Nonprofit: Exactly. Can I ask you to speak more about approaching donors who are either internationally focused, but based in the US or donors who have focus on both?

Donor: I think the two things I've learned since I've switched hats that I didn't even know until a few years into being a donor is, first, try and develop a relationship with the donor as a peer and as a champion, so they can champion you to others. Of course you can't control that or make that happen the same way with different groups. Maybe some foundations that will be easier to accomplish than with others and maybe some temperaments will work better than others. When that happens, then you don't have to even do as much fundraising because you have a person or a few reputable people stepping up to do it for you.

The other thing that I didn't know then that I know now is to engage donors as thought partners and not as check writers, because a lot of people have been working in the field for many years and have knowledge to share. A lot of nonprofits have a tendency to want to put donors in a box and hold them at arm's length. I understand why and I, myself, did that dance, but donors want to contribute and there are ways to channel that in a way that doesn't compromise the mission, but accelerates it. You can invite them to speak on panels you organize. Let them be on a review board for your strategic planning or your strategic paper. Invite them on a field trip or something like that. The more you can engage them as field advisors and have some openness to what they say I think that's a really good way to build good partnerships.

In my last job, I sometimes felt artificial because I was trying to think of questions that donors could advise us on and maybe you would have to create something, but that is a way that engages the donors and makes them want to get deeper into your organization and want to do more. That will not only help you with that organization, but help bring in others. For a national organization trying to fundraise from international donors, it's about making the initial contacts and showing up at some international forums, including trying to get on speaking panels of international meetings using a domestic case where you could see a couple of different donors at once on the panel and then set up coffee for a few others to further discuss the issue and use that time to highlight how your domestic work ties into their international mandate.

Nonprofit: Thanks. That makes a lot of sense.

Me: I think there are some great ideas there, but I am also aware that more donor involvement into a nonprofit causes other problems outside of veering off mission. Sometimes the donors are in total alignment with the mission, but have some radical or even misguided ideas about how that mission should be reached, and saying no is not always that simple.

Nonprofit: Yes. We have encountered this a lot in our work. One of the things we won't do is put forth victims of trafficking as poster children for our fundraising efforts, both literally and metaphorically. We won't do salacious pitches. We won't talk to people about children chained up. We will talk about the realities of trafficking. As you can imagine, there are groups that do use those tactics. There are also some groups that will do some rescue missions and some vigilante style activities that we will absolutely not touch.

And then there are some things where we have a philosophical disagreement. We have one donor who is really wealthy (laughs), but is laser focused on this one idea in his one community. We just can't do what he wants us to do, because we have a national scope. Because of the context in his community, his approach actually wouldn't be effective. We disagree with what he wants to do and think it would be a waste of time and money. It is very tough to have this conversation with him as a peer when we know it is very likely he can pull out his funding if he disagrees.

Donor: I know from my experience you never want to see a donor walk away because of differences that have nothing to do with the mission. I would say one way to make sure this doesn't happen is always keeping the context of who would benefit from his support and why that is so important, even if his interests are narrower. I don't know the issue specifically, but you could communicate to him that if you are successful in your mission, the need for his approach may not be necessary in the end. You can try and sell him on the idea that national includes all of the nation, including his little area. But individual donors can be difficult about these things.

Nonprofit: Exactly. Well, one last question to that point. Do you ever find people too rigid on how they communicate on what they do? They would say, 'We do this' and maybe the funder would say, 'Well, that's interesting, but is there this add on or have you thought about it this way,' but the organization says, 'No, we do this.'

I would think that would actually be an advantage when an organization is very clear in its strategy and its focus, but does it ever feel rigid?

Donor: Yes. And I would say often when you're talking to more junior people especially. It feels more rigid, because they only know their particular technical piece.

Nonprofit: Right.

Donor: Whereas when you talk to the Executive Directors—if they're good—I think they have the imagination to expand and say, 'Oh, well I'm working on x sector, but maybe this other sector offers some overlap to do something there,' but they still have the discipline to say, 'no, I'm getting pulled too far from our core strengths and you're asking me to do too much at the moment.'

In the middle, in an ideal world, there is this rich collaborative conversation of thinking and imagining and exploring. That's when it works out really well. You can definitely go too far in either direction, where you see organizations become overly bendable and you can see organizations get overextended and move away from their core strength or go the other way and be too narrow.

●●●

Conversation 02:

Getting multi-year grants for any nonprofit is often a difficult task. Trying to accomplish that while working in a conflict area can feel like trying to catch a unicorn. When that region is the Middle East, catching the unicorn feels like a much easier proposition. Uncertainty over the length and severity of a conflict means that nonprofits have no real way of knowing how long specific programs will need to run. Uncertainty in the stability of the region and the lack of a clearly defined leader to support means that donors cannot map a proper entry and exit strategy. This usually leads to the bulk of grants in these areas going to humanitarian efforts and not to support more systemic change.

One area outside of the Middle East that is most affected by the conflict is undoubtedly Europe, and yet philanthropic euros have been refocused domestically to deal with the rising refugee crisis. To examine this further, I paired a European funder with a local nonprofit in the Middle East who is facing these described problems and possibly more.

Me: (To the donor) Keeping in mind the context and the region we are discussing, what are some hard truths about fundraising that you think nonprofits should know from the donor perspective, from your perspective?

Donor: Ah, there are so many. At our foundation, we do try to think about how difficult fundraising is for nonprofits and we recognize that resources are super limited. There is this impossible goal of sustainability and I think many donors who have been in the business for a long time understand that sustainability without private funding for most advocacy-oriented NGOs or NGOs who are interested in affecting policy and practice is an unrealistic goal.

If I'm allowed to flip the tables a little bit, I have come in recent years to be a critic of the private world of philanthropy, because most of the money that is given out to nonprofits is in some way perpetuating some of the root causes that we are all trying to fight against. Oftentimes, the trustees who are making decisions about how resources are allocated have blind spots because of self-interests, because of the circles that they move in that don't allow them to see that there are inconsistencies in how they're going about their work. I think the hard truths about fundraising is that donors have to deal with as much as nonprofits, if not more.

Nonprofit: Thank you for saying what you shared because I feel the same way. Sustainability is impossible. We have demanding requests for sustainability and of course we make up stuff, well not make up stuff, but on the grants applications, we write all the things that are even remotely related just to fill in the sustainability section. My organization works in the emergency context, but mostly on man-made crises. There are so many variables that sustainability is really a wild card. We are always hoping that the root cause of the problems would end, which is war. Then there would be no need for us to continue this work. We struggle with how to show sustainability when we are just as ignorant about how long the emergency will last as everyone else.

The other thing is the reports that go with the grants. It seems like there is a lot of bureaucracy. Some donors want to get too much in the details which can be burdensome. Sometimes even within the same donor organization, we reach an agreement and then the legal departments makes it really difficult to do anything.

Donor: Mhmm.

Nonprofit: So it takes forever to finalize.

Donor: Do you get money from us? (Laughs) Because that sounds like us. Our legal department putting up more demands on grantees than the Program Officers.

Nonprofit: We do have these conversations with donors. One of our board members is a lawyer, so we have this internal resource that we make a lot of use out of. In fact, we do have a lot of contacts within our board and circle of supporters who can and want to work for us. Sometimes, though, the demands are really unrealistic and stretch beyond our own resources. We can't imagine any organization signing off on them. We push back with the donors in our conversations. We have set very high standards for what we would do for the money we get, so that makes it even harder.

Donor: I imagine that it took you some time before your organization was able to reach that level where you could be in a position to negotiate at all with donors.

Nonprofit: We have diverse funding streams, from individuals to some corporations with some foundations mixed in. I would say our current foundation funding counts for about 25% and the individuals make up 50%. The individual funding is mostly crowdfunding style or individual giving. Because of the emergency context, a lot of people give, but it's a lot of work and not very sustainable. There are a lot of people giving $100 a year and for us, that adds up to $400,000 on average.

In a way, there is a lot of risk and uncertainty with that, but there isn't the paperwork (laughs)—

Donor: My question was more along the lines of the power imbalance between funders and organizations who are trying to raise money. In most cases, when an organization is just starting out or young, they're not in a position to negotiate, to understand what should be their red line for receiving funding. You said you had developed some standards in your organization—

Nonprofit: Diverse funding allows us to draw that red line. I was trying to explain before that because the bulk of our funding currently and in the past had come from the crowdfunding model, we could be choosier with how we engage traditional donors. The composition of the board allows us more freedom as well, and just being confident about what we do makes it easier. Of course, we don't know how that will change as we look to expand, because we need to expand and crowdfunding can't cover everything.

Donor: Just as an aside, I have recently learned of a review site for foundations called Glass Pockets, which I think is wonderful. People are able to leave anonymous reviews on foundations and their experiences with foundations. I believe that transparency in the foundation world is severely lacking, so an initiative like this is needed. It is being spearheaded by some nonprofit leaders from California and Minnesota, but as a European donor, I would love to see it go international. The more people have an understanding of how foundations engage with stuff like, 'Don't bother with this foundation because they're just gonna make you jump through hoops and jump over hurdles just to get $5,000' or 'This foundation was great because they helped with our capacity building.'

The more organizations are able to navigate this very, very dark space, I think the better off we all will be.

Nonprofit: That's great. I would love to know more about that. Another thing that maybe you can reflect upon, because I still can't seem to figure it out: the letter of inquiry vs. the grant application. The letter of inquiry...it feels like you need a personal connection and it's very hard to meet everyone, so how do I, as a person who runs an organization, meet everyone so that the letters of inquiry would work?

Donor: Hmmm. You can't meet everyone, but I would disagree that a letter of inquiry requires you to have a personal connection. Like everything in life, it's about understanding who your audience is. It may be unrealistic, but that's just a fact of life that we in the donor world expect organizations to have done some of the basic research. Who are the foundations that are in your space who are likely to give you funding or fund similar initiatives to the type of work you're doing?

Unfortunately, the reality is that foundation staff are often already overstretched. In my experience, it's the minority of staff who are doing the active looking for people who they've somehow missed. Otherwise we're so busy dealing with the grantees who we've already established a relationship with that it's hard to look beyond that. So organizations that are searching for money have to do this lay of the land to see who might be a good potential funder. Then you have to look at the type of language that's going to appeal to them.

For us, we do the same thing in asking for letters of inquiry or just concept papers first and that's purely because of the human capacity element. If someone can tell us in a two to three page note what the idea is, what the problem is and how they propose to deal with and address that problem, then that says a lot. That's when we would invite a longer grant application. We also recognize that this privileges those who have good communication skills, good language skills who know the grant and foundation lingo better than those who don't, who might be closer to the ground, working with communities and not understanding the policy foundation wonky language that we use. Or even just the language aspect of it, not having a grasp of English or a major European language could be a barrier. Try to be sensitive to the barriers.

Having an open mind is very important. For you, it's not about needing to meet everyone, but needing to understand who your most likely relationships can be. That's the advice. You have to prioritize which of the foundations that are most likely to give you some solid funding and then try to invest in those relationships.

Nonprofit: Thank you.

Donor: Does that help at all?

Nonprofit: It does. It's just a lot of work, though. (Long pause) Most of the foundations have specific interests, so you're not really sure about how to engage—and it depends on the foundation obviously. It is hard measuring how broad they would be willing to get out of an area of interest when the core of what they normally fund and what we do are very similar. It is hard scripting the language that we think might appeal to them. Yeah.

That's why I wonder whether there is any place in the professional development space that all the donors go to that maybe you can recommend, if there is a conference, maybe like the Global Philanthropy Forum—I don't know. Someplace where you can meet someone and have a conversation, even if it's for a few minutes, but it gives you some idea of how they work and how we work, and then we can see if there is an alignment and enough energy behind it to pursue it.

Donor: Well I actually—as a matter of fact—met EJ at a donor convening of European Human Rights funders and there are a few here in Europe. There are many more in the United States than there are outside the United States. In the European space, there are only a handful. That space is far more developed in the US. I was recently at a convening that was geared towards Social Movement activists and Social Movement funders, so funders who are interesting in funding movements and not just professionalized advocacy. It was very interesting because it was the first time for me where there was a conscious gathering where funders and nonprofits were meant to be on equal footing and that no sessions were closed to either funders or grant recipients.

It was very uncomfortable. It even came out in the meetings. There were some representatives of nonprofits who said anytime they tried to start talking about the work that they did with funders, the funders would get that glazed over look in their eyes that said, 'Uh oh, here comes the pitch. How do I get myself out of this situation?'

But it was really good to have this dynamic aired within the convening because it's real. It happens all the time, but I think the more we can understand that for those of us who consider ourselves Social Justice activists and Social Justice funders, the more we can see that we all play a little tiny role in a much larger interwoven tapestry, the better off we are. Even if my foundation might not be able to give you funding, because the work that your organization does is outside of our priorities, I might know some funders who would be interested in your work.

The more that we are sharing that information and breaking down the high levels of competition that exists at the nonprofit level—and I always say that it exists at the foundation level, too. Many foundations like to gloat that they're supporting all the key actors who have done A, B and C, but it takes a lot more than that to make the real social change that we want to see. I would hope that you have connections and convenings that you're attending with other groups in your sector where you're sharing some of this information with each other. Who are the reliable good funders who have really helped your organization and who are those who have not? Those conversations do take place in the donor-sphere.

Me: I want to ask a question of the nonprofit while there is a moment for me to do so. I know you're located in the US, but the work that you do is completely based in the Middle East. As you've said and we've discussed before, you're trying to go from a crowdfunding model to a foundation relationship model to account for the majority of your budget. How do you find donor engagement as a Middle Eastern nonprofit? How would you describe the experiences you've had going to donors from that perspective and what are some of the precepts they may have had?

Nonprofit: Thanks EJ. I think it may be useful to give an idea of how and where we work. We work in the refugee space, specifically with Syrian refugee nationals who have been displaced outside of Syria and within. I find myself constantly having to work on definitions of what it means to be a Syrian refugee. Given the media narrative and all the attention to refugees in camps, many people are not aware that most of the refugees are living out of camps, in urban areas. We advocate for the people struggling in the temporary shelter in Germany just as we do for the people still in Aleppo. Defining these people first and then their needs second is a huge challenge. We sometimes struggle the most with definitions for donors, who come with their own definitions as facts, not ideas. Many times they are wrong ideas.

Another struggle for us is that some donors prefer to work with the larger international organizations, which I don't think is particular to the Middle East, but I think the fear of working with more local organizations in this region is higher than possibly any other region in the world. Donors want to work or want us to work through Save the Children or UN Agencies, which we understand, but we are not a tiny organization that needs the kind of oversight that a CBO or grassroots might need. We do great work and at a much lower cost and I would say higher efficiency than those agencies in our specific targets. Entering that big donor-sphere, it's just harder when they already have those relationships.

Donor: But there are some foundations that take some measure of pride in not giving money to the large international, highly institutionalized organizations. They like to believe they are getting money to organizations that are closer to the people they are serving. Have you managed to find that community of organizations?

Nonprofit: We do receive some grants from donors like this. It's an area we want to grow and we haven't found enough like that. It's sort of a Catch-22, because we try to keep our fundraising costs low, but at the same time, if we don't have the resources to find and engage these donors, we can't find these investment opportunities. So the answer is yes, we try to find more, but I'm sure we could do much more.

Donor: And going back to EJ's question, have you found any peculiarities dealing with any foundations and your work being in the Middle East? Or is it the general refugee crises that we've been in for, I guess, the last few years that is the main problem? How has that shifted the way that your work has gone and the fundraising as well?

Nonprofit: I think it really does depend on where the foundation is located, because there are some foundations out of the Middle East, too. We have been very cautious not to take money from foundations that are linked to governments or political processes in certain countries that may impact the political side of the crisis. We want to keep our integrity and promises we have made to our beneficiary group that we serve, so where the funding comes from is very important. I think that could be an answer in relation to the Middle East, because then we need to look at the money invested and if that same foundation funds other things that are not in line with our values or goals.

Donor: Well one thing that I am encouraged and heartened by is that there is much more emphasis in the foundation world on openness and transparency. You probably wouldn't come across these resources on your own, but I can share them with EJ who can pass them on to you, but there is an initiative to try to make the foundation world more transparent. In terms of funding priorities and where groups are funding, there are maps and there are lots of initiatives listed. It's meant to be a one stop shop to help give you information about the funding landscape so that you wouldn't have to devote too much more of your human resources in figuring this out.

Nonprofit: Thank you very much for that. That would be great. One thing to also add maybe on the Middle East note, we were discussing a fundraising policy update—internally—of what to do. One of the board members suggested that we don't take any money from organizations or foundations who had funded or contributed anything to manufacturing weapons. We thought it sounded great. Of course we say that and it sounded good, until another board member noticed that we actually have received money like this. It was an interesting situation for us, because we do want to get that money to strengthen our programs—it's a lot of money. The company has a strong reputation and great brand recognition, so if others see that we have received money from them, others would be encouraged to give to us who might otherwise think of us as too risky or unfamiliar. But then, what is the tradeoff we are willing to accept?

Donor: That is such a tough call. It's really great that your board has raised it, but just for yourself as the leader, you need to know or have an idea where that money comes from before you make any policy decision of whether that cuts off a vital source of funding or whether the principle matters more. I think it's wonderful you're having a conversation like this with your board. These are similar conversations we're having in the funding world. It matters more in some ways where the money comes from than how it's given out. I think these are all really important conversations to be having. Where did your board come down on deciding whether or not to ban taking money from weapons manufacturers?

Nonprofit: The whole fundraising policy has been in a place where we haven't been able to finalize (laughs). It's been a process with a lot of back and forth it seems like it has been pushed to our annual meeting for finalization. My board is very active and meet regularly, but this is one issue we haven't been able to complete in those monthly calls.

Donor: Well good luck with that.

Nonprofit: Thank you.

Me: I just have one last question of you both before we finish. I know from my own experience from working with other nonprofits in the region, well not just in that region, but in conflict and post-conflict areas in general, is when grantees want to go to a donor and discuss the possibility of a multiyear grant, even when they have no idea how long the situation on the ground will continue. Obviously when you're talking about war, war can more or less end at any moment.

When you're going to a donor and asking for a three year or even two year—although most nonprofits would prefer something closer to five years, but again, you never know how these things will go—what kind of conversation do you construct when you're asking for that kind of multiyear grant? You have the security blanket of crowdfunding, but you also have the instability that goes along with it, where it could be quite robust one year or even two but then disappear altogether if something else comes along, either another conflict breaks out or a newer idea comes up.

On the flip side, to the donor, how do you look at that as a donor when someone is asking for a long-term commitment for a situation that could drastically change or end at any given moment?

Nonprofit: To be honest with you, we haven't been successful at all in getting multiyear grants. We've certainly asked for them. I think first it was because the organization was younger, but even now that we've been around for more than five years, donors seem more comfortable getting annual pitches. There's also the problem on our side in terms of the changing facts on the ground. By the time we get the money to implement our plan—the plan that the donors agreed to support six months ago—everything could have changed. So it becomes hard to say, 'What you funded us for this year is not exactly how we planned, but can we also have a grant for two or three more years of uncertainty?'

Of course we don't say it like that, but I think that is how donors hear it. I think we have to become better at talking about the risks of working in conflict areas without being afraid we are painting too negative a picture and scaring donors away.

We know we are lucky to have the external resource of crowdfunding to allow us to maneuver more through the changing landscapes, because if we were only foundation dependent, that would be crippling. But like you said, we know we can't rely on that and it doesn't cover everything we need, especially to grow.

Donor: Yeah, I just think that it depends a lot on the foundation and the relationship that you build up with a foundation or any donor for that matter. On a practical level, what we tend to do is we won't give a multi-annual grant to a new grantee. We want to see and get to know each other. It's kind of like dating, so before we commit to a longer term relationship, we would give a one year grant to see how that organization is able to think and work and how they choose to build the relationship.

Only after that—and of course there are always exceptions to this rule, but in general this is how we operate—would we then give a multi-annual grant if we think that your organization is doing good work and they have a solid understanding of they are trying to accomplish over the longer term. None of the problems that we're working on are solvable in a year or 18 months. Acknowledging that and acknowledging how fluid the environments that we're working in are—that plans need to change—is the best way forward. Unfortunately, I think too many foundations stick to their long frame and they want to see you do Activity 1 to Activity 4.5 with no flexibility.

Fortunately, there are some foundations who don't think like that, who do realize that we are working in a very, very turbulent time and there are all types of factors that are beyond our control. They want to see organizations shift and be able to change and adapt to how the world and events are moving. Finding those foundations is really key, especially for you, because you are working specifically in an emergency context.

That makes it doubly difficult for you to look for and find multi-annual funding. Being able to craft a narrative of how long it takes and how much work it takes to go from emergency to stability is key. You can't just pull out when the war is ended, because you leave a vacuum that will lead to chaos. In the lives of the people that you're working with, the commitment has to be for a longer term. Otherwise you leave the work half done. So I would advise crafting the story of the ground and the people you serve on it, based on who you're talking to, that a job half done is a job that is not done.

●●●

Conversation 03:

A couple years ago, I was leaving my office for lunch and ran into someone who was a top-level staffer at one of our grantee partners. He was suited up quite nicely and I asked him the occasion for the spiffy look. He told me that he had left the nonprofit world entirely and had joined the corporate world. Of course, my mind immediately went to why he left and I am not shy about asking why, so I did. He assured me that he loved the organization and was sad not to be a part of it in the same way. He told me he felt he could do more from the corporate side. I pressed him a bit more, as I can do, and without his saying much more, I realized he was burned out.

He and I had spoken prior about the stress of nonprofits having to perform two very stressful jobs at once—satisfying beneficiaries and satisfying donors—under less than ideal conditions. The picture painted of nonprofits is often one shrouded in suspicion, more focused on fundraising than mission completion. A more accurate or at least a more common description I've seen is that of the enthusiastic bright mind who wants to bring acumen and energy to the nonprofit sector, only to be defeated by process and bureaucracy, not from hostile governments or brutal conditions on the ground, but from donors.

I have heard some true horror stories from nonprofits about donor behavior and the only reason those stories are not appearing in a dedicated chapter in this book is to safeguard those nonprofits from retribution. Every twenty-five seconds in the nonprofit world, there is someone in an office rehearsing the 'Who's coming with me' scene from Jerry Maguire, while trying desperately not to flip out. I'm kidding, but not really. One voice I desperately wanted to capture within this format was one of those bright minds who was fighting desperately against the dimming of their shine. It was equally, if not more important to pair that person with someone with a tremendous wealth of experience and knowledge about the entire field of philanthropy to provide honest and informed feedback. I'm quite lucky to know more than a few of those people and one of them happily agreed to the following conversation.

Nonprofit: I ran a nonprofit for over ten years and recently handed the leadership reigns to a successor. In many ways, the reason I transitioned out or left earlier than I otherwise would have liked to or intended was because of my frustrations with fundraising, as well as my interactions with donors. I'm not sure all those things can be avoided. Some of these things are just the natural, kind of neurotic things that happen when some people are giving money to other people to do things with. But there is a lot of stuff I think can be avoided.

Maybe before we dive into this, I can highlight some of the things that drove me away to provide some framing for this conversation.

Donor: OK.

Nonprofit: First and foremost, what I perceive across the board—from individuals to big foundations—is the inability to fully grasp the nonprofit that also functions as a social enterprise. Funders who bought into our mission and bought into our quality of work, I felt, misunderstood that we were trying to run ourselves like a business or didn't know how businesses like ours work. They didn't know how to support us as a business and nonprofit, and this came up in a variety of ways.

Donor: So this is a social enterprise?

Nonprofit: It's a nonprofit, but it's also a social enterprise.

Donor: So it's a social enterprise that's setup in a nonprofit model, not a hybrid.

Nonprofit: Well, we generated income, but our focus was more on the nonprofit side.

Donor: OK, I get it.

Nonprofit: So there is a lot at the service levels that donors don't really get. General operating is always the first that's spoken about, but there's an entire context around why that's important that donors don't understand. Assume that nothing I say is a blanket statement, because there are always exceptions. It's not just that we need more general support. It's more granular than that. For example, it's hard enough that I have to fundraise the salaries I need for staff in chunks of 10% or 15% increments of grants, but if there is uncertainty about when a grant cycle starts, when it begins and what the odds are of getting it, I don't know when that money is coming in, but I still need to hire people. And it takes me three months at least to post a job, do the interviews and then to onboard someone. Then, I have to submit a report at the same time for a grant renewal, because if I don't submit on time, there will be a gap between the end of the grant period and the renewal, which means a gap in receiving funds. And yet when they are late with payments, they want the same understanding they are unwilling to give to us.

Something that should be as simple as hiring someone just becomes another hoop to jump through. Putting aside the 12% cap for a moment, I need a fund that allows me to hire really good people and really good people are what's gonna make our sector survive in the long-term. So I guess I'd ask you to reflect upon that first.

Donor: That's a lot.

Nonprofit: I know. I just threw a ton at you.

Donor: Yeah. Well, first there's the issue of understanding the difference between a nonprofit and a for-profit. We, as donors, have a luxury of time that we forget that our grantees don't have. There's a real-world clock that we don't even get.

Nonprofit: That's an awesome way of putting it. We are on this clock, both programmatically and financially. And donors institutionally find it hard to understand that.

Donor: We are slow as hell. There's absolutely no urgency to the way we work and it's very scary. A mentor to me who runs another really large foundation wrote a report on this. She says that at her very first foundation, she was stunned by the amount of inactivity. People would just mosey around the office and it wasn't until the board book came through that there was this frenetic activity. She said that foundations were more corporate than any corporation she had ever worked for and she had come from the corporate foundation world into more traditional philanthropic institutions. She realized after that stint that she either had to conform or run her own house. Now she runs her own house.

Nonprofit: Of course, and many—not all—but many for-profit companies are much more action oriented, much more impulsive than traditional foundations.

Donor: Exactly. I'm working on this research project now with another institution around knowledge, learning and talent that a group of CEOs from European and US foundations have asked for. They are asking for this research, but what cracks me up is that in this issue around learning and talent, we don't prioritize learning. Everyone's so hot on social enterprise, but do you know how a business operates in order to effectively fund it?

I recently had a discussion about boards and leadership and evolution of leadership and people don't even know organizational life cycle. It's like we value knowledge, but we don't actually ever use it.

Nonprofit: That's a great point, but I would challenge that only to say that there are some great leaders in nonprofits who have the knowledge, but we can't even keep them.

Donor: Oh my God, that's the other thing. There are so many people—good people—leaving the nonprofit sector because donors are unknowingly pushing them out. There's a great TED Talk by Dan Pallotta and he says that we will nickel and dime someone who is trying to cure a disease, but we will exalt someone who makes $50 million from a violent video game. It's just crazy how we have allowed our thinking to become.

And then the other thing is that donors will ask nonprofits to think in a more innovative way. People can't do that kind of thinking if one, they are worried about bills at home and two, they don't even have the space to create innovatively. You want people to be brilliant and fabulous, but you don't want to pay them. That's not fair.

Nonprofit: And it's better in a way to hire fewer people, but hire the ones that are really, really good.

Donor: Then you probably end up stressing them out or overwhelming them and then they leave because they burn out.

Nonprofit: What we have to do is reduce the expectations of funders of what can happen in a year. We do Human Rights work and we know some funders who are amazing, who will say, 'We know this is going to take time.'

One donor gave us a massive planning grant. We didn't do anything but learn with that grant and it made our projects so much better.

Donor: But wait, what did you say about expectations? You mean, not your work, but—

Nonprofit: The expectations of our programmatic work. So, for example, we had this grant and our funders expected us to get a certain project completed as if we were contractors, with these project-focused grants and their expectations were wildly unrealistic. The metrics that are set are also unrealistic. We all know it and dance around it, and it's ludicrous.

Donor: But here's the thing and don't get me wrong, working that way is very hard to do, but there is going to have to be a pushback on the part of nonprofits. They will have to coalesce to say to donors, 'The way you're funding us is kind of ridiculous.'

I literally raised this same question around reimagining how we fund a couple of years ago at a donor conference and I kid you not, there were crickets. We talked about grantees. We talked about laterals or government organizations. We talked about everyone and how they failed except for us. So I asked, at what point are we going to reflect on the way we fund and whether or not that's actually impacting the success of our programs? Crickets. There was total silence. It's funny because the conference organizer asked me right then if I thought anyone was actually going to answer that question and even with that, silence.

Nonprofit: That's actually a perfect segue into issue number two for me. Issue number one is not understanding or investing in organizations and developing talent, etc. so that we can properly run it. Issue number two is that there is no accountability for funders. Zero. None, except the IRS. The IRS provides some legal accountability, but that's it. There are no ethical standards. There are supposed to be best practices, but often, those best practices are what slows things down to begin with.

Donor: The process.

Nonprofit: Yes, the process.

Donor: That same foundation I was speaking about before is going through their process now and how they get rid of doing nothing until the board book comes. It's the luxury of time. I was speaking with the COO and she was saying that when you have time, you just come up with shit. You don't even know why you're coming up with it. You create a process and call it best practices because it justifies your position when you are not making grants.

Nonprofit: Yes, and that actually relates to another thing. I'm just gonna call out some funders here because you're really hitting on the problem. So there's lack of accountability for process and there's lack of accountability for substance. With the process, it's the worse. Each foundation has their own application process and the amount of needless garbage that I have devoted entire teams to generate is ridiculous. I know that my foundation contact reads it, but that person submits a fucking one-pager of what I have to write to the board. And everything in the report I have to submit is stuff the Program Officer already knows about us.

I know how this works, but some of these things are beyond comprehension. Government grants I actually understand. I understand we are accountable to congress and there is a lot of accountability and oversight. At least there's a good—or at least understandable reason why that sucks. There's no reason in a private foundation or especially a family foundation why this should be so bad.

We've been treated so poorly and have wasted so much time that it's soul crushing. One funder—a wonderful funder in terms of who they fund—strung us along forever. We did a concept note. We did a big proposal and revised proposals. We did financials and revised financials, which all took months of time and money we really didn't have to waste. At the last stage, they rejected us at the board level for reasons they knew about and could have informed us about before the concept note even went out. They should have just told us no from the start. It would have been fine. We get a ton of nos. That's how it works. We could have moved on to find a better fit.

Then, in our conversations with the Program Officer, we're told that everything is closed doors, so they can't give us any information about why we were rejected. The surface level reasons they gave were both factually inaccurate and heavily implied—or blatantly told us—that we were never a good fit from the start. So, to me, this is unethical.

Donor: It *is* unethical.

Nonprofit: This is why I say there are no ethical standards or best practices that make it easier or better for grantees. The best thing that could happen in situations like that is if more grantees are rejected sooner.

Donor: I still can't get over the fact that they let you get so far in the process. They should have never accepted your proposal in the first place. There's clearly a lack of initial vetting process.

Nonprofit: But why are there even proposals or why is that the metric? The Walton Family Foundation, they only ask for a one page note asking about what are your goals and objectives.

Donor: At my last foundation, we actually eliminated the interim report, because I went to my board and asked, 'Are you even reading these? If not, why are you making grantees do them?'

We only had eight questions on our application. That was all we needed to know if they were a fit we were willing to explore. Before we even started talking to people or figuring out who we were going to ask for proposals, we sat down and worked out what our capacity was for giving. If we were going to do five grants, then we were going to ask seven organizations for proposals. We were not going to ask fifty people to do proposals when we know we only have five grants. That's ridiculous.

We do at least want to have choices and be able to compare and figure out where it is we can be the most helpful. But with everything you said, it just speaks to all the work that still needs to be done. I sit on the board of a philanthropic group and I've said in our board meetings that philanthropy is in for a reckoning. I don't know when or how it's going to come about, but it is coming.

Another colleague of mine who is General Counsel for a large foundation tells me that he worries about it at the federal level. People are not crazy. People are getting tired and exhausted. Anyone can just go on someone's website and see what they say they support, but then go look at their grants—how do they justify that disconnection? Many of these foundations can't even make connections to their own missions and what they are supporting, but expect their grantees to do a better job of it. Oh, by the way, with exponentially fewer resources.

Nonprofit: That's why the win rate is nowhere near as high as it should be.

Donor: Exactly. The donor who runs The Foundation Center wrote a piece, I believe for the Stanford Social Innovation Review and I think a blog on the foundation's website. He basically said that foundations gather information for the appearance of rigor. There's no rigor in our decision making. When you talk about rigor, when is the last time anyone has done an actual rigorous academic report? That's rigor. When you just have stats, that's not rigor.

Nonprofit: Where there's peer review.

Donor: Exactly. We're not doing an IRB (Institutional Review Board) level assessment, nor do we really need to.

Nonprofit: It's actually going in the opposite direction. Look at what MacArthur Foundation is doing with this 100 Million and Change project. It's absolutely ludicrous.

Donor: Exactly. You go from crazy rigid to crazy open. It's all about money and being focused on its power instead of the power of great leaders on the ground.

Nonprofit: It's the biggest abdication of accountability for the work. I think the foundation world concerns itself with the wrong things. What doesn't help is organizations like Guide Star and Charity Navigator, because they provide terrible incentives. OK, so I'm gonna unleash my potty mouth and say I'm sorry in advance. This fucking overhead thing? You know how much time is wasted on this? It's insane and just forces people to lie. And everyone lies. Everyone says the overhead is 12% and you make it up somewhere else in the allocations. Well, you don't lie, but you structure your programs—

Donor: No, you actually do lie and it's our fault. The donor at my former foundation would tell grantees that no one has a perfect budget for salaries so don't even bother doing it.

Nonprofit: But you should care about outcomes. If someone has 80% overhead and they're 'wasting all this money' to people who only see the money, but the outcomes are great, then that's what should matter. Imagine if Mark Zuckerberg went to Marc Andreessen and said, 'I've got this really cool idea to connect people around the world called Facebook' and Andreessen sees that the company is going well in the beginning, but says 'Well, you're overhead is above 14%, so we're not going to invest in you.'

It's just crazy to me.

Donor: You're right, and I refuse to use the term, indirect services.

Nonprofit: It's all direct! Do you know what happens if you're limited to 5-10 people to run a nonprofit successfully? You have senior staff doing admin work. So the question is—to address those crickets you heard at the conference you just talked about—if there is no accountability for donors or no bar association—if you will—for funders, how do we change that? The power dynamic is staggering, because I can bitch and moan all I want, but donors have the luxury of selective hearing.

Yeah, funders want to fund us because we're hot right now, but there will come a point when we won't be and yet our influence to change things will be the same, which is not much if at all. The power dynamic is never not going to exist. They have the money. We have the ideas, but there are always more ideas than money. I don't even know how many good ideas there are, but the only current qualification for determining a good idea is having the money. I just think the system is so structurally flawed that I don't know what the solution is.

Donor: I don't know what the proper definition or the psychological term is for how donors work, but we're crazy. (NGO laughs) There's a level of insanity and I kid you not, the definition of crazy is doing the same thing over and over again and expecting a different result. The only difference is that donors come up with cool new names for doing the exact same thing and expect new results.

There was a report on the future of foundations and there was a CEO compilation done where they asked CEOs of foundations to do their own assessment of the field and their work in general. These are leaders, all CEOs. What was crazy in the findings is that while they all overwhelmingly agreed that they don't do enough or they could do better as foundations, when asked if they were willing to change, 40% said no.

Everybody is scared of everyone else. Boards are afraid of the public. CEOs are afraid of their board. Program Officers are afraid of their Directors. We are run by fear. I'm sorry, but this is supposed to be fun. We shouldn't be afraid of the potential we have the power to turn into reality. We should embrace it. At the end of the day, this doesn't have to be as complicated as we make it out to be with no clear victories after changes to our strategies.

My very first boss said to me, 'Should philanthropy be thoughtful and deep? Yes, but is it rocket science? No.'

Nonprofit: So maybe this is a way of pulling some of this stuff together, at least to address these questions around entrepreneurship, risk and fear. I feel like the foundation world, like you said, they are acknowledging problems and are doing some thinking around—

Donor: No, they are giving the appearance of knowledge.

Nonprofit: That's it, the appearance of knowledge. So this is a subtly different point and I'm applying it to the venture capital world and the Marc Andreessen types. If you listen to them, you often hear them say something akin to, 'Yeah we don't really care about the type of technology. We want the best and brightest entrepreneurs.'

So some foundations—and this is where I think Echoing Green and other similar foundations get it right—decide to focus on developing the brains behind the programs and not just developing the programs. Most other foundations are obsessed with program areas and subject matter.

Donor: At the sacrifice of actually helping institutions.

Nonprofit: Even when they say they don't sacrifice, they do, instead of investing in entrepreneurs. And the Macarthur initiative is just weird. It is going to the extreme. The board is now trying to become the NGO by picking these super narrow program areas. It's like they are saying, 'We're only going to fund issues around bail in eight cities' and that's their entire criminal justice program.

In a place like Nigeria, their Human Rights grants are just focused on the issue of police corruption, so then every NGO suddenly opens up a police corruption program not because they are experts or have the capacity to address police corruption in a meaningful way; they're just chasing the money that they desperately need. Don't get me wrong, police corruption is an important issue, sure, but why not take that money and invest in what the people see as the biggest Human Rights issue in their area, not what an internal strategic review dictates?

Donor: Not only that, but something like police corruption is connected to so many other things that, if they are also not funded or addressed, will make it impossible for real change to occur.

Nonprofit: Totally. And this comes back to talent and attracting the best people to the sector. I'm not saying it's all about entrepreneurs. We need great entrepreneurs in addition to great workers. This move in philanthropy is wildly anti-entrepreneur, because if you have a good idea, the money is no longer available. The boards and staff of the foundations have supplanted the entrepreneur's role in ideating. So, could the foundation world find a way to step back and say, 'We're not gonna do all the sexy stuff. We're just going to fund the best talent in more general areas' and will that work? I don't know if this is the answer, but from my perspective, it feels very much like philanthropy is more anti-entrepreneur and anti-Social Entrepreneurship, at least in the philanthropic world. In the for-profit world, it's a whole different ballgame.

Donor: Well, I don't know. First of all, donors can do whatever they want to do. But we are fooling ourselves to not think that when we fund things in the beginning, we are not funding leaders. Don't get confused, like we said before, there is no rigor, so when you decided to make that grant, you were swayed or persuaded by a really charismatic leader. Even if the idea may have been a little wonky. We kind of ignore that part and give praise to the program and not the brain behind it because we don't want to be seen as falling for something more superficial and less evidence-based.

Nonprofit: It's like they are trying to avoid embarrassment, but it becomes embarrassing for totally other reasons.

Donor: Right, so I don't even think some donors can actually identify when they are investing in an entrepreneur or a smart idea, and helping them take that to the next level, whether that be a social enterprise or a nonprofit.

Me: Before we finish, I wanted to pose a question to you both, based on this conversation. One of the things I hear a lot from many people, mostly from nonprofits, is the difficulty in not just finding support for technical work, but difficulty in celebrating its importance. We go to these forums that give really big awards that celebrate organizations that offer us something we can look at, smile at or cry at.

Donor: Mhmm. It drives me crazy.

Me: Sometimes you have an organization that is so technical that there is no way to elicit that same kind of response.

Nonprofit: You mean it's not emotive enough.

Me: Yes. The process is not emotive, but the end result will have significant impact, often at a level that will effect more lives, but still lacks that moment that has people reaching for their handkerchiefs. How do you speak to that from your respective fields? I've seen money wasted on trying to make this work look more attractive and digestible to other donors, so are there solutions? What are your thoughts? I guess I'm looking to you as a donor first. Is there something nonprofits can say or do to improve the donor experience and their own experience with donors?

Donor: That's a super interesting question that has come up for me a lot lately. I was just at a little convening a few days ago and a grantee went off on the misguided conversations around innovation, scale sustainability and impact, and rightly so. And these words drive me crazy. We treat these words like crayons and tell our grantees to paint a picture of success for us.

Meanwhile, there is someone over there creating a masterpiece of success with tools we're not used to and because we can't explain it, we don't support it or we don't deem it a real success.

And these words, for one, people don't even know what they mean. To your question, I don't know if I can tell you how to better describe the work when the language behind it is so screwed up. Donors have yet to sit down and define these words for their institutions, so they are sharing these words, but not sharing any meaning behind them. And going back to what I said about success, we don't know how to picture it. We don't know the right specific questions to ask our grantees, therefore we have them do all this paperwork.

Nonprofit: And have them distort the work they are doing just to placate for a grant.

Donor: Exactly. So, to answer your question, I don't know. It's kind of scary.

Nonprofit: I think about the Skoll awards, when a group like Landesa won. Their work is highly technical and seemingly boring to the layman. It took them a long time, but they found a way to communicate what they do in a way that caught the attention of one of the biggest award donors. This goes back to donors funding what they want to fund versus funding what's needed, but at some point, someone invested in or funded communications for Landesa and look how that worked out for them.

Donor: It's very true. It's about messaging and branding and storytelling, all of those things.

Nonprofit: It's also matchmaking between ecosystems of grantees. Again, something the venture capital world does incredibly well. They invest in a portfolio where one business helps create more customers and revenue for another business. I think even if something is highly technical, it can be more easily explained. Well, not always, but most times, there is a way to get around the technicality, and that comes with communications, which comes with investing in communications by donors.

And I'm aware that this means that there are possibly fewer grantees if more money goes into making great nonprofits greater. This is the tradeoff. There are fewer dollars to go around to other nonprofits when there isn't enough already.

Donor: But if we actually gave in a way that was more powerful and multidimensional, they may not need more of our donor dollars in the long run. We don't even talk about gaps or if we should be working to fill those gaps instead of overfunding programs we like by using our grants like steroids.

I am hard on my sector, but I stay in it because I know we have the potential to do better and I refuse to let them settle for what we have now.

Final Thoughts:

So you've read that there is not enough funding. You've also read that there is plenty of funding. You've seen some donors say not to use nonprofit jargon, but you've also seen donors admit that not knowing the lingo could hinder the chance for a grant. No one seems to know where we came up with 15% as the standard cut off for core operating nonprofit costs, but many donors still agree that this number is necessary to oversee nonprofit spending...except when it isn't. As a nonprofit, you'd be forgiven if you were trying to map out a direction for your organization with the rubrics of this book, but occasionally misplaced north on your compass.

But then again, I gave fair warning from the outset. The ED of that very first nonprofit I engaged no doubt came to our meeting with a plan. It was a plan that I imagine had worked for him in prior meetings with donors. He should have had multiple options when that plan didn't work, as should all of us. Yes, his first choice was to dismiss my potential input for his organization, but after that plan also turned out to not work so well, he listened. He asked questions. He (hopefully) learned from the flaws in his plan A and plan B and we had a conversation not based on rehearsed notes or a pass/fail style metric of grant or no grant. He gained resources and a greater understanding of how to present his organization.

The human element of engagement between nonprofits and donors is both the core and the wild card of how we interact with each other. All sides involved ask for more humanity to be included in the process, but that means inviting human behaviors like bias, mistrust, trusting too easily, laziness, eagerness, empathy and apathy. We can create materials that make us all appear inviting and easy to approach, but that is not always representative of the actual interactions in our space. No matter what is showcased or said on a well-polished website, no one can predict how these behaviors will manifest themselves in a real person-to-person context.

This explains why I hear the names of the same two or three corporate foundations when I ask nonprofits to candidly reveal their best donors, while others have cited individual donors and family foundations as causing the most frustration, second only to government donors. It isn't always about the organization, but the people behind them. We are those people. As donors, we represent the best intentions and endless possibilities of philanthropy, but when we don't come to the table at our best, we are not just failing the person in front of us who is relying on our best, we risk failing all those intentions and possibilities.

As this comes to a close, there are many thoughts that come to mind about all the contributions that have been harnessed, whether or not they made the final cut. To add anything more to what people have contributed would only be redundant, so I won't bother. Instead, I would like to share some behind the scenes reflections and a few reminders to consider as one begins the daunting task of digesting this all.

My first reflection would have to be from the previous chapter. There were six donor/nonprofit anonymous conversations, although I only chose to showcase three of them. I paired people based on many factors, including an increased difficulty in trying to find a synergy, just in case the conversation devolved into a long-term direct pitch. However, in all of the conversations, donors found ways to offer resources to their nonprofit counterparts, either directly during the conversation or after. This further bolstered my personal beliefs that when not pressed to fund, donors are willing to provide resources beyond direct funding, and donors also understand more and more that they don't have to become experts on the ground, but can be more effective in becoming experts in who else is funding great work on the ground.

The amount of donors who, in their advice across the chapters, said to challenge them and not be afraid was surprising and encouraging. I think, for nonprofits who feel the tension from donors—whether it's in an attempt to pitch or simply in engaging throughout a grant process—this sentiment does not come across well. That's because donors are afraid. They are afraid that you won't treat them as humans. You won't represent yourselves as humans. You haven't done your homework. You won't take no for an answer before you even ask the question. So when they are saying don't be afraid, what they also mean is don't make me feel afraid either.

Another reflection that came through clearly is that more donors than we might think are aware of their flaws, even if they are not forthcoming about them in the immediate moments when they happen. Donors have their own reflections on how they perform their roles. Some of these flaws and missteps have gone on to vastly improve how donors engage the space. Some have not. The donors who shared their stories certainly have learned from their experiences as bad donors in ways that have since benefited countless numbers of organizations collectively. The lesson learned here is that today's bad donor can be tomorrow's reformed donor with the proper reflection.

As I take the chance to praise those rehabilitated donors, something must also be said about the donors who are still not aware of their flaws. As previously mentioned, there was originally a chapter that focused on nonprofit experiences, including negative ones, which was scrapped in order to not put nonprofits under any undue grief or retaliation. There are questionable mistakes that new or uncertain donors make that are understandable and/or forgivable. There are also mistakes that are much more serious and can leave a grantee in a worse situation, as shown in the 'I was a bad donor' chapter, but all of those experiences have gone on to create more insightful donors.

However, to the obstinate donor, to the donor who takes a video meeting half-naked in pajamas and then proclaims, 'I'm the funder so I can dress however I like,' to the western individual donor who, based on a few secondhand experiences funding in a couple of African countries on the entire continent, can tell an African leader of a local NGO that Africans don't value the importance of education, to the donor who makes sexual advances or innuendoes to the young representative of an organization who is trusting that you will not abuse your position of power or possibly that person, and to all the donors who can't leave your biases at the door, please don't walk through it.

You can be part of the problem and part of the conversation, but only if you are looking to work on fixing the former. Of all the words that have multiple subjective meanings that can be left to interpretation, respect is not one of them. Chances are, though, if you are taking direct meetings or attending any type of convening where nonprofits are present, then you want to be involved in doing good. But doing 'good' doesn't start or stop with money.

And what are the lessons for nonprofits to learn when encountered by bad donor behaviors? It is difficult to give one definitive answer when the problems range so broadly from the professional to the personal. The first thing to know is that you can walk away from a bad situation with a donor, no matter the situation. The fear that many nonprofits expressed to me is that they could be cutting off a potential supporter when resources are already low and other donors might be harder to find.

I didn't want to make this book about stats, but I wanted to point out a few things. According to the National Center for Charitable Statistics

(NCCS), there are over 100,000 philanthropic foundations in the United States alone. That does not include high net worth individuals who give in more clandestine ways. This also does not include the thousands of foundations located in Canada or the other 130,000+ philanthropic foundations in Europe or the hundreds of philanthropic grant-makers in Africa. I haven't even touched upon the Middle East, Asia, Oceana and Latin America. All this is to say that as much as you think you don't have options to look elsewhere, you do. Not everyone will be a good fit, but anyone who makes you feel uncomfortable in your efforts to fundraise is already not a good fit.

The second piece of advice is to be vocal. If you are not comfortable with a donor at any point, organizationally or personally, say it. Whether the discomfort comes from pressure to shift organizational ideologies or from a comment that detracts from the main goals of partnership, voicing it once it happens lets the other party know that you do not agree with where things are going or have already gone. If the power dynamic still makes you uneasy, talk to your closest donor ally for support and advice. If something needs to be said or brought up, they could be willing to do so on your behalf. This is also another way good donors can be more than just grant-makers.

That serves as a bit of a segue into my final reflection on this process: ambassadorship. The amount of times a donor gushed over a grantee or a nonprofit they loved even if they didn't directly support them was refreshing, especially given its volume. This speaks to people on both sides understanding that the endgame for relationship building does not always have to be direct funding. The percentage of unaligned donors I spoke to either for this book or in general who offered potential partners for our foundation after I spoke about our focus had to be over 80%. In many cases, the same names came up, and right after the organization was mentioned, it was always quickly followed by, 'You should speak to.... He/She is great.'

It goes both ways. Nonprofit friends and colleagues have introduced me to several donors who turned out to be eventual co-funders. When we are doing things the right way in relationship building, there is a natural bond and an unencumbered rapport that forms, independent of mission alignment. What is aligned is how organically we present ourselves and how well we represent why we are in this.

As for the reminders, some are more about how to view and absorb all of this feedback, which leads to the first one:

Whether or not you agree with the contributions, the people who spoke to me, emailed me and connected me with others all did so for the purpose of trying to improve the space. No one was paid anything for offering their advice. Their motives were all the same, even if their feedback differed, at times dramatically.

●

Take nothing personally. I remember how offended I used to be when the barista at my favorite coffee shop or the guy who would sign me in almost every day at the gym never remembered my face or name. Now, older and more overwhelmed, I sometimes forget people while we are still speaking. I regularly get that feeling of dread when someone looks at me with familiar eyes while my memory just shrugs its shoulders at me, leaving me to fend for myself.

Much of the staff I spoke to from foundations came from a former life in the nonprofit sector. They would repeat how things that drove them crazy on the implementing side about donors made total sense after making the switch. Not everything, but some things. A decision that doesn't go your way or a criticism that may seem targeted may not be. It's only constructive criticism if you choose to build upon it.

●

This is not a self-help book. Well, it's not meant to be a self-help book. It really is about reflecting upon who you help, as well as who can help you help them, and making that process as less frustrating as possible.

●

Take to heart the title of the first chapter, why are you in this? Remember to first, do no harm. Think about your contribution to the sector and if there is anyone or anything that could be harmed by your implementing theory. However, don't construct a plan that is so focused on harming no one that it also helps no one either, not significantly at least.

•

The support you offer should mirror the same support you would want if in the same position. We speak a lot about hierarchy between donors and nonprofits, but we shouldn't support anything that reinforces a 'less-than' relationship between beneficiaries and implementers.

•

As much as I said this book was meant to be as much about tangibles as possible, don't forget the role gratitude should play in your work and your life, no matter where you fit in this space. Being aware of what you're grateful for really can be a great asset in reminding you what you're fighting for.

•

Remember to listen more and fear less. Instead of waiting for your turn to speak, dig in to the conversations, for they can offer something richer than money. A replicable strategy. An entry point. A connection to more aligned support. It isn't just the devil living in the details. Opportunity has a nice home there as well.

I have already spoken so much about fearing less. This is just one last reminder.

•

Last, but not least, everything you say and do professionally in this space matters. As much as we talk about risk, we don't spend nearly as much time on responsibility. No matter who we are, our words and actions have impact, both within and beyond our control. How we give or receive a pitch, how we engage and how we partner gets remembered, repeated, reviled and revered. We are in the business of life. Everything we do in pursuit to improve or save it—good or bad— plays a role in how successful we ultimately will be.

Made in the USA
San Bernardino, CA
03 July 2018